THOMAS FITZSIMMONS

THE EXTRAORDINARY LIFE OF AN ORDINARY MAN

A
MEMOIR

Copyright © 2023 Thomas Fitzsimmons
All rights reserved

When the Gods wish to punish us, they answer our prayers.

Some of the names have been changed.

Contents

Prologue	1
Chapter 1	8
Chapter 2	21
Chapter 3	29
Chapter 4	34
Chapter 5	39
Chapter 6	45
Chapter 7	53
Chapter 8	63
Chapter 9	78
Chapter 10	88
Chapter 11	95
Chapter 12	99
Chapter 13	103
Chapter 14	108
Chapter 15	118
Chapter 16	127
Chapter 17	134
Chapter 18	141
Chapter 19	154
Chapter 20	164
Chapter 21	172
Chapter 22	179
Chapter 23	185
Chapter 24	189
Chapter 25	194
Chapter 26	201
Chapter 27	206
Chapter 28	215
Chapter 29	222
Chapter 30	232

Chapter 31	240
Chapter 32	245
Chapter 33	250
Chapter 34	258
Chapter 35	265
Chapter 36	270
Chapter 37	278
Chapter 38	287
Chapter 39	293
Chapter 40	304
Chapter 41	311
Chapter 42	318
Chapter 43	327
Chapter 44	333
Chapter 45	338
Chapter 46	344
Chapter 47	346

Prologue

"You're a loser." Donald J. Trump stormed around the Trump Castle's high-roller hotel suite in a jealous rage, huffing and puffing and angrily kicking furniture. Enraged that Bill O'Reilly (from *Inside Edition*) had been calling his paramour, Marla Maples—my fault, according to Donald, since I'd inadvertently introduced O'Reilly into the Trump inner circle.

"I keep telling you," Marla said, "Billy's not interested in me."

"Billy?" Donald sneered. "So now it's 'Billy'?"

"Everyone calls him Billy."

"I don't call him Billy." Donald looked at me. "You call him Billy, Tom?"

"No, but..."

"He's interested in Kim Knapp," Marla said, exasperated at having to explain for the umpteenth time that she was planning to fix up O'Reilly with her "guru" and spiritual advisor. But Donald didn't believe that. Perhaps he heard something incriminating on the bug he'd placed in Marla's NYC apartment. Or was it the fact that, since Donald was sexually obsessed with Marla, he assumed that every man was?

"You're a real loser," Donald continued to rant. His unruly, tusk-like eyebrows gave him a demented, threatening look. "A total fuckin' disaster."

"Why do you do me like that?" Marla Maples cried, tears now streaming down her blotchy beauty-queen face.

"You fucking Billy, Marla? Huh? You fucking him?"

"I'm not," Marla sobbed. "Why won't you believe me?"

"'Cause you're a fuckin' whore."

Marla's tears stopped. Her face flushed. "What did you call me?"

Uh-oh.

Donald saw what I saw and knew what was coming. As Marla's former fiancé, I also knew what was coming. My instincts, as a former New York City cop, were to intervene, save my former singles-bar wingman from a much-deserved ass-whooping. But I knew from experience that refereeing a violent domestic dispute was a good way to get hurt. Besides, over the years I've been tempted to kick Donald's ass on more than one occasion.

"Say it again," Marla screamed. "I dare you."

Donald's face turned the color of spackle as he braced himself to suffer the wrath of a Georgia peach scorned. He looked my way, his expression imploring me to intercede.

No way. I shook my head. *You're on your own, pal.*

Resigned, Donald turned to face Marla. The cocky sneer vanished from his famed, bee-stung lips. "Let's not get mentally irregular," he said and held up his hands in surrender. "Just take it easy." Which was, in Trumpspeak, his way of giving an inch, making peace. Not because he had overreacted, as usual, or had hurt someone he professed to love with his childish, quick-cutting scorn. It was because he knew all too well the consequences of pissing Marla off. Regardless, Donald would never apologize. Ever. Instead, to my horror, Donald changed tack and did what he always did: doubled down.

"You're a sleaze," Donald said. "A major sleaze."

That did it.

Marla picked up a crystal vase and flung it across the room. Donald ducked. The vase, the price of which could pay my monthly rent, shattered against a richly papered wall.

"You'll pay for that," Donald said, inspecting the damage. "You crazy bitch."

That's when Marla lost it. Literally. She slapped her own face. Hard. Once. Twice. Three times. Spittle flew from her mouth. Snot from her nose. Red finger marks appeared on her face.

Holy shit.

Marla growled.

Donald stepped back. Covered up.

The blue-eyed beauty queen attacked. Let go with a stinging salvo of Three Stooges slaps and punches. Donald blocked most of the blows. Enjoying a weight, height, and reach advantage over the scrappy former Miss Hawaiian Tropic, Donald could have done her serious harm. But this time, to his credit and my relief, he did not hit her back.

"I hate you!" Marla lunged and tore clumps of hair from Donald's oft-plugged scalp.

Donald freaked. "Not my hair!" He zigged and zagged around Marla, dashed across the room, putting a large dining room table between them.

"Knock it off, you two," I shouted before this battle got out of hand and one of them seriously injured the other. When I was a cop, I'd seen my share of violent domestic disputes. These two set new standards for wackiness.

Donald finger-combed his hair, then stuck his chin out, taunting Marla like a six-year-old. "C'mon, hit me again. Let's see what you've got."

Marla's response was another chilling growl. She hiked up the spaghetti straps of her $15,000 red designer dress and circled the table, trying to catch Donald. "Stand still, asshole."

"C'mon, wimp," Donald said, managing to keep just out of Marla's reach. "Let's see what you got. Hit me again."

I groaned; Donald stuck on stupid.

Donald had turned forty-five years old that June weekend, 1991. We had just returned from his birthday party at the Taj

Mahal in Atlantic City, an eight-by-one-mile hambone-shaped New Jersey barrier island. It was to be an auspicious occasion. And not just because it was Donald's birthday and the casino's first anniversary. He had planned to announce to the world that he and Marla were engaged. But he didn't. Convinced that his beloved was screwing around with Bill O'Reilly or someone else, he suffered one of his chronic, volcanic mood swings and changed his mind. Marla was understandably heartbroken, baffled, but more importantly, embarrassed.

We were having a late-night room service snack in a luxury, two-bedroom suite that Donald had rented for Marla's mother, Ann Ogletree, whom he'd flown in from Marla's hometown of Dalton, Georgia, for the birthday/engagement weekend. Donald had also flown in Marla's father, Stan Maples, his wife Deena, Ann's husband David Ogletree, and Marla's grandparents, Laura and Arnold Locklear. Dozens of Marla's friends had also arrived for the festivities from as far away as California, most on Donald's dime. Marla's personal hairdresser and makeup artist were in tow; again, compliments of Donald. The entire entourage was staying at Trump Castle, registered under my name, Thomas Fitzsimmons. I didn't know it at the time, but over the years Donald used my name often to register his various lady friends, reporters he'd encouraged to write favorable stories, or shady characters he covertly associated with. I never saw the hotel bills, which were always paid by the Trump Organization.

"You've made me look like a fool," Marla cried, "in front of my entire family."

Donald sneered. "You don't need any help with that."

Oh, boy.

I slipped off my blue cashmere Dunhill suit jacket, hung it on the back of a chair, rolled up my shirtsleeves in case I was forced to referee. Regretting that I hadn't accepted my dear friend, Larry Hagman's—of *I Dream of Jennie* and *Dallas* fame—invitation to spend the week with him at his oceanfront home in Malibu. Or "the happiest billionaire" Malcom Forbes's standing invitation to party on his mega-yacht, *Highlander II*, which was moored across town from my Manhattan apartment on the Hudson River.

"Stand still, you chicken," Marla said.

I edged forward, ready to move fast if I had to and wondered for the umpteenth time why these two self-absorbed, nutty adolescents bothered to stay together. Marla, with her wide-set blue eyes and thoroughbred body, could have almost any man she desired. Men brighter, more accomplished, and even richer than Donald. Similarly, Donald's perceived wealth, power, and surgically induced good looks kept him in constant demand by gold diggers of the fairer sex. Did they love each other as much as they professed in public? Yes. I think they did.

"Prick," Marla shouted.

"Whore," Donald shouted back.

Marla raced around the table, dove, managed to grab a piece of Donald's suit jacket sleeve, and slapped-punched away. Donald used his fleshy arms to cover up, backed into a wall, and did a pretty good rope-a-dope, further frustrating the Georgia peach. She let out a nails-on-a-blackboard scream and clawed his neck.

"Hey!" Donald scurried away, feeling for blood. "No scratching."

A door opened. The action stopped.

Marla's mother, Ann, attired in a silk robe that she wore recklessly low over wonderful cleavage, high-heeled into the room, pretending to be unaware of the knockdown, drag-out brawl taking place in her suite.

Ann, at forty-eight years old, a distant cousin of actress Heather Locklear, was an exotic beauty in her own right. Her full, shoulder-length raven hair, high cheekbones, and large almond eyes hinted at her mixed English and Lumbee American Indian roots; lineage she was embarrassed by and vehemently denied.

"Pour me some champagne, Thomas?" Ann said.

I grabbed an open bottle of Dom Pérignon from a sterling silver ice bucket, poured, and handed her a flute.

Part of me expected Ann to put an end to this insane squabble. But I knew that her mission in life was to ensure that Marla married a rich man: Enter Donald J. Trump.

"Your daughter is a fucking disaster," Donald said, still feeling his neck for blood. Absolutely certain of Ann's gold-digging ways, he spoke to her any way he pleased. Ann would stick her tongue in a light socket if he asked her to.

Ann raised a perfectly tweezed eyebrow. "Now, Donald," she said in a saccharine-sweet, Southern drawl. "You know Marla has no interest in Bill O'Reilly."

"How would *you* know?"

"Oh, I'd know."

"What? You think she tells you everything?"

"Well, now you're just being silly, Donald," Ann said diplomatically. She sipped her champagne. "You do understand why we're all upset that you didn't announce your engagement like you promised you would."

"If I ever *do* announce my engagement to *her*..." He finger-combed his hair, adjusted his tie, and made the mortal mistake of taking his eyes off Marla. "It's only because I'll make her an instant star. And I'm a star-fucker."

Donald sensed movement. Instinctively he raised his right leg. The kick missed the family jewels. Caught him squarely on the thigh.

"Ooff," Donald croaked. Grabbed his leg. That hurt.

I stood there, frozen. This was not good.

Ann, watching her privileged future wither before her very eyes, whimpered softly, did a Norma Desmond, and collapsed dramatically onto the couch.

I made my move, rushed to get between Marla and Donald before she did more damage. "Marla, stop. Enough already."

"You bitch." Donald was limping in circles, fighting to breathe.

"You prick," Marla cut back. I grabbed her around the waist, pulled her over to Ann, who locked her daughter in a bear hug.

"You," he said to Marla. "You get out of my hotel."

"Fuck you," Marla screamed and fought to break Ann's hold. But Ann squeezed her squirming meal ticket, fighting for both of their financial lives.

Donald hobbled across the room, opened the door, and fled the suite. I grabbed my suit jacket and followed. Marla's primeval shriek echoed down the hall. The all-too-familiar sound sent a prickle up my spine.

Chapter 1

THAT NIGHT, NOT WISHING to be caught up in anymore Donald-Marla drama, I shared a Trump helicopter back to Manhattan with Jack Nicholson, Anjelica Huston, Robin Leach of *Lifestyles of the Rich and Famous*, et al. Woke up early the next morning in my high-rise apartment. Made a pot of coffee. Sat at my six-pound Zenith laptop—one of the first laptops sold—which I'd purchased for the sole purpose of writing books, screenplays, and eventually—since socializing with the likes of Donald and other celebrities, famous and infamous, had provided me with a treasure trove of provocative material—my memoirs.

Which gave me an idea.

I lifted the laptop lid, pressed the power button, waited for the system to boot, and decided that, because of the wild and crazy events of the last few months, it was as good a time as any to begin outlining my memoir, maybe write a chapter or two; not that anyone but family and friends would read it. Although, if I did muster the discipline and focus it would take to complete such a daunting task, I planned to send the tome to Michael Collyer, esteemed A-list entertainment attorney, chairman emeritus of the National Academy of Television Arts & Sciences, pseudo-agent, mentor, and dear friend. Collyer, who I'd met through ex-NYPD detective Sonny Grasso of *The French Connection* fame, had read a draft of my first novel, *Confessions of a Catholic Cop*, and was a fan. Ironic, since the Sisters of Charity at St. Barnabas elementary school in the Bronx—where I endured the vicissitudes of a parochial education—told my parents that I was ditchdigger material, an academic and developmental lost cause.

I took a sip of my first cup of black coffee. Turned back to my computer. Slipped in a floppy disk. Opened Word Perfect, one of the first word processing programs. Typed the heading *My Memories*. Keyed to the next line and typed *Chapter One*. I leaned back. Drank more coffee. Stared at the screen. Fidgeted. Yawned. Stretched. Wrung my hands. I had no idea what to write next.

I got to my feet, stuck my hands in my pockets, and paced my 1,100-square-foot apartment, trying to organize my thoughts. I'd read dozens of memoirs and recalled that most started with the author's birth, their family circumstances (usually dire), and progressed chronologically—as good a way to start as any. I picked up my coffee cup, swallowed a mouthful, and let my mind wander.

I was born on February 20, 1948. A gallon of gas was 16 cents. The Cleveland Indians had won the World Series. *Gentleman's Agreement* (Twentieth Century-Fox) won the Academy Award. I was raised across the street from Woodlawn Cemetery, in the Irish section of the north Bronx, one of five, the offspring of first-generation Irish immigrants. My formative years, many of which were spent in notorious pubs like the Mayo Inn and the Woodlawn Tavern, where I was exposed to a disparate clientele of undertakers, sanitation workers, gravediggers, construction workers, sandhogs, cops, firefighters, and erstwhile IRA heroes, were idyllic, uneventful, and mostly drama-free. That was because my parents were sober, moral, and hardworking. Granted, my mother Madeline, a homemaker, and Thomas Sr., a NYC cop, weren't perfect, but they really tried to be.

Although there was the traumatic ordeal of attending St. Barnabas Catholic School, suffering the wrath of Irish nuns who, in those days, had no idea how to deal with students afflicted with learning disabilities. Not that it mattered after all these years. My psychological and physical wounds have healed. I harbored no hard feeling toward the nuns. One reason was that my three sisters, Maureen, Patricia, and Carol also attended St. Barnabas and were A students. Plus, in those days the nuns knew virtually nothing about ADD, ADHD, and dyslexia. Nor did my mother or father. The fact that my parents held the nuns — all clergy, for that matter — in unreasonably high regard and, as a result, believed their theoretic assessment of me being an academic lost cause, was an unfortunate product of their own strict Irish Catholic upbringing and generation.

You see, in those days, where you sat in a classroom was based on academic achievement. The first few rows were reserved for the brainy A students like my three sisters. The B students took up the next and largest block. The C and D students —D being hopeless—were relegated to the last few rows at the back of the room. My twin brother Robert was a C. I was a D. And so, I sat in the last row, last seat. As a result, I endured not only the mortifying, life-altering experience of being labeled one of the dumbest kids in school, but the occasional assaults of taunting bullies, the relentless wrath of the nuns, priests, and my parents. Sometimes it seemed that the whole world was angry with me.

And so, I spent a stifling eight years at St. Barnabas feeling isolated, caged, gazing out the window toward the all-girls high school, hoping to get a glimpse of sophomore Mary O'Connor. Even then I knew she had an awesome rack. Come to think of it, that sort of sums up my entire academic career: an intellectually and emotionally stifled walking gonad, obsessed by the fairer sex.

I stopped pacing. Glanced out my windows and recalled graduating—just barely—from St. Barnabas and then DeWitt Clinton High School with a GED. Having no idea what I wanted to do with my life, I joined the military. Best thing I ever did.

I'll never forget those swashbuckling Navy days. Serving aboard the *USS DeLong* DE 684, *USS Cony* DD 508, *USS Purvis* DD 709, *USS Topeka* CLG 8. Sailing the Caribbean and

Mediterranean Sea, enjoying liberty call in Gitmo, Italy, Greece, France, and Spain. The free-for-all brawls in the bars and on the docks of Naples and Marseille. The women I'd encountered. The vacationing Canadian schoolteacher I'd met in Malta, who followed me from port to port for six months. Returning to the States. Meeting my first wife in Boston. Then, after being honorably discharged, joining the NYPD. An understandable career choice, since I came from a police family—think the TV show *Blue Bloods*. The fact I couldn't sing or dance was another reason. But it was more than that: I truly wanted to protect and serve. To defend the defenseless. Put the bad guys in jail.

The fact was that, even now, I sometimes missed being a cop. The prestige that came with carrying a gun and badge in the number one police force in the country, 42,000 officers strong, was part of my heritage. My father retired after almost forty years on the NYPD. My father's brother retired after thirty-seven years. I had an uncle who served for forty-two years. My twin brother and two of my nephews were police officers. Most of my close friends were still current or former law enforcement officers.

I poured another cup of coffee. Remembered graduating from the Police Academy and, after a short stint in a low-crime precinct, being assigned to the South Bronx, the most violent region in the city of New York. The South Bronx's notorious 41st Precinct, Fort Apache, was where I would have the privilege of working with the bravest and most dedicated men I'd ever know. Men who, considering the low pay and horrendous working conditions, saw being a New York City police offer not as a job, but a vocation.

I recalled my first day at Fort Apache: It was August. The temperature hovered around 98 degrees. The humidity was at least 90 percent. I had nosed my 1965 VW bug into a vertical parking space half a block away from the 41 Precinct station house. I killed the engine, stepped out into the muggy afternoon air and, even though the area swarmed with convicted car thieves,

I didn't bother to lock up. Rumor was that the last person caught breaking into a cop's car was escorted to the 41 basement and nearly beaten to death.

Carrying my uniforms and other police paraphernalia, I crossed the cratered street, swatted at a formation of dive-bombing horseflies, and breathed in the neighborhood stench. Heat radiated off the soft, tire-rutted blacktop. It would solidify as night and slightly cooler temperatures claimed the Bronx ghetto.

I wove though a crowd of sullen, shirtless young men and foul-mouthed, provocatively attired adolescent girls who were dancing to boom box salsa music. Kids on skateboards streaked down the sidewalk. A well-fed middle-aged couple exchanged slaps and harsh words in Spanish. Several cats fought a stray dog over a scrap of food. Fire engine sirens wailed in the distance. There was the faint odor of smoke.

I walked past clots of colicky stoop dwellers guzzling cheap wine and noticed that the station house was the only building on the block that did not have a stack of rotting garbage piled in front of it.

The neo Florentine 41 precinct station house was built around the turn of the last century. The bulky, flat roofed fortress was covered with ugly concrete slabs. There were bars on the windows and, because angry mobs still sometimes stormed the station house, there were thick steel shields behind the bars.

Shrill voices forewarned me to sidestep a group of irate civilians as I entered the stuffy – there was no air-conditioning— beehive-active 41 precinct and headed to the desk officer. The cavernous, grimy, and dimly lit space was painted institutional green. One glance at the worn-out wooden floor told me that peeling paint chips had recently rained down from the ceiling.

"Police officer Thomas Fitzsimmons," I said to a harried sergeant sitting behind the desk, "reporting for duty." The sergeant adjusted the angle of an old, cruddy desk fan that was blowing directly on his face and graced me with a sour look. "Fitzsimmons?"

I nodded.

He checked some paperwork. "Roll call. Upstairs. Second floor."

"Welcome," the roll call man, Rocky T., said when I introduced myself. "Who'd you piss off?" He regarded me suspiciously. "You a drunk? Violence prone? You get caught shaking down street peddlers? You had to do something incredibly stupid to get dumped in this shithouse."

"I'm, er, new. Just off probation."

"A rookie. That explains it." Rocky checked a roster. "I'm gonna team you up for the day with Richie G. His regular partner retired."

"Richie G.," I repeated.

"Look, kid," Rocky said. "Richie G.'s a hell of a terrific guy. Just don't believe anything he says. And I mean *ever*. Capisce?"

I didn't know how to respond to that.

"Locker rooms up on four. Take any empty locker. Good luck, kid."

I climbed to the fourth-floor locker room. Found an empty, battered locker. Tore down half-a-dozen pornographic photos of fat women that were Scotch taped inside the door. I stored my gear and was changing into uniform when I heard someone several lockers away say, "Richie G., my man...."

Richie G.? My ears perked up. I looked down the aisle.

"I see you still carry an old six-shooter." A young, skinny cop was pointing at Richie G.'s holster, which contained a six-shot, Smith & Wesson .38 revolver.

"Automatics can jam." Richie G., a mocha-skinned, five-foot-ten, lean rooster of a man, buckled his gun belt, which he wore low, gunslinger style. Then shoved a backup gun, a two-inch .38, into a waistband holster.

"Not if you keep 'em clean."

"Oh, yeah?" Richie G. closed and locked his locker door. "Couple of years ago, I respond to a bullshit landlord-tenant dispute with a couple of other uniforms. We walk into the tenement and two pit bulls attacked."

Half-a-dozen cops in various states of dress had stopped to listen.

"Yeah?" the young, skinny cop said.

"The dogs charge, leap for our throats. One of the uniforms pulls his automatic, it jams. I pulled my .38 and BAM! BAM! Kill both dogs. One shot apiece." Richie G. paused for effect. "Midair."

"Midair?" the skinny cop said. "Wow! Those had to be the luckiest shots ever."

"Luck, my ass." Richie G. stuck a blackjack in a rear pocket. "I'm good." He picked up his nightstick and strutted out of the locker room.

"That was bullshit," a dark-skinned black cop, slipping on his uniform shirt, said.

"What's bullshit?" the skinny cop said.

"Richie G.'s whole story."

"How do you know?"

"You gotta be kidding," the black cop said. "Look, pally, no one—and I mean no one—could shoot two charging pit bulls dead, midair."

"So, he was putting me on?" the rookie said.

"No," the black cop said. "He was lying."

I smiled at the memory. Richie G. and I had become fast friends and sector car partners. Working with him had been a hoot. Yes, he was a world-class BS artist, but he was also one of the best cops I ever knew. I considered writing about one of the first radio runs I'd responded to with Richie G.

It had been another one of those stifling, foggy, rainy summer days. We were working a midnight to 8:00 a.m. tour. Central dispatch was holding around seventy-three jobs. Which meant that seventy-three reports of robberies, burglaries, larcenies, gunfights, and sexual assault had yet to be answered:

"Central to forty-one Ida," came over the radio.

I picked up the transmitter. "Ida."

"Ida, respond to an assault in progress at nine-forty-six Hoe Avenue. That's nine-forty-six Hoe."

"Ask them how old that job is," Richie G. said.

I asked central when the job was called in.

"Five hours ago," central responded.

Richie G. scoffed.

We arrived at the scene: a block of mostly burned-out tenements that resembled photos I'd seen of bombed-out Berlin after World War II. Pulled to the curb, expecting that the complainant who'd called 911 and perpetrators would be long gone. But realized at once that we'd stumbled onto another crime in progress. A small, unruly crowd had gathered on the sidewalk in front of the ramshackle tenement.

As we exited the car, a sweaty fat guy shouted at us in broken English, said that a man had assaulted a young girl and pointed to a dark alley that led to a backyard.

"He went that way."

The father of two daughters, Richie G. snapped to. "Where's the girl?"

"Upstairs with her mother," the fat guy said.

Richie G. used a handheld radio to call for an ambulance. Then asked the fat guy what the assailant looked like.

"Mid-thirties. Five-foot-five. Wearing Army fatigues. He ran down that alley."

"You go around back," Richie G. told me. "I'll count to sixty…."

I put my coffee cup down, sat at my computer, leaned forward, cracked my knuckles. Placed my fingers on the computer keyboard and began to type.

The morning rain soaked the South Bronx an hour before dawn, purging the oil-slick streets and littered sidewalks, shrouding me in misty shadows as I climbed the hurricane fence and dropped into the empty courtyard behind a Hoe Avenue tenement. I pulled my NYPD-issued .38. Scanned the area for signs of guard dogs: chains, leashes, fresh excrement, gnawed bones.

There were none.

I took a deep breath, then picked my way through piles of scorched furniture and fetid kitchen trash that must have been thrown from the apartments above. I heard a noise, turned, and saw a furious Hispanic man come racing from an alley, into the courtyard with a baseball bat in his hand.

"Freeze!" I pointed my weapon.

"Drop the bat!" My partner Richie G. was suddenly behind the guy, his gun extended, his finger on the trigger. "Drop it! Hands in the air."

The guy glanced back at Richie G., then at me; we had him in a crossfire.

"Do it," I said.

The male reluctantly dropped the bat, put his hands up.

I kept the guy covered as Richie G. spun the guy around.

"Hector?" Richie G. holstered his weapon. Picked up the baseball bat. "Fuck's going on?"

"Ricardo Ramirez," Hector raged. "He attacked my daughter, Maria."

I lowered my gun.

"Ramirez?" Richie G. said. "That piece of shit's out of prison?"

"He's been hanging around the block for a week."

"Really?" Richie G. took a thoughtful moment and said, "Come with us."

We sat Hector in the rear of the police car. As an ambulance arrived, we pulled away from the scene, south on Hoe Avenue, hunting Ricardo Ramirez.

"There he is," Hector shouted not five minutes later. He was pointing to a man sitting in a darkened PS 75 schoolyard, smoking a cigarette.

Richie G. hit the gas.

"Where the fuck you going?" Hector exploded. "That's Ramirez."

"I didn't see anyone." Richie G. grinned.

One block later, Richie G. slowed and pulled to the curb. Put the car in park. Turned around and, still grinning, handed Hector his bat. "Have a nice day."

Hector hesitated. Looked at me. Looked at Richie G. Took the bat. "Thank you." He opened the door, stepped out, and double-timed it back to the schoolyard. Richie G. shifted to drive, tapped the gas.

"Ricardo Ramirez," he said, "has been arrested for sexually assaulting kids as young as six years old at least three times. We lock him up, the courts let him go. He'll never stop." He turned onto Southern Boulevard. "Which means it's time for a little street justice. If the courts won't do their job, it's up to us to protect the kids."

"I have no problem with that."

"You'll have even less of a problem once you and your wife have kids."

"That's not gonna happen." I lowered the sound on the police radio. "We're not getting along. I'm thinking of moving out."

"A trial separation?"

"We're beyond that."

"You were gonna tell me this, when?"

"I just told you."

I pushed back from the computer. Got to my feet, walked over to my window, and gazed to the northwest toward the George Washington Bridge and the New Jersey Palisades. I wondered what had become of my first wife, a New Hampshire beauty queen. Had she remarried? Was she happy? I hoped so.

I was a nineteen-year-old sailor, assigned to the guided-missile cruiser, *USS Topeka* CLG 8, which was being decommissioned in the Boston Navy Yard when I met the blue-eyed, blond-haired knockout in a Back Bay restaurant. Spotted her sitting at the upstairs bar with her roommate. Mustered up the courage to claim the stool alongside her and say hello.

A Hampton, New Hampshire native, Diane Elizabeth Hawthorne had been high school homecoming queen and —she was quick to inform me—a direct descendant of *The Scarlet Letter* author Nathaniel Hawthorne. Thinking back, while the girlfriend I'd left behind after joining the Navy had been attractive, I'd never been in the presence of a breath-stealing beauty before. Although Diane's eye-popping looks belied her reserved, prim and proper manner. I recall being surprised when she seemed to be receptive to my bungling advances. Took a chance and offered to buy the two roommates a round of drinks. The bartender set us up. We toasted. By the third round Diane, an entry-level secretary in an insurance company, gave me her phone number. What followed was a hormone-fueled, whirlwind love affair. Sunset walks, picnics and concerts along the Charles River and the Boston Commons. Rendezvous for a drink at places I couldn't afford, like Locke-Ober, the Union Oyster House, and Anthony's Pier 4. Listening to live music until the wee hours in the pubs in Kenmore Square. Crazy as it sounds, we dated for only three months before, much to the consternation of her tight-assed, Yankee father, we eloped. Got married in a civil ceremony in Newport, Rhode Island. A Navy buddy, Dominick Porco, was my best man—oh, the folly of youth. We moved to 59 Pickney Street, a studio apartment on snooty but glamorous Beacon Hill. Lived there until I was discharged from the Navy. Diane wanted us to stay in Boston. But I wanted to join the NYPD. And so, I dragged her kicking and screaming to a five-floor walk-up in my hometown. I was sworn into the NYPD a short time later.

I don't recall how long it took, but once out of her element, my usually reserved bride became an emotional wreck; insecure, high-strung, combative with abandonment and trust issues. She also didn't handle her alcohol well.

"Who died and left you boss?" she'd bark after a few vodka tonics, having had enough of my adolescent "Me Tarzan, you Jane" attitude. We argued about everything from choices of restaurants, music venues, movies, to my friends; she thoroughly disapproved of my friends.

"You don't understand," I explained to her repeatedly. "Richie G.'s not just my partner, he's one of my best friends. I trust him with my life."

"I don't care," Diane said. "I don't want that nigger in the house."

Talk about irreconcilable differences.

There were other issues, of course. Nathaniel "Nate" Hawthorne, her alcoholic and suicidal father—he'd made two attempts—was an avowed Protestant who hated Irish Catholics. Hated me. Then there was her punk kid brother, who referred to cops as pigs. Diane had stopped me from putting him through a wall more than once.

In the end, I realized that I was in over my head. I had no idea how to handle someone with deep-seated emotional problems; I knew I'd never make Diane happy. I began to look for excuses not to go home. Worked as much overtime with the NYPD as possible. No longer cut any slack to borderline criminality. I locked everyone up, much to Richie G.'s delight. Became one of the top "collar men" in Fort Apache. Eventually, I packed my bags. Moved in with a cop buddy.

Diane's plan was to move back to Boston. Which was fine with me. I even drove her to the airport. That self-serving good deed led to a life-changing chance encounter with a group of attractive, wild and crazy young stewardesses who would help me out of my post-divorce funk and introduce me to the airline-employee saturated Kew Gardens section of Queens—a mere twenty-minute drive from Fort Apache. There I would revel in the singles scene and, for the first time, come face-to-face with diabolical, high profile, criminal infamy.

Chapter 2

THE GREAT PIERRE HOTEL ROBBERY was still on the news when I moved into a Kew Gardens' "stew zoo." (An apartment rented by groups of stewardesses). The $3 million (worth $27 million today) heist would later be listed in the *Guinness Book of World Records* as the largest, most successful hotel robbery in history. New Yorkers were griping that the subway fare had been raised to — gasp! — 35 cents. And the Black Liberation Army, emboldened by liberal politicians' war on cops, assassinated two police officers, Gregory Foster, and Rocco Laurie, in the East Village.

It was during my first few months in the Silver Towers, a 420-unit, white-glove doorman building that, besides meeting dozens of young, attractive, and carefree airline stewardesses, I met superstar thoroughbred horse trainer and future high profile murderer, Howard "Buddy" Jacobson. Not that the high school dropout and former merchant marine was living there. Jacobson spent his time at his 300-acre horse farm on Long Island, or Vermont ski lodge, or his two tenements on Manhattan's Upper East Side. But his ex-wife, Joan Miller, and two sons, David and Douglas, were residents, and Jacobson visited often. Buddy and I would attend many of the same airline parties in the various stew zoos and singles bars—Salty Dog, 10 Downing Street, Pep McGuire's—scattered around Kew Gardens. It was in one of those bars that I'd first meet Jack Tupper, an acquaintance of Buddy's who would become a tragic figure in both our lives.

A bunch of us off-duty cops were attending a rousing beer bash at the Forest Hills Town House; there were three stews for every guy. Buddy Jacobson, who always dressed like a homeless person, and I were hitting on a couple of American Airlines stews when I was approached by two cop friends, Norman K. and Kyle S.

"We're heading up the road to the Sherwood Inn," Norman K. said. "A couple of friends of mine own the place. Some wiseguys are trying to take it over. Things could get hairy."

"Whose car we taking?" I said.

"Isn't that Jack Tupper's place?" Jacobson said.

Kyle S. and Norman K. said it was.

Jacobson smirked. "We wouldn't want anything to happen to Jack." He ran a hand though his shaggy, uncombed hair. "Now would we?"

"Meaning, what?" Norman K. challenged him.

"Nothing."

Since I'd witnessed Jacobson's brash ruthlessness when it came to matters of the heart, I figured the snide remark had something to do with him and this guy Jack Tupper competing for women. From what I'd read in the newspapers, Jacobson's arrogance and questionable ethics were among the reasons he was no longer training racehorses; he'd been run out of that business.

The Sherwood Inn on Lefferts Boulevard turned out to be a short walk. Norman K. and Kyle S. lit cigarettes — I never smoked in my life — as we buttoned up our coats and shrugged up our collars.

"Gotta make a stop first," Norman K. said.

Kyle S. and I waited outside, backs turned to a brisk March wind, as Norman K. entered a liquor store. Came out a few minutes later with two bottles of rye and two bottles of vodka.

"Bringing booze to a restaurant?" I said.

"Jack ran out," Norman K. said.

"No way," Kyle S. laughed. "How's that even possible?"

Norman K. just shrugged. "That's Jack."

The Sherwood Inn had the look of an old English tavern. A moonlighting stewardess we knew was working the door. She greeted us warmly, asking if we wanted a table. We said no and headed to the crowded, smoky bar, squeezed in between a group of firefighters we knew and an elderly couple visiting from Ireland. Tony Bennett crooned over the sound system that he'd left his heart in San Francisco.

Norman K. handed the store-bought booze to the bartender, an infamous 495-pound bookmaker, Fats Thomas. The Pulitzer Prize–winning *New York Daily News* columnist Jimmy Breslin, who I'd heard was a lifelong friend of Fats, was sitting at the bar with several known racketeers. Their female companions looked cartoonish with their heavy makeup, bouffant hairdos, and tacky cocktail dresses, overdressed for a neighborhood pub.

"Isn't that Donald Brown?" I pointed to a thirtysomething, well-dressed, deeply tanned guy sitting at a table with two attractive ladies. I knew Brown as an amiable, quirky, frantic character from the neighborhood. Also knew that he was a major drug dealer—hash and marijuana only. No hard stuff.

"That's him." Norman K. lit another cigarette. "He's one of Jack's partners."

I let that sink in. An infamous bookmaker as a bartender. Racketeers as customers. A drug dealer as a partner. No wonder the Mob thought they could take over.

Someone began to sing "Happy Birthday." A table of six rowdy stewardesses we knew from Silver Towers were whooping it up in the crowded dining room. A singing waiter delivered a birthday cake, candles blazing. Half-a-dozen birthday balloons tied to the back of their chairs festooned the table.

At the end of the bar, Jack Tupper, a commanding, fit and tough-looking six-footer, applauded along with the rest of us after the birthday song. Attired in an expensive-looking blue blazer and open collar dress shirt, his eyes swept the restaurant, making sure no customers were being neglected.

"Hey, Jack," Norman K. said.

Shaking a few hands and schmoozing along the way, Jack made his way over to where we were sitting and greeted Norman K. and Kyle S. enthusiastically.

"Say hello to Thomas Fitzsimmons," Norman K. said.

"Thanks for coming, Thomas," Jack said as we shook.

Norman K. said, "The crew of assholes from last week, they been back?"

Jack shook his head. "Not yet."

"A bunch of them came in. Drunk," Norman K. explained to me and Kyle S. "They got loud. Chesty. A couple of them laid their guns on the bar, out in the open."

"You were here?" I said.

Norman K. nodded. "They realized I was a cop. Backed off."

"We got lucky," Jack said.

"What about those guys?" Kyle S. gestured to the racketeers and their painted ladies sitting with Jimmy Breslin.

Jack shook his head. "They're from a different crew. Friends of Fats."

We ordered drinks and I scoped out the place. It was English Tudor cozy. A decent size. Lots of wood. Oval wine barrel–type fixtures sticking out from one wall. Low sherry-colored lighting.

"They ever tell you what they want?" Norman K. said.

Jack shrugged. "Twenty-five hundred a week for protection, or else."

At 2:45 a.m. a group of suit and tie–clad, central casting wiseguys burst in and bellied up to the now almost empty bar. The firefighters, elderly Irish couple, Jimmy Breslin, and the racketeers were long gone. The wiseguys said a loud and cheerful hello to Fats and then ordered drinks. I looked across the room to where Jack and Donald Brown were sitting at the table with the inebriated stewardesses. Jack, his eyes on the wiseguys, had gone visibly pale. Donald Brown seemed to shrink into himself.

I elbowed Norman K. "Know them?"

Norman K. nodded. "They were Pep McGuire's regulars when Fats worked the bar. The young one's Henry Hill. Tommy DeSimone's the big guy. The boss is Jimmy 'the Gent' Burke."

None of us had any idea at the time, but they were part of the Mob that would commit the infamous JFK Lufthansa heist in 1978 — billed as the biggest cash robbery in United States history. The robbery, the proceeds of which were never recovered, was glorified in the Academy Award–winning, 1990 Martin Scorsese movie *Goodfellas*. Ray Liotta would play Henry Hill. Five-foot-four Joe Pesci assumed the role of the burly, six-two Tommy DeSimone. Robert De Niro portrayed Jimmy "the Gent" Burke.

Criminals know cops when they see them; it's in their DNA. And so, the wiseguys eyeballed Kyle S. and me — they already knew Norman K. — trying to figure out if we were on duty, or off duty enjoying a few cocktails, or there on Jack Tupper's behalf. After a while, they quieted down, spoke among themselves in muted, conspiratorial conversation.

About an hour later I checked the time, decided I'd had enough to drink, that the Mob guys wouldn't make a move on Jack with us there. I was thinking of excusing myself, heading home, letting Norman K. and Kyle S. handle things, when all of a sudden Tommy DeSimone—the Joe Pesci character—shot to his feet, pointed at Kyle S., and yelled down the length of the bar, "What the fuck're you lookin' at?"

Everyone froze. The other Mob guys swung around and stared angrily at us, backing up DeSimone's play, although it was obvious to me that they had no idea what DeSimone was up to. Not that it mattered. They'd back him no matter what.

"Me?" Kyle S. said.

"Yeah, fuckhead," DeSimone said. "You."

Now, understand that Kyle S. had a quirky sense of humor belied by a short fuse and unpredictably violent temper. I'm not exaggerating when I say that, if provoked, Kyle S. was capable of anything. And I mean *anything*. Norman K. and I focused our attention on DeSimone's crew, watching their hands. I was thinking things could go sideways fast when Kyle S. surprised everyone by saying:

"I'm looking at you, handsome." Kyle S. smiled at DeSimone. "I think you're cute. If I was a broad, I'd go for you."

Holy shit.

I held my breath, waiting for DeSimone's reaction. He glanced at his posse. A couple of them shrugged. He tossed back a shot of booze. Slammed the shot glass down on the bar and glared at Kyle S. —who wiggled his eyebrows and blew DeSimone a kiss.

DeSimone broke out laughing. His Mob cohorts nervously followed suit. The tension in the room evaporated. Conversations resumed.

Tony Bennett, or maybe it was Jerry Vale, began to sing, "Al Di Là."

I relaxed my gun hand.

"Fats," DeSimone said to the bartender. "Set 'em up. And buy my new fuckin' friends over there a fuckin' drink."

We spent the next few hours hanging with the wiseguys. Buying each other rounds of drinks. Making small talk: the fucking Mets, Knicks, Jets, and Giants. Who favored what make and model of car. Where was the best place to meet women in Manhattan. Where to get the best Italian food in Queens. All and all, the night ended peacefully without further incident.

"If it weren't for the fact that those guys are murderers," Donald Brown said, gesturing to the wiseguys as they stumbled out of the bar, crossed Lefferts Boulevard, and climbed into their cars, "we could all be friends."

"Are you nuts?" Jack said. He switched off the bar lights. Ushered us, along with Fats Thomas, his waiters, and other employees outside, then used his keys to lock the front door.

"At least," Kyle S. said, "they won't bother you again."

"Let's hope," Fats Thomas said, waddled down the street and got into his car.

I sucked in a breath of cold air and scanned Lefferts Boulevard. Eyes and ears alert for sounds or sudden movement just in case our "new friends" decided to double back and ambush us.

"See you around," Jack said as he, Kyle S., and Donald Brown walked west toward the Forest Hills Town House. They would most likely stop at the cop-owned Salty Dog on Metropolitan Avenue for a nightcap. Norman K. and I headed east toward Queens Boulevard and the Silver Towers.

Loud, angry voices.

"Oh, hell." Norman K. pulled me into a movie theater's doorway.

"What is it?"

Norman K. pointed.

Across the street, two women and a man were staggering along Austin Street—probably coming from the Austin Ale House —and stopped at the corner. The women were really going at it. Cursing each other. Getting physical. A tall, strapping guy was doing his best to get between them, calm them down.

"Hey," I said, straining to focus my boozy eyes. "Isn't that John G. from narcotics and…"

"Claire," Norman K. said. "That's Claire. His partner."

"Isn't Claire…?"

Norman K. nodded. "My sister. She and John G. are an item. Or were. The other broad's Ellen. Jack Tupper's ex-wife."

"Guy I just met?" I gestured back to the Sherwood Inn.

"The same," Norman K. said.

I let that sink in.

Claire suddenly shouted that Ellen was a man-stealing whore. Ellen said that Claire was a slut that fucked half the cops in Queens. Ellen shoved her. Claire snapped, pulled a .38. Pointed it at Ellen Tupper's head.

"Oh, shit," I said.

"Don't move," Norman K. said.

John G. started begging and pleading with Claire to stop. Put the gun down. Please put the gun down. "Claire. Don't do this. Please."

Norman K. said, "Claire shoots Ellen, she'll probably shoot John G. too."

I looked at Norman K. He wasn't kidding.

It was then that lights flicked on in several high-rise apartments. Curtains parted. Windows opened. People stuck their heads out, looking down to the street.

"Someone's gonna dial nine-one-one," I said.

"Forget that," Norman K. said. "Remember Kitty Genovese?"

Back in the wee hours of March 13, 1964, Kitty Genovese, a twenty-eight-year-old bartender, was stabbed to death outside the Austin Ale House. Fifty feet from where John G., Claire K. and Ellen Tupper were arguing. Reportedly, thirty-seven witnesses saw or heard the brutal attack. Not one had called the police or come to the victim's aid. They didn't want to get involved. Only in the last month, twenty-five-year-old Sandra Zahler, a licensed cosmetologist, was beaten to death in the apartment house across the street from the Genovese murder scene. Again, neighbors said they heard screams and a "fierce struggle," but did nothing. Bottom line: No one was about to call the police in that Queens neighborhood.

Claire reluctantly lowered her weapon.

Ellen collapsed to the pavement in tears.

John G. snatched Claire's weapon. Stuck it in his pocket.

"Let's get the hell out of here," Norman K. said.

Our heads low, hands in our pockets, we emerged from the movie house doorway. Backtracked past the Sherwood Inn, taking the long way home to the Silver Towers.

Chapter 3

"Got a minute?" Jack Tupper said to me a few months later. I was seated at the bar at the Sherwood Inn. A cop friend and I were yucking it up with two probationary stewardesses who hailed from Dallas, Texas. Mine was a heartbreaker with a toothpaste commercial smile. My cop friend's was a curvy munchkin. The place was packed. Clouds of cigarette smoke hung in the air. Fats Thomas was bartending. Buddy Jacobson, looking like an unmade bed, was seated at a table with a group of stews. The Rolling Stones were lamenting that they couldn't get any satisfaction.

Jack gestured that I should join him outside. I told the ladies I'd be right back. Wondering what was on Jack's mind—had he heard about Claire K. pulling a gun and threatening to murder his ex-wife? Had the future Lufthansa heist gang—Henry Hill, Tommy DeSimone, and Jimmy "the Gent" Burke—resumed their attempted shakedown?

The Stones' music faded as Jack and I stepped out onto Lefferts Boulevard. The weather was a clear, crisp 65 degrees. There was very little pedestrian or vehicular traffic.

Jack lit a Marlboro Red and took a long pull. "It's Yolanda." He blew out the smoke. "I think she's cheating on me."

"Sorry to hear that," I said, wondering why Jack was confiding something so personal to me. I mean, I didn't know him that well or that long. Sure, Jack, a one-woman-man kind of guy, had introduced me to the then love of his life, Yolanda, a

Pan Am flight attendant and RN who spoke a couple of languages. An exotic beauty, she was a stylish, outgoing flirt I didn't take seriously.

"I want to catch her in the act."

"What?" I said. "Like dating another guy?"

"In bed with him."

"What the hell for?"

Jack shrugged. He looked off, an odd expression on his face. "Will you do it?"

"Do what?"

"Break into her apartment. Take pictures."

I looked at him. He was serious. "You nuts?"

"Maybe." Jack shrugged. "A little."

"Have you talked to Yolanda?"

"No."

"Why not?"

Jack sucked in a lung full of smoke. "Will you do it?"

"Of course not. Want some advice?"

"No."

"Talk to Yolanda."

"Thanks for nothing." Jack dumped his cigarette, ground it out with his foot, and walked back into the bar. I followed him in, saw that my heartbreaker with the toothpaste commercial smile had taken up with a firefighter friend.

I heard a few weeks later that Jack confronted Yolanda about her infidelity. After a heated argument she dumped him for the other guy. Jack took it hard, lapsed into a spiraling depression, and was hospitalized for a short time. I didn't know it at the time, but Jack's obsessive behavior toward lovers was a harbinger of things to come.

Though Jack and Donald Brown later sold the Sherwood Inn — I don't think they ever made a profit — I saw Jack often. We frequented many of the same parties and bars in Kew Gardens' stew zoos. We also patronized the same Manhattan restaurants and bars that were frequented by the city's most glamorous females; TGI Fridays, Adam's Apple, and Maxwell's Plum where, around the time Jack sold the Sherwood Inn, I'd first meet and befriend Donald Trump.

An upscale, glittering watering hole, Maxwell's Plum—with its outlandish Art Nouveau decor, kaleidoscopic stained glass ceilings and walls, Tiffany lamps galore, and a menagerie of ceramic animals — was the undisputed showcase of New York City's singles scene. A gilded international celebrity hangout, Maxwell's was packed nightly with young, beautiful models, actresses, and leggy stewardesses.

One evening a boyishly handsome, thirtysomething guy in a dark business suit entered Maxwell's Plum, scanned the crowd, then hustled over to three hotties seated at the bar to my right; the same three that Kyle S. and I were eyeballing.

"Hi," I heard the guy stammer to the women. "My name is Donald Trump."

I recognized Donald's accent as Brooklyn/Queens and him as a Maxwell's Plum regular. And I could tell by his awkward manner that there was no way he'd score with the three ladies. Kyle S. and I traded conspiratorial glances and made a move.

"Good to see you again, Donald," I said as Kyle S., and I claimed the stools on either side of the ladies. "How've you been?"

Donald gave me the once-over; we'd never met.

"I'm Kyle. That handsome guy in the blue suit is Thomas. And I see you've already met Donald." The elegant, twentysomething Southern belles — a blonde, brunette, and redhead — introduced themselves. Said they were high school teachers from Tennessee visiting NYC for the weekend. Kyle told them we were in the restaurant/bar business. We never told anyone we'd just met that we were cops.

"May we buy you ladies a drink?" Kyle S. said. "You too, Donald."

I guess Donald liked our act because he decided to play along. After all, there were three of them and three of us.

"I'll have a virgin Mary," Donald said, his eyes on the blonde.

Two rounds of drinks later, Kyle S., his tie loosened like a lounge singer, was serenading us with a pretty good rendition of the Jay Black classic, "Cara Mia," when Donald interrupted.

"See the article about me that ran in last month's *New York Times*?"

Kyle S. stopped singing. There was an awkward silence.

"We didn't," one of the ladies drawled. Donald reached into his suit jacket pocket and handed us photocopies of an article written by one Judy Klemesrud and dated November 1, 1976.

The article—DONALD TRUMP, REAL ESTATE PROMOTER, BUILDS IMAGE AS HE BUYS BUILDINGS—featured photos of Donald sitting in his Upper East Side, three-bedroom apartment and getting into a silver Cadillac with a set of vanity license plates bearing his initials, DJT.

Klemesrud wrote: *He is tall, lean and blond, with dazzling white teeth, and he looks ever so much like Robert Redford.* The article said that Donald started working in the family real estate business when he was only twelve years old and that he had graduated first in his class from the Wharton School. He claimed that he was worth more than $200 million and that he had recently made a financial killing in California, where he claimed he owned a Beverly Hills mansion. *"I've probably made $14 million in California over the last two years,"* he was quoted as saying.

I finished reading the article, handed it back. "I guess you can afford to buy a round of drinks, then?"

Donald beamed. "Of course."

The Southern belles were most impressed. And thinking we were Donald's friends, impressed with us. We all scored that weekend.

From that evening on, whenever I was in Manhattan and the opportunity presented itself, I'd team up with Kyle S. and Donald to infiltrate the dense packs of females that frequented the singles bars on the Upper East Side. As a matter of fact, over the years, Donald and I wound up dating several of the same women. Who would have guessed that in the not-too-distant future, he'd become engaged to and eventually marry my former fiancée, Marla Maples.

Chapter 4

The recession, which started in the early 1970s, along with an oil and steel crisis, caused an economic shift in America. Major cities, like New York, were operating in the red. Mayor Abe Beame planned to lay off 8,200 city employees, 1,500 of them police officers. Already overworked, underpaid, and frustrated with the revolving-door system of justice, I was beginning to have serious doubts about remaining a cop.

Then skyrocketing fuel prices triggered airline layoffs. I felt left behind during the next few years as I watched the Kew Gardens stewardess population dwindle and many of my friends make the move to Manhattan's Upper East Side. Which was where the action was. But rent in Manhattan was high and a police officer's pay was low. We'd been working without a contract for years, and the city was not negotiating in good faith. A cop with four kids was living below the poverty level. Every family man I knew held down two jobs. (My partner, Richie G., drove a yellow cab forty hours a week.) Which meant that for me to be able to afford Manhattan, I'd have to get a second job, or quit the NYPD and find a more lucrative way to make a living.

I thought about asking Donald for a job, but I knew squat about the construction trades. Jack Tupper had offered me and Norman K. a piece of a new Manhattan restaurant/bar that he was prospecting. But I had no source of financing. Buddy Jacobson offered me a gig managing the Vermont ski lodge. But I had no relevant experience. Jacobson said that didn't matter, that I could always learn the ropes. I was pretty sure he'd offered the same position to several others before me. I thought about a career as a private investigator, but I had no idea how to acquire clients and my head and heart wouldn't be in it.

I became anxiety ridden. Couldn't sleep at night. At the 41st Precinct, Richie G. commented that I was becoming too short-tempered with the citizenry, too ready to use my fists—that, coming from the likes of Richie G., was a wake-up call.

To help me deal with the pressure, I decided to focus on getting in the best physical shape possible. Jack Tupper, Kyle S., Norman K., and I began a routine of running three to five miles a day around Kew Gardens' Forest Park. We lifted weights. Boxed. But my focus shifted when a crazy they dubbed "the .44 Caliber Killer" started terrorizing the city.

Even though the crimes were committed in Queens, a goodly number of us Bronx cops volunteered our off-duty time hunting the deranged killer. Civilians, like Jack Tupper, assisted us by accompanying unescorted female restaurant/bar patrons home at night. Jack and I actually wound up in short-term relationships with a pair of American Airlines stewardesses that we'd escorted to their Kew Gardens apartments.

It's difficult to impart the fear that gripped the five boroughs during those days. For a year the .44 Caliber Killer's crimes were in the news virtually every day. Son of Sam would wind up shooting or stabbing thirteen victims: killing six, wounding seven. He would leave a bizarre handwritten letter at one crime scene, then write a letter to *New York Daily News* columnist Jimmy Breslin — who had been a regular at the Sherwood Inn — taunting the police for their failed efforts to capture him.

In the end, Son of Sam was caught by old-fashioned shoe-leather police work. Baffled and desperate, police began checking parking tickets issued at the various murder scenes — a long shot, to say the least — giving special attention to license plates registered to other localities. Fortunately, Son of Sam had indeed received a parking ticket at the scene of his last and final murder. A police background check revealed that one David Berkowitz of Yonkers was a US Army veteran and fit the serial killer's general description. He was arrested at his home without incident and readily confessed to all the crimes. Then two oddball things happened in quick succession.

I was notified that the NYPD's Internal Affairs Division, IAD, had begun investigating me for dealing drugs and guns in New Jersey. A big laugh since, not counting Newark Airport, I couldn't recall ever having been in New Jersey. But after receiving copies of the actual allegations, I was pretty sure I knew who the informer was.

Remember those two American Airlines stewardesses that Jack Tupper and I dated? To say that mine was angered when I stopped calling her—I couldn't deal with her unfiltered rudeness to restaurant waitstaff, among other issues—was an understatement. She went bonkers, threatened to tell the NYPD that, since we'd once smoked a joint together, and Jack had turned her and her roommate on to some coke, I was a drug dealer. But when Jack Tupper's name was mentioned, I began to wonder if the investigation had something to do with my connection to Jack and the drug dealer Donald Brown. Although, admittedly I saw the investigation as one big joke, I made sure that I was represented by a union attorney when I was interviewed by two moderately hostile IAD investigators. I cooperated fully. Volunteered to give blood and urine samples.

A few months later, after the IAD investigation had petered out, I was stunned to receive an official IRS summons in the mail. What the hell? I tore open the envelope. The one-page letter stated that I was being audited. Which didn't make much sense, since cops are civil servants and are issued a W-2. Our very limited deductions are standard and never questioned. But I soon found out that their interest in me had nothing to do with my tax returns and everything to do with Jack Tupper.

"Not to worry," the IRS auditor said with a warm, friendly smile. "It's a numbers game. We have to audit a number of police officers every year."

He was in his forties, graying at the temples, dressed in a suit and tie.

He opened a folder, asked questions about my deductions, uniform purchases, cleanings, and maintenance. Bullets for the shooting range.

"I see you live in Kew Gardens," he said. "I used to live there. Frequented a restaurant called Sherwood Inn. Know it?"

"Sure," I said. "I was sorry to see it close."

"Know Jack Tupper?"

"I do. Good guy."

"Tell me what you know about him?"

I stopped. Regarded the auditor. "What do you mean?"

"You know his partner, Donald Brown?"

I saw where this was going. "Sure. But not well."

"So, you know Jack better?"

"Look," I said, getting annoyed. "Jack's a friend. We work out together sometimes. We've dated roommates. I don't know anything about his business."

The auditor backed off. "No reason to get defensive. I'm just making conversation."

"Let me ask you a question," I said. "You really IRS or DEA?"

The guy hemmed and hawed, continued reviewing my tax return, but never answered my question.

"You have tax problems?" I asked Jack a few hours later. We were in Forest Park, stretching, preparing for our run. Waiting for Kyle S. and Norman K., who was always maddeningly late.

"No," Jack said. "Why?"

I told him about the IRS agent that asked me questions about him.

"What'd you tell him?" Jack said, somewhat alarmed.

"Hell do you mean? I told him the truth. We're friends. I don't know shit about your business."

"That's all?" Jack was skeptical.

"Yeah," I said. "That's all."

Chapter 5

"Pull up ahead," Richie G. said, seething. "Park at the hydrant."
"Why?" I said. "What's going on?"
"Just do it!"
It was mid-January, about five past midnight. The temperature was a bone-chilling 5 degrees. Richie had just stepped into the passenger side of my VW bug, a bag of junk food and sodas in hand. We were stopped in front of a bodega on Intervale Avenue, on our way to a "fixer"—we were working a midnight to 8:00 a.m. tour, assigned to guard a high school that had been burglarized with inane regularity. Not that we were complaining. We were looking forward to a stress-free night off the mean streets, putting our feet up and relaxing alongside a steaming radiator.
I shifted to first gear, tapped the gas, and pulled to the curb.
Richie G. kept his eyes on the rearview mirrors.
I knew better than to ask any more questions. Knew my partner well enough to know that someone in the bodega where he'd purchased the junk food had disrespected him in some grievous way. And they were about to pay the price.
Street justice.
I thought for a moment about jamming the car in gear and racing away from the scene, defusing the situation before the violence began. After all, Richie G. had told me that I'd grown short-tempered, so he'd have to understand. Right?
But Richie went rigid as two burly thugs strolled out of the bodega. Coats and collars zipped up. Watch caps pulled down

over their ears. They stuck their hands in their pockets, braced themselves against the winter wind, and walked in our direction. Richie G. stepped out of my car. He was on them in an instant. Cracked the taller thug across the face with a right cross. A rib-breaking uppercut put the shorter one down on the frozen sidewalk.

"Let's go," Richie G. said as he stepped back into my vehicle.

There was chaos at the 41st Precinct when we arrived the next evening. Seems that two men, accompanied by superior officers from Internal Affairs, were in the station house screaming they'd been brutally assaulted on Intervale Avenue by a uniformed police officer the evening before. Claimed that they could identify him. A lineup was being held in the first-floor sitting room.

I bolted to the fourth-floor locker room. Took my time changing into uniform. Waiting impatiently for Richie G. to show up. Knew that if he stood the lineup and was identified I could very well be arrested and charged as an accessory.

I overheard Richie before I saw him. He was bragging to a couple of rookies in the next aisle about the time he engaged in a running gun battle with a team of Bronx bank robbers. A face-to-face gun battle reminiscent of the shoot-out at the O.K. Corral.

Truth was that Richie was present when two masked gunmen barged into the bank, fired shotguns into the ceiling, and ordered everyone to lay face down on the ground. But Richie took no police action. He dropped down to the cold tile floor like everyone else. Didn't identify himself as a cop until the robbers, $20,000 richer, were long gone. Why he continued to retell outrageous, verifiable BS stories would always puzzle me.

"Hey, dog breath," Richie G. said to me as he came whistling down the aisle. He dialed the combination to his locker, slipped out of his coat, hung it up.

I lowered my voice. Checked to see that the rookies couldn't eavesdrop. "We have a problem." I closed my locker. Locked it. "Those guys from the bodega ...?"

"Are morons," Richie G. said. "They got the timing wrong." He went on to say that the thugs were claiming that they'd been assaulted around 11:00 p.m. Positively. Which meant that yesterday's four to midnight tour were standing in the lineup.

"We didn't turn out until midnight." Richie grinned. "So, we have nothing to worry about."

"Hope you're right," I said.

"I'm right."

We remained out of sight, in the locker room until the lineup was completed.

I sustained a back injury about five months later making an armed robbery arrest.

It was a sweltering July day. We were prowling down Whitlock Avenue, which paralleled the overhead Bruckner Expressway. Hit men sometimes dumped their victims amid garbage and abandoned cars, in the foreboding darkness under the overpass.

Richie G. spied a mocha-skinned hooker wearing an obscenely short dress and six-inch stiletto heels. She nasty-strutted across the avenue, gave us an eyelash-singeing stare, then moved on, hips waving adieu.

"Wow." Richie was bug-eyed. "You see that?"

"I'm a former altar boy. I'd be struck blind."

"She wants me."

"She wants everyone."

Richie tapped the horn.

The hooker gave him the finger.

"Maybe I should get her phone number," Richie said. "The two of us could bang her like screen doors in a hurricane."

"I don't do threesomes. You know that."

"Not *us*, you idiot." Richie swung the car into an oncoming lane. Cut back. Hit the accelerator. "Me and the beast." He grabbed his penis.

My shoulders sagged and I groaned with remembered boredom. "Oh, yeah. How could I forget the beast?"

"Women don't forget. Oh, no." Richie's smile broadened. "You can ask my wife. I'm not bragging. Just telling the truth. Face it. I'm a great lay. And I'm cute." Richie honked the horn and screamed at a slowpoke driver to get the fuck out of his way. "Just look at this face. Women see me, they want me. It's a curse I've had to live with all my life. And I'm hung like a T. rex. I got a tongue I could lick a fly off a wall with from six feet."

"And you're modest," I said.

"Physical perfection, matched with deep humility."

"That's it." I smiled tolerantly.

We turned onto Longfellow Avenue. Block after block rolled by. Every crumbling building had a fire escape, and every fire escape window was gated in an attempt to keep the predators out.

Richie slowed to avoid scores of children, who pranced and splashed in a gushing stream of water, courtesy of an illegally open fire hydrant. By law, we were supposed to close the hydrant, thereby maintaining the lifesaving water pressure in case of yet another tenement fire.

Richie stopped the car. "We should shut that off."

I looked at the children, who were shrieking with joy, momentarily relieved from the mosquito-drenched heat and humidity. I shook my head. We drove on.

I checked out the mass of humanity along the avenue and wondered how the slumlords got away with it: hot-bedding the tenement apartments. Renting the same squalid, un-air-conditioned dwelling in eight-hour shifts to three separate immigrant families. Charging each the full rent, of course. The other sixteen hours, the off-shift families had no place to go.

Many congregated on the streets, played cards, dominoes. A few drank the heat of the day away, drowning their poverty and aimless lives in cheap booze. While others resorted to indiscriminate sex and sporadic acts of wanton violence.

Richie turned onto 165th Street.

We spotted a known youth gang member shove a citizen into a tenement doorway and hold a knife to his throat. I told Richie to pull ahead, park out of sight beside a double-parked delivery truck.

"He's gotta be stoned," Richie said. "Pulling a stunt like that in broad daylight."

We slipped out of the car. Using the swarming pedestrian crowd as cover, we approached the doorway. Richie pulled his gun, stood to the side, and gave me a nod.

"Hey." I charged. Drove my shoulder into the punk. The knife flew from his hand as we crashed through a vestibule door. Hit the ground hard. I felt the muscles in my upper back snap. Not good. Richie came in behind me, rolled our prisoner over, and cuffed him.

He looked down at me, offered a hand. "You okay?"

I shook my head.

"I'll get you an ambulance."

After an x-ray, a doctor at Jacobi Hospital said I'd sustained a serious whiplash injury. As a result, I was temporarily transferred from the 41st Precinct, placed on desk duty at One Police Plaza in the building maintenance division. Spent the next few months working in a clean, air-conditioned office in civilian clothes.

Although I found that I missed Richie G. and others in our squad, I did not miss the ghetto. The very thought of one day returning to Fort Apache, putting on the uniform, dealing with the endless violence, unrelenting poverty, and despair, twisted my stomach.

One night after work I met Norman K. and Kyle S. at the Salty Dog. Kibitzed with a few regulars. Purchased drinks for several stewardesses. After finishing my third Irish whiskey, I said good night to everyone, drove home, checked my mail, unlocked my apartment, and felt a welcome blast of frigid air. I stripped off my clothes, got under the covers, and decided I didn't want to be a cop anymore. I lay there in the safety of the cold darkness, stared at the ceiling, and listened to the hum of the air conditioner.

Chapter 6

THERE WAS NO ONE I could talk to about my decision to quit the NYPD. My family would think I'd lost my mind. Richie G. would say I was going through a phase. Then there was the reality that I still had no idea how I'd make a living.

Out of desperation, I decided that maybe I should give school a try. Using the G.I. Bill, I enrolled in Stony Brook University, signed up for night school, and chose business as a major. But after only a week I found myself unable to sit still in class and pay attention. I was still suffering from those childhood learning disabilities.

I stopped going to class. Slacked off on my physical fitness routine. Spent more time partying in the pubs than I used to. Woke up one morning after a Halloween party to a dreadful hangover, an unfamiliar female dressed as a Catholic nun lying on one side of me; a frequently pierced, tattooed circus freak who called herself Ophelia on the other side. I decided things couldn't get worse. That was when fate tossed me a lifeline.

A chance meeting at a dinner party with a movie press agent would change my life.

Kyle S., who'd fallen in love with and married an Eastern Airlines flight attendant, invited me to a Christmas party at his apartment in Queens, where he introduced me to Chuck and Lynn Jones. Chuck, a former Marine and Vietnam veteran, was the East Coast head of publicity for Avco Embassy Pictures.

Kyle S. and I regaled Chuck with NYPD war stories. Which Chuck said would make a good movie. I told him that I was thinking of writing a book based on my experiences. Chuck said he'd like to read it and then embarrassed me by saying he thought I was heroic "leading man" good-looking and asked if I'd ever considered modeling or acting. I thought he was kidding. He gave me his phone number, said that if I ever wanted to give it a shot, he'd help me get started.

I called Chuck a few days later. Told him that I was most interested in modeling and acting. That week he arranged for me to meet a professional photographer friend of his who would shoot my model's portfolio. To say I was excited was putting it mildly.

I put on one of my best suits, and met with the photographer, Alex Wasinski at his sun-filled, industrial-style studio on West Twenty-second Street. The walls were covered with poster-sized photos of advertising campaigns he'd worked on: Gillette, Budweiser, Salem cigarettes, Maybelline makeup, etc. Robust, well cared for potted plants grew in front of large windows. Alex, an ox of a man, greeted me as I walked in, shook my hand, and gestured to a chair in front of his large desk. An affable former Marine who served with Chuck in Vietnam, Alex explained the portfolio shooting process—it would require at least one full day. I was expected to bring several changes of clothes. We agreed on a price. Then he broke out a bottle of Russian vodka to celebrate. He poured me a vodka, rocks, twist, and suggested I stick around for a while.

"What for?"

"I'm casting an ad for a lingerie company. Having a go-see."

"A go-see?"

"That's when models come to the studio. Show me their portfolios. The ones who are right for the job try on the lingerie. I shoot a Polaroid and send it to the client." Alex drank some vodka. "The way you're dressed—" he gestured to my suit— "they'll think you're the client."

I liked the sound of that.

For the next few hours, I sipped vodka, watched a parade of flirty, shockingly immodest, beautiful models from half-a-dozen model agencies parade though the studio.

I was in heaven.

"Did you choose one?" Alex said.

"Huh?"

"When I shoot your portfolio, you'll need a female to pose with."

A week later, at 10:00 a.m. I arrived at the studio with a dozen changes of clothes, everything from business suits, casual wear, tennis outfits, bathing suits. The model I'd chosen as my partner—a freckled, ravishing redhead born and raised in London, England —was already in the studio, attired in a plush terry cloth robe, sitting in front of a makeup mirror, having her hair and makeup done.

Alex ushered me to the fitting room, where a stylist, an elderly, matronly Irish woman named Helen Smith, relieved me of my wardrobe, hung it on hangers.

Alex inspected the clothes.

"Put the bathing suit on first."

Alex walked out and pulled the fitting room curtain closed behind him.

I looked at Helen, waiting for her to leave so I could change.

She didn't budge.

Okay. I began to strip down, then realized I had my gun. What the hell was I going to do with my gun? I was about to summon Alex, figuring I could trust the former Marine to safeguard my weapon, when the redhead pulled the curtain aside and entered the fitting room.

"Cheerio," she said. Helen handed her a bikini. The redhead slipped out of the robe and stood there naked. I gaped. She graced me with a coy smile, looked down, and her eyes bulged. She pointed at my .38

"He has a bloody gun!" She grabbed her robe and fled.

The stylist laughed.

"Give it here," Helen said. "I've a brother retired out of the 103 precinct."

I felt a wave of relief. I unloaded the .38 and handed it over.

We spent most of the day shooting. A long, surprisingly arduous, and arousing process. Posing as my significant other, the Englishwoman sat on my lap; hugged me, kissed me, hung all over me. The sight of her long, bare legs, her tiny waist and enticing cleavage; her sweet breath and scent intoxicated me. Not surprisingly, I fell in love. But she blew me off after the shoot, told me she had a boyfriend. Sigh…

About a week later, on a Friday around 5:00 p.m., I was back in Alex's studio inspecting contact sheets of my photos—twenty miniature photos per page—while Alex busied himself setting up a makeshift bar, stocked with all sorts of booze, beer, and wine. As I sat there trying to choose the most flattering photos for my portfolio, I was delightfully distracted by the bevy of networking models who came and went. A few hung out for a while. Most had a drink, flirted with Alex before leaving him a "comp card," which consisted of several photos, in different outfits, on a mailer. Their hope was that he'd call them for future modeling assignments. As the evening wore on and the parade of models slowed to a trickle, Alex mentioned that impromptu gatherings at his studio were a weekly occurrence. That, as long as I contributed to the booze supply, I was most welcome to attend. I knew then that Alex and I would become fast friends.

I made an appointment to see Chuck Jones at the Avco Embassy offices on Third Avenue and Forty-first Street and showed him the photos Alex and I had chosen. He scrutinized them, chose a headshot.

"I'll show this to a producer I know," Chuck said. "He's casting an action picture. I'll see if I can get him to give you a small role that will qualify you to join the Screen Actors Guild. You can't work in movies or TV without a SAG card."

Good to his word, Chuck convinced the actor/producer David Broadnax to book me for a small role in a never-to-be-released feature film, *Sharpies*. A fun, rather intimidating experience.

Nervous as hell, I showed up at the shooting location, which was in an old diner on Eleventh Avenue in the Forties. Overwhelmed by the comings and goings of the film crew; the lights, cables, the barking of orders, I was handed a one-page script. Taken to a wardrobe trailer, where I changed into a Hells Angels–style biker costume. Greeted there and coached by an extremely affable director. My role, he explained, was to enter the eatery, have a short conversation with a waiter, "spy a rival biker" sitting in a booth across the room, rush to a pay phone, and call for backup. Next, an assistant director came and guided me back to the set, showed me the blocking; tape was affixed to the floor that told me where I was to walk, stand, stop, and deliver my one and only line: "You see Mad Dog lately?"

"Action," the director said. I felt the blood leave my head. Stood frozen.

"Action!" he repeated.

Someone shoved me from behind. I lurched into the restaurant, not remembering what I was supposed to say or do. I stuttered, stammered, and tripped over my feet. "Sorry," I said.

"Cut. Let's go again."

Nervous as I was, we finished in five takes.

The very next day I raced over to the ultramodern Screen Actors Guild office on Broadway, pay stub from *Sharpies* in hand. As I entered the building lobby, I experienced feelings of guilt. Felt that making clandestine plans to quit the NYPD was, in a way, betraying my family legacy and brother officers.

But walking out of the SAG offices, I knew that a new world with endless possibilities had opened up to me. I could see a path out of my dispiriting life as a cop. I pictured myself posing for magazines like *GQ*, *Esquire*, *Playboy*; acting in cigarette and shaving cream commercials, dating bejeweled women. I decided that this was the perfect time for me to make the big move to Manhattan. I phoned Jack Tupper, who was already living on East Seventy-fourth Street and knew a few building superintendents. We met at the All-Ireland Pub on Eighty-second and Third Avenue.

The All Ireland was one of the last Irish buckets of blood—where puking fistfights were the norm—remaining along Third Avenue on the Upper East Side. Not my choice of a meeting venue, but Jack was considering buying and renovating the place in order to compete with the more upscale bars popping up on the avenue; Churchill's, JG Melon, Harpers, among others.

Jack was sitting at the bar with his nose in the *Daily News* when I walked in shivering from a cold, windswept rain. I slipped out of my sodden wool Navy peacoat and hung it on the back of a stool and sat down. "Still selling life insurance?"

Jack nodded. "And bartending at Churchill's on weekends." He gestured to a large cardboard box on the floor beside him. "Selling leather coats too." Jack folded the paper in half, put it aside. "Heard you were modeling. Hell's that about?"

"Money. Women."

"Yeah? How's that going?"

"It's not until I find an agent. Which is another reason I want to live in Manhattan. All the photographers and agents are here."

Jack reached into his pocket. "Here's a list of apartments in the area and the names of the building owners or superintendents." He handed me a piece of paper. "They're All Ireland customers. Tell them I gave you their info."

"What about your building?"

Jack shook his head. "Nothing available."

I scanned the list. "Buddy Jacobson?"

"He's three blocks north. Remember he bought a couple of tenements? He did a major renovation. Converted the two buildings into one. Added a couple of floors. I heard he did a pretty good job." Jack ordered us drinks. "Although I hear the water pressure sucks. And hot water is hit-and-miss."

"So why would I bother going there?"

Jack grinned. "His renters are mostly stewardesses and models. And he opened his own modeling agency. It's on the first floor."

The bartender set down two bottles of beer.

"So, what do you think of the All Ireland?" Jack gestured around the dilapidated pub. It was dark. Smelled like stale cigarettes and sour beer.

"It's a toilet."

"That it is," Jack laughed. Then went on to describe a costly renovation. "We upgrade, get rid of the rumdums." He pointed to three waxwork drunks sitting at the other end of the bar, staring off into space. "Business will increase by seventy percent." Jack drank some beer. "Give any more thought about being one of my partners?"

"I'm a professional customer, Jack. I don't know shit about running a bar."

"I know all there is to know," Jack said. "We could make this place a singles bar, another TGI Fridays. The location's great. We'll serve the best food. Hire good-looking bartenders that will attract the ladies. Give drink and food specials to the stewardesses and models. Place could be a gold mine. All you'd do is sit back, charm the women, and collect your share of the profits."

Call me a skeptic, but common sense told me Jack's plan was yet another one of his schemes. He was always talking about big-money deals. I remember thinking that, when he and Donald Brown owned the Sherwood Inn in Kew Gardens, they were more interested in the glamour part of the business, of being playboys, and not the everyday nuts and bolts.

"I'd love to buy in, Jack," I said. "But I can't. No moola."

"Maybe down the road," Jack said. "When you become a rich and famous model."

"From your lips," I got to my feet, "to God's ears."
"Hey." Jack looked me over. "What size are you. Forty-two?"
"Forty-two long."
He reached into the cardboard box, pulled out a black leather jacket. "Try this one on."

Chapter 7

I walked down East Eighty-fourth Street, carrying my new leather bomber jacket draped over an arm. I stopped in front of Nicola's restaurant, a celebrity haunt that I'd dined in once or twice. I looked across the street at Jacobson's building. The storefront was indeed occupied by a model agency; *My Fair Lady* was stenciled on a window. Catchy name. Using a hand to shield my eyes from the rain, I scanned up the seven-floor building. Like Jack said, Jacobson had combined two tenements. The light-colored brick looked new. Each apartment in the structure had a small wrought-iron balcony, a plus to city dwellers.

Two young model types came hurrying down the rainy street, collapsed umbrellas, descended a couple of steps, and entered My Fair Lady. A few minutes later, a group of different models, using newspapers to cover their heads, exited and headed toward Lexington Avenue.

A double door to the left of the model agency opened. Buddy Jacobson himself pulled out two large trash cans, dragged them across the sidewalk, and set them at the curb. The glamour of Manhattan hadn't changed the former superstar horse trainer. He was scrawny as ever and scroungy in dirty workman's clothes.

"Hey, Buddy," I said as I crossed the street.

It took a moment for him to recognize me. "Thomas," he said, shaking my hand. "What brings you around?"

"I'm looking for an apartment."

"Yeah? Come with me."

I liked the three apartments he showed me. They had walls of brick and old barnwood planks. Pegboard floors. Wood-burning fireplaces. Glass doors that led to the balconies. We rode the elevator up to the seventh floor, where he'd built five penthouses. As we discussed rent, he led me into his apartment 7D which, although cluttered with construction debris, was spacious and impressive. I looked out onto a large, private promenade that sported a swimming pool and a wooden-walled handball court. I was a pretty good handball player as a kid.

I turned to Buddy. "I like the one-bedroom you showed me. Can you do better on the rent?" It was then that I noticed two odd-looking items resting carelessly atop a pile of magazines. It took me a moment to realize they were stun guns. What the hell was Jacobson doing with stun guns? Leftover tools from his horse training days? Not that I thought that electrically shocking thoroughbred horses was ever sanctioned in the racing world. Although from what I knew about Jacobson, it might not have mattered.

"The two-bedroom is good for a roommate. That would cut your rent in half. Besides, you'd be one of the only single guys in the building." Jacobson's smile revealed small, yellow teeth. "Most of the other apartments are occupied by models."

I surely liked the sound of that.

But I didn't care for Jacobson.

Having observed him over the years, I knew that he could be an overbearing alpha male, proprietary and aggressive when it came to women. The kind of guy who'd show up at a party I'd organized and try to charm groups of women into leaving with him, going to a restaurant, or back to his place. And I'd heard rumors about how he had problems with almost everyone he did business with. Thinking he was always the smartest guy in the room, he'd engage in questionable business practices; like when he was a horse trainer. He didn't pay his bills on time. Although he spent freely on beautiful women.

The Extraordinary Life of an Ordinary Man

A Brooklyn native, Buddy was born on December 10, 1930, into a thoroughbred horse racing dynasty. Although his father was a relatively successful hat salesman, his mother's three brothers, Hirsch, Eugene, and Sidney, all trained thoroughbreds. Uncle Hirsch was known as the greatest horse trainer of his day. Apparently, Jacobson inherited his family's love for the racing business, because he dropped out of high school to join his uncles. Started at the bottom, mucking out their stables in the Hialeah racetrack, north of Miami. Working his way up, he obtained an assistant horse trainer's license, and got lucky when a horse owned by a well-known owner/trainer David Schneider became ill. Unable to pay his mounting personal medical bills, Schneider took a chance and asked the unknown trainer for help.

Elixir, a once-celebrated mount, had suffered a career-ending bowed tendon only the year before. But Schneider, refusing to accept the veterinarian's dire diagnosis, took a full twelve months to nurse it back to uncertain health. Jacobson accepted the challenge. Elixir first won a $15,000 stake race. Without consulting Schneider, Jacobson then entered Elixir in the prestigious $50,000 Tropical Park Handicap. Even though Elixir was cast several classes below the favorites, and it was common knowledge that the horse was washed up, he pulled off an extraordinary upset and won by four and a half lengths. Provided with a much-needed financial windfall, Schneider thanked Jacobson and then fired him. Not that Jacobson cared. Elixir's miraculous comeback win made him a trainer in demand. Owners assumed that the young, brash Jacobson knew what he was doing.

Within a few years, he was training over fifty horses for more than a dozen owners. In the years that followed, Jacobson became the sport's most dominant trainer. In 1963, 1964, and 1965 he was America's most successful trainer. The New York Turf Riders Association named him trainer of the year, the leading trainer in America three times and New York state five times.

However, he would do anything to gain an edge. They reported that he was the first to shoot cortisone into a horse's joints. That he drugged and ran "sore horses." Palled around with shady characters. The New York Racing Association (NYRA) eventually found enough irregularities with Jacobson's business dealings — committing fraud by underreporting the actual sale or purchase prices of houses and pocketing the difference — that they suspended him, denying him stabling.

"Well?" Buddy said. "You want the two-bedroom?"

"I'll have to think about it," I said.

"Let me know soon."

After a few weeks, I settled on a temporary, dreary, second-floor studio apartment in a five-story tenement walk-up at 438 East Seventy-seventh Street. But the rent was affordable, the location great. Within walking distance were some of the hottest singles bars in the city; several owned by working models and frequented by celebrities.

When I wasn't working in the NYPD's building maintenance division, I put most all of my efforts into acquiring a legitimate model agent; there weren't many. I did all the research. Garnered advice from active fashion photographers and models that I met while partying in East Side model hangouts like Fridays, Harpers, Jim McMullen's, JG Melon, Rusty Staub's, and Churchill's where Jack Tupper still bartended; Herlihy's, Daly's Dandelion, and P.J. Clarke's, and of course Maxwell's Plum.

I purchased a customary model's portfolio, a large, flat black attaché case or "book," which I filled with representative Alex Wasinski photos and lugged around the city. Every agent I met with said that since I didn't have any tear sheets — actual print ads torn from magazines — I wasn't ready for an agent. A catch-22, since I couldn't work as a model without an agent, but I need an agent to get tear sheets.

After months of frustration, I got creative and finally figured out a way to generate my own print-ad tear sheets without having to actually book a modeling gig. I scoured magazines like *GQ*, *Esquire*, *Glamour*, and *Cosmopolitan* to locate ads that would work with the photos in my book. I razored out the ad's photo and placed the remaining frame over mine. Then Alex took a photo of the finished product.

I remade the rounds, showed the model agents my tear sheets. Within weeks every major agency in the city—Ford, Wilhelmina, Zoli, and Stewart—agreed to represent me. I signed with the largest and most prestigious, Ford.

I met with my new agent, former successful Ford model Joey Hunter, then president of Ford's men's division. Joey showed me around the agency's East Fifty-ninth Street converted four-story town house. I recall that during our meeting, he was bemoaning the shocking heart attack death of "the King" Elvis Presley at age forty-two. Joey introduced me to the men's division's six bookers. A couple of them agreed that I was a perfect daytime soap opera actor type. When I confessed that I had no acting experience, Joey advised me to enroll in renowned acting coach Bob McAndrew's acting class.

Formerly head of Lucille Ball's new talent program at Paramount Pictures in Hollywood, Bob's students included Raul Julia, Christopher Walken, Sela Ward, John Stamos, Corbin Bernsen, Tom Selleck, and Sam Elliott.

I met and auditioned for Bob. Enrolled in his West Fifty-fifth Street film acting class, where I met a who's who of beauty pageant winners, glamour girls, and supermodels like Melanie Cain who, I was surprised to discover, was Buddy Jacobson's longtime girlfriend. Surprised because Melanie was beautiful and Buddy… well, Buddy was a toad.

I spent the next year working hard at learning the craft of acting. Rehearsing and acting in scenes with some of the world's most attractive and talented women.

I performed a scene from *Casablanca* where Ilsa confronts Rick in his office, demands he hand over the letters of transit at gunpoint. Bob paired me with a former Miss Alabama, who after we'd spent a week rehearsing, and performed the scene in class to rousing applause, she pulled me into the lavatory and had her way with me—did this beat being a cop, or what?

That evening after class a bunch of us—Bob McAndrew, Sela Ward, Corbin Bernsen, Miss Alabama, and Melanie Cain among others, met for drinks. Stopped by Churchill's pub, where Jack Tupper was behind the stick, filling in for another bartender. We ordered beers and burgers and, when Jack wasn't busy flirting with Melanie, traded bills for coins that we fed into the jukebox.

"Hey," I teased Jack, noticing that he was touching Melanie in a most familiar way. Thinking it was a good thing Buddy Jacobson wasn't around, because there was more than flirting going on. Melanie was beaming. And I hadn't seen Jack this cheerful in a very long time. "How about some service down at this end of the bar."

"Hold your horses," Jack said. "I'm coming."

"Before Saint Patrick's Day," I said, "you shanty Irish bug."

"I didn't mean it to happen," Jack was telling me a few months later.

"I'm listening."

"I couldn't deal with my roommates anymore, so I broke the lease, sublet an apartment in Buddy's building. Temporarily, you understand. Just till I found another place." We were having lunch at JG Melon on the Upper East Side. The place was crowded as always. We'd scored two choice stools at the bar by the window overlooking Third Avenue. Ordered a couple of burgers and beers.

"It had to be four months ago." Jack drank some beer. "I ran into Melanie in Buddy's building. We started talking. Got along. Had a lot in common. We began jogging together during the evenings. She started telling me about her problems with Buddy. How controlling he was. That she wanted out of the relationships.

They've been living together for five years. She's his partner in My Fair Lady."

The bartender set down our burgers.

"I didn't know that." I wondered for the umpteenth time what the hell someone as beautiful and sweet as Melanie saw in a devious old dirtbag like Buddy. I mean, no one would put those two together. He had to be twenty-five years her senior.

"Long story short," Jack said. "I fell in love with her. She feels the same." He shrugged. "She broke up with Buddy. Moved in with me."

I took a bite of a bacon cheeseburger. "Wait." I chewed. Swallowed. "She moved in with you?" I was incredulous. "In Buddy's building? You've gotta be shitting me."

"It's a problem. I know. But we're looking for our own place."

"I'd look harder, if I were you."

"We've been staying at a hotel most of the time. Figure, out of sight, out of mind. But Buddy won't let go. He's stalking us. Calling us both at all hours. Even having us followed." Jack gestured outside to a shady-looking character who was leaning on the corner fire hydrant, smoking a small black cigar. It was obvious by the way the guy dressed and the way he held his smoke that he was a foreigner, Italian or Greek. I recalled hearing somewhere that Jacobson had hired foreign construction workers on the cheap when he was renovating his building. Was the guy outside connected to Buddy? Or was Jack, a two-hundred-pound tough guy, paranoid?

"You sure?" I said.

"I'm sure."

"You think Buddy would do something stupid?"

Jack smirked. "He does, I'll break the little cocksucker in half."

"So," I said and drank some beer. "Why you telling me all this?"

"You know Buddy. You know where he hangs out. What if you ran into him?"

"You want me to tell him to back off, leave you guys alone?"

"Just make small talk. Feel him out. Ask him how's business. How's Melanie. Yada yada. See what he has to say."

"I can do that."

About a week later I spotted Buddy eating dinner at his usual table in what had become one of my favorite Italian restaurants, Nicola's on East Eighty-fourth Street. The upscale, high-priced eatery was across the street from the seven-story apartment building that Buddy owned, and where Buddy, Jack, and Melanie now lived; in the same building, on the same floor. As a matter of fact, Jack and Melanie's apartment was across the hall from Buddy's penthouse.

Buddy saw me and waved me to his table. As usual, he was entertaining models. I figured that the four fresh-faced teens had most probably signed contracts to be represented by My Fair Lady.

"You want something to drink?" Buddy asked as I sat.

I ordered a dry vodka martini, up, lemon twist. Buddy introduced me to the girls.

"So," I said as I scanned the familiar, moneyed crowd. Noted that I, and every other guy in the place, was wearing a business suit. Buddy was dressed, as usual, like a derelict in paint-stained workman's clothes. "What's new?"

"Melanie dumped me." Buddy shrugged, seeming to take it in stride. "I can't blame her. I was an asshole."

The waiter set down my martini. Left me a menu.

"Yeah," Buddy continued. "She's better off."

I studied his face, looking for signs of deception.

"We're still friends," Buddy continued. "She's still my partner in My Fair Lady. Did you know she's my partner? We started the agency together."

I said I knew.

"Well, she's dating Jack Tupper now. A great guy. He'll treat her right."

I sipped my martini.

"Yeah, Jack's the best. He'll do the right thing. Not like me. I was an idiot."

"No hard feelings?"

Buddy said "No." That he still considered Jack a friend.

"Some guys would be pissed at a friend dating his ex," I said.

"Not me." Buddy leaned toward me, lowering his voice conspiratorially. "No way I'd lose a pal over some piece of ass." He gestured to the four models. "There's plenty more where Melanie came from." Buddy sat back and tapped my menu. "You hungry?"

I declined dinner. Finished my martini. Figured Buddy seemed sincere about his current relationship with Jack and Melanie. Which is what I reported back to Jack Tupper.

"Buddy's a pathological liar," Tupper said. We were sitting at the bar, in another Irish bucket of blood called the Carlow East on Lexington Avenue, watching a Yankees game. "He called Melanie yesterday begging her to take him back. Give him another chance." Jack said that Buddy continued to corner Melanie in their building's hallways, lobby, and basement laundry room. "He leaves notes under our door. Sends flowers, letters, cards. Tells Melanie he wants to marry her. When she said no, Buddy threatened suicide." Jack took a long pull on his beer. "Late last night the asshole called me. Offered me a hundred grand, cash, to give Melanie up. I tape-recorded it."

I thought about that. "When're you guys moving?"

"Melanie's out looking at apartments now."

"Once you guys move," I said, "Buddy will back off."

"You don't know Buddy."

A week later, Jack Tupper was dead.

He'd been shot seven times. His face had been sliced up with a knife. His head was bashed in. His body was bludgeoned, burned beyond recognition, and discarded in a Bronx garbage dump. (Which would one day become Trump Golf Links at Ferry Point). Thanks to an accidental eyewitness, Buddy was arrested for the murder within hours.

The murder in the penthouse incident caused a front-page media frenzy. After a long, lurid, sensational trial that alluded to call girl rings, drug dealing, death threats, FBI and Mafia involvement, Buddy was sentenced to twenty-five years to life. Although he would manage to escape by swapping clothes with a visitor and evade a nationwide manhunt, he was recaptured and returned to prison.

Chapter 8

It was around this time that I met my second wife, Eastern Airlines flight attendant Constance Williams. I was sitting at a round table in the rear of Herlihy's on East Seventy-seventh Street—owned by Ford Model Steve Herlihy—with a group of New York Jets that included quarterback Richie Todd, when the green-eyed, blond and beautiful Southern belle walked in. Accompanying her was a pretty, brown-eyed flight attendant from Mississippi who was dating one of the Jets. They sat at our table. Someone made the introduction.

Constance was effervescent with a butter-wouldn't-melt-in-her-mouth manner and a thick, sweet-as-molasses Southern drawl. Unlike her girlfriend who, after a few cocktails, became loud and redneck sloppy, Constance was chatty but ladylike. Since lately, I'd been meeting mostly angry women who'd been screwed over by commitment-phobic or unfaithful men, Constance was a welcome ray of sunshine. I'd finished my third beer when Constance said she had to meet another girlfriend at McMullen's—owned by Ford model Jim McMullen—over on Third Avenue. I offered to escort her.

We had a drink at McMullen's bar. Constance's other flight attendant friend, a big-haired, big-eyed, big-boobed brunette from Galveston, Texas flirted with actor Ben Gazzara, who was seated alongside us. They seemed really into each other. So, Constance and I excused ourselves, taxied down to the West Village, caught a set at the Blue Note jazz club. Then stopped by the Lion's Head, a celebrity dive bar, for a nightcap. A not quite sober author, Norman Mailer—who I knew from another celebrity watering hole, Elaine's—bought us a round. Comedian Jackie Mason wouldn't leave Constance alone. I bought Mailer back a round. Dodged the slobbering Jackie Mason, paid our check. Cabbed it up to a new club that only just opened. We partied the night away at Studio 54. Hung out with Mick and Bianca Jagger, Cher, Andy Warhol, and owner Steve Rubell. Then ate breakfast at the Green Kitchen on First Avenue and Seventy-seventh Street. Wound up back at my apartment around 7:00 a.m. That's when it dawned on me that I'd never met anyone like Constance before. She had none of the sharp edges, surly attitudes, anger issues or gold-digging ways of many New York women. She was sweet, kind, innocent and, unlike most of the hard, manicured quaalude queens who saw a kitchen with pots and pans and ran the other way, she loved to cook. Which brings to mind an evening she'd cooked a meal for me and her six female roommates, was doing dishes, complaining that her hands were red and rough from washing dishes at home and on the airplane. Thinking I was doing something loving, I showed up the next day, not with flowers, candy, or a trinket, but with a pair of Playtex HandSaver rubber gloves. Constance accepted the gift graciously. Her roommates were appalled. (I'm still reminded of that faux pas some fifty years later.)

Regardless, six months later we eloped. Tied the knot in a civil ceremony in Hollywood, Florida. Celebrated afterwards with close friends at a hot tub party at my mother's brother, Uncle Eddie's place. When we returned to the city, I moved from my dreary East Seventy-seventh Street apartment and rented us a large studio in an upscale doorman building on East Forty-seventh Street, one block from the United Nations.

Although as a married man I stopped with the occasional acting class trysts, I never missed a class and, as a result, became comfortable performing in front of an audience. Ford was submitting me for everything. The casting agents were beginning to take notice and request me by name. Then I booked several TV commercials for local banks and car dealerships. Which got my agent, Joey Hunter's attention. When he received the casting call from WNBC for a host for a new TV show, I was one of the models he picked for the audition.

"They're trying to capitalize on the success of other magazine format TV shows," Joey told me. "You'd be perfect."

The *Now!* audition, which was held at 30 Rockefeller Plaza, was the fourth or fifth audition I had scheduled that day. I arrived on set completely relaxed, anxious to get the audition over with because I had two more auditions scheduled immediately afterwards.

A perky casting agent escorted me into a room where a half-a-dozen people—a producer, director, writer, and network executive—were seated. But there was no script for me to memorize. No direction of any kind. I was told to stand in front of a camera. The camera was turned on. The casting agent said, "Tell us about yourself."

And so, I did. Prattled on about being raised Bronx Irish Catholic. Told a few funny stories about what it was like to grow up with an identical twin brother—yes, we sometimes switched girlfriends. I recounted and dramatized a few of my adventures while in the Navy: being caught in the Atlantic Ocean by a hurricane, fighting off muggers on the docks in Marseille, France. Told them that I was still an active member of the NYPD. But instead of telling them about the horrors of the ghetto, the poverty and violence, I told them about the eight babies I'd delivered. Finished off by saying, "At least five of those Hispanic kids' middle name is Fitzsimmons." Everyone laughed. Walking out of 30 Rock, I felt good about the audition. Although, I never thought I'd hear from WNBC again.

I booked the WNBC gig a few days later. Signed a two-year contract at ten times my puny cop salary. After which, I presented myself at the personnel division at One Police Plaza, resigned from the NYPD. And never looked back.

Chuck Jones and his wife Lynn threw a party to celebrate my retirement from the NYPD and my landing the WNBC gig. Their Forest Hills Gardens home was filled with TV and movie people when Constance and I arrived. It was where we would first meet Bill O'Reilly. He attended as a guest of my guest, WNEW's *PM Magazine* cohost Danielle Folquet. (Dani would later marry Lee Louis Mazzilli, the former major league baseball player, coach, and manager.).

As Dani introduced Constance and me to the six-four O'Reilly, I had no doubt that he and I would become fast friends. I mean, here was another Irish-American in my age range, who was hosting *7:30 Magazine*, a WCBS show like mine, and whose Irish roots were Cavan on his father's side—like mine—and Northern Ireland on his mother's side—like mine. I'd also heard that his grandfather was NYPD.

"Hey, O'Reilly," I said with a shit-eating grin. "My network's better than your network." Dani and Constance giggled.

O'Reilly looked like he'd swallowed a hairbrush.

"Joke, O'Reilly," I said. "Joke?"

"Oh," he said sourly, looked off, and didn't say anything more.

I regarded the boorish Long Island native and realized that my instincts were wrong: O'Reilly might look like a "regular guy," but he obviously had issues. And I could tell just by looking at him that he wore women's underwear.

Just kidding.

I avoided sourpuss O'Reilly for the remainder of the evening. While Lynn Jones served us hors d'oeuvres, I think it was Chuck who brought up the idea of the four magazine format shows joining forces and doing a series of shows together. O'Reilly scowled at the idea. Dani and I promised to pitch it to our producers. But when I arrived at 30 Rock on Monday, I realized that the *Now!* show was in trouble. Ratings were poor. Not surprising since the show's main host—that's me—was inexperienced. The producer had never produced a TV show before. The writers had never written for a show before. Then there was the fact that I never fully committed to the show. I didn't attend editing sessions or story conferences. Only showed up to do my on-camera segments, then hurried off to other auditions or to meet with Constance and socialize with our friends. We shot another few segments—which is how I would first meet multimillionaire magazine owner, motorcyclist, balloonist, and self-proclaimed "capitalist tool" Malcolm Forbes – before the network cancelled the show. Afterward, I was too preoccupied and embarrassed to realize that my career wasn't the only thing in trouble.

My marriage to Constance had been one big party. Dining out most nights and frequenting the hottest clubs. Traveling the country on free airline passes; weekends in Montreal, New Orleans, Acapulco. We also spent a lot of time with her parents. who— unlike my first wife's austere, humorless folks—were fun-loving, salt of the earth types.

But when Constance worked, she insisted on flying "trips" that kept her away from home for days at a time and left me on my own. No matter how many times I asked, I couldn't convince her to fly turnarounds, which would put her at home every night.

"If I fly turnarounds, I'd have to fly New York to Miami and put up with rude Yankees," Constance complained. "I'd dread going to work. I'd hate my job."

"We're married," I pleaded. "I want to spend time with my wife."

"I'm not flying turnarounds."

Which meant what? Was her job more important than our marriage?

And so, Constance left me alone a lot. I became lonely. Angry. It was only a matter of time before we split. Although

Constance would eventually move back down south, she wished to remain in our East Forty-seventh Street apartment for the time being, which was fine with me. I moved uptown to an East Ninety-sixth Street high-rise.

It was difficult dealing with the post-breakup funk. But thanks to Chuck Jones and David Broadnax, the producer behind *Sharpies,* I landed a costarring role in a low-budget horror film. Spent a much-appreciated month shooting on the island of Jamaica, where I met fellow thespian, Abscam scandal alum—her congressman husband at the time was convicted on charges of bribery and corruption—and future Princess Rita Boncompagni Ludovisi of Italy. Rita Jenrette was a Texas-born *Playboy* cover model-turned-Italian-princess by marriage. She was also, as I recall, talented, bright, and an all-around "good dame." That month of Red Stripe beer, sun, and surf spent with Rita and the other cast members was one of the most therapeutic and fun experiences of my life.

On the way back from Jamaica, I stopped off in Florida to visit my parents, and break the news about my impending divorce. Which is when I met the woman who would become the first real love of my live.

I'd left my parents in their Deerfield Beach condo and was on my way to Fort Lauderdale Airport, heading back to NYC. My mother and father took the news of my imminent divorce in stride. Although they had liked Constance well enough, it was my second marriage, second divorce. Killing time before my flight back home, I'd stopped off for a drink at Sweetwater's in Boca Raton with a cop buddy of mine. It was midafternoon, so the restaurant was practically empty.

"Hi," the bartender, a brunette Ava Gardner look-alike said. "I'm Djuna. Can I get you gentlemen anything?" We ordered two beers. Spent the next half hour making small talk with the sexy, funny, and wry Pennsylvania native. She told us about her life as a full-time bartender and full-time physical therapy student. Obviously, she was intelligent, hardworking, motivated, and I could tell she had a wild side.

Oh, goodie.

"I've a flight to catch." I checked the time. "I'll be back to visit my parents in a few weeks. I'd love to get together." Djuna gave me her phone number.

Back in New York I couldn't get the feline, brown-eyed brunette bartender out of my mind. I phoned her two days later. Began our relationship over the phone. A few weeks later I took her to a romantic dinner at Sea Watch on the ocean in Fort Lauderdale. Wound up back at her apartment, a tidy one-bedroom just west of Federal Highway. Realized she was a wild and crazy fashionista when she put on a champagne-fueled fashion show for me. Modeled everything in her wardrobe, from formal gowns, sexy cocktail dresses, to loungewear complete with Hollywood slippers. When I woke in her bed the following morning, I knew I was in love.

The passionate affair—think red-hot, jungle sex—lasted for about two years long-distance. I flew to Florida as often as possible. We partied nonstop at tiki bars, hot tub soirees, and happy hours, all the while searching southeast Florida for the perfect margarita. Spent one of the most romantic weekends of my life when we flew on a Chalk's Airline seaplane to the island of Bimini.

After Djuna graduated from physical therapy school, I moved her into my NYC apartment. We were madly in love, saw romance every day, everywhere, in everything. Our future had no limits. Or so I thought.

The honeymoon ended soon after we cut back on the partying and settled into the grind of everyday life. Djuna working long hours at Metropolitan Hospital as a physical therapist, me grinding away at writing, acting, and modeling. Djuna became morose and depressed. The romance dissipated.

So did the sex. We stopped havening fun. I couldn't figure out why. Was she ill? Was her unhappiness my fault? Was there something she wasn't telling me? One thing I'd knew about myself: I couldn't live with a depressive. Untreated depressives, like alcoholics, drug addicts, and gamblers destroy lives.

"What's wrong?" I asked her. "Is it me?"

"It's not you."

"You've changed."

"Not really."

"What's different? Talk to me."

It took some time before Djuna confessed: "I knew the kind of woman you'd fall in love with. So, I pretended to be that woman, thinking that when you found out what I was really like, you'd be too much in love with me to leave."

Huh? "So, you conned me, deceived me?"

"All's fair," she said, shrugging, "in love and war."

She was wrong about that.

Our breakup was gut-wrenching.

Djuna stayed in the city, moved into her own apartment. I moped for months. Questioned why I kept making bad choices when it came to women. Why I couldn't enjoy a lasting relationship. What was I doing wrong?

It took me a while before I started dating again; there were several quick flings with models in my acting class. A half-a-dozen booze-fueled, 3:00 a.m. one-night stands with women I'd met in P.J. Clarke's, Studio 54, or Elaine's. But I wasn't really connecting with anyone. That is, until I met Marla Ann Maples.

I'd first met Marla Maples in the spring of 1985.

Plain talking, Democratic incumbent Mayor Ed Koch was about to be reelected to a third term with 78 percent of the vote. Violent street and subway crime were epidemic and yet crack — a solid, smokable form of cocaine — was only beginning to infest the inner city; the worst was yet to come. While the feds were busy prosecuting the Mafia's five families, the Bloods, Crips, MS-

13, Ghost Shadows, Flying Dragons, and other youth gangs were establishing footholds, spraying major cities with their unsightly territorial graffiti.

I recall that I was in my twenty-fifth-floor Normandie Court apartment, on the southern Harlem border, waiting patiently for a wack-a-doodle Rockette who had picked me up the previous evening at Elaine's, to finish showering. I seemed to recall her corralling me as I walked into the lovingly seedy establishment around 2:00 a.m. Randy? Brandy? Candy? I do remember she said she loved the rodeo, was into calf roping and barrel racing. She said she was born and raised in some place called Montana. My phone rang.

"Hello?"

"I know a lady you should meet," my good friend, entertainment attorney Paul Derounian, said. "Marla Maples. She's a nice girl."

"Not interested," I said without hesitation. Granted, I'd become cynical, wary of "nice girls" and serious relationships. But after two divorces followed by the soul-crushing Djuna breakup, I preferred to play the field, protect myself by not getting involved.

I heard singing, cocked an ear. Randy, Brandy, or Candy was belting out, "Mama Don't Let Your Babies Grow Up to be Cowboys."

"C'mon, coach," Paul insisted. He always called me coach. "She's a knockout."

I reminded myself that Paul was for real. Every woman I'd seen him with actually *was* a knockout.

"Really, Paul," I said. "I'm not interested in meeting anyone new."

"Look, coach. We'll have a few drinks. Some dinner. Then, if you don't like her, you can split. I'll buy. It's all on me."

"My last blind date looked like André the Giant in a dress."

"It's not a blind date," Paul lied. "Not really. And you'll be doing me a favor. C'mon. Do this for me. Seven-thirty at Wilson's."

"Wilson's?" Since I'd once dated a beautiful, Goth barmaid at Wilson's who now hated my guts, it wouldn't have been my first choice. But Paul did say he was paying.

All at once, I heard the shower being turned off. The singing stopped. A moment later, the bathroom door flew open. Miss Montana sashayed into the room, a fluffy white terry-cloth towel draped provocatively around her torso.

"Giddyap, cowboy!" she hollered, whipping the towel off and twirling it over her head like a lasso. "*Yeee-haaawww!*" She flung the towel across the room.

"Who's that yelling?" Paul said.

"See you at seven-thirty," I said and hung up.

O.J. Simpson once asked me what type of women I liked. At the time, we happened to be standing on the balcony in Studio 54, gazing down onto the dance floor. O.J. was ogling two young women I'd met through Princes Diana's future fiancé, Dodi Fayed: a stunning Wilhelmina Agency model named Denise Brown and her younger sister, Nicole. The sisters were dancing together, gyrating suggestively to pounding disco music. On a couch behind us Andy Warhol was snorting coke with the usual suspects: Truman Capote (who read some of my short stories and always encouraged me to keep writing), Bianca Jagger, Halston, and Jack Nicholson.

"My type?" I had to lean close to O.J. to be heard. "Whoever's nice to me."

"I hear you, brother," O.J. said. We exchanged high fives.

In my experience, many beautiful women, whether as a defense mechanism, insecurity, or they thought playing hard to get was clever, were mean. Especially if they'd recently broken up with a lying, cheating, commitment-phobic asshole guy. Thus, when I walked into the now defunct Wilson's on West Seventy-second Street, I was ready with an escape plan. If Marla Maples was one of those mean girls, snarky, or if I felt no connection, I'd have a drink, remember a previous appointment, and bolt.

As I walked into Wilson's, I scanned the bar area for the Goth barmaid I once dated. Didn't see her. Made my way to Paul's table, a corner four-top.

"Say hello to Terry English," Paul said as I sat. "Terry's actually from Hawaii. She's a former Miss Hawaiian Tropic, like Marla Maples. She's in town looking for a model agent."

"Welcome to the Big Apple," I said.

A waiter came by, and I ordered a dry martini. Up. Lemon twist.

"Do me a favor," Paul said. "Get Terry an interview at Ford?"

I gave Terry the once-over. At the time Ford, the most prestigious and successful modeling agency in the world, was known for its white-bread models. Terry was an exotic beauty, all right, but way too ethnic for Ford. "Sure, Paul. I'll see what I can do."

My martini came. I took a sip.

"There's Marla now," Paul said.

I followed Paul's gaze. Saw the maître d' practically genuflect as a statuesque blonde in a clingy white cocktail dress swept into the restaurant. The maître d' spoke to Marla for a moment, then pointed to our table.

"Sorry I'm late," Marla said breathlessly. Her voice was deep South, sweet as honeysuckle. "My granddaddy's been ill."

Paul and I rose to greet her.

"You already know Terry English," Paul said.

"Oh, my, yes," Marla said. "From the pageants."

The two women hugged.

"Thomas Fitzsimmons," Paul said, "meet Marla Maples."

We made eye contact. Exchanged pleasantries. Shook hands.

"Marla is an actress and model," Paul said as we all sat. "She worked in a Stephen King movie. She just screen-tested for the soap *Loving*."

I tried to appear appropriately impressed.

"Marla, Thomas is a Ford model. A writer. A television personality. He hosted his own TV talk show on NBC. Has a slew of national TV commercials running…"

Well, this was embarrassing.

"He co-stared in a horror movie. He's producing his own film."

"And I'm a legend in my own mind," I quipped.

Marla burst out laughing.

I liked Marla.

A waiter appeared. Marla ordered white wine.

"Tell me about your movie?" Marla said to me.

Paul said, "It's about clairvoyant twin cops. Thomas is an ex–New York City cop. His identical twin was also a cop."

"Sounds fascinating," she said.

"It's called *Blue Gemini*," Paul said. "He's also writing a novel, *Confessions of a Catholic Cop*."

The waiter set down Marla's wine. "Any studios or publishers interested?"

I waited for Paul to respond. When he didn't, I said, "There's some interest."

"Tell her about your meeting with the Cannon Group," Paul said, then addressed Terry and Marla. "They produce Chuck Norris pictures."

"I pitched the movie to a producer at Cannon," I said. "The guy looked fourteen years old. I made the mistake of saying the stories took place in the Fort Apache section of the South Bronx. The producer says, 'Fort Apache's been done already. Paul Newman did it.'

"I tell the guy, 'No. You don't understand. My script and book aren't *about* Fort Apache, they happen to take place in that part of the Bronx.' The kid looks at me like I'm speaking Vulcan and repeats, 'Fort Apache's been done already. I don't wanna do it again.' End of meeting." I sipped the martini. "Now I'm looking for private investors."

"Any investors yet?" Marla said.

"A client of mine," Paul said. "Dodi Fayed."

Marla shuddered. "Dodi Fayed's a creep."

Whatever *ears perking up* means, mine did. Marla was speaking about my most promising investor. At the time, I'd known the Egyptian-born jet-setter and part-time movie producer socially for more than five years. I'd partied with Dodi at Studio 54 and Régine's and been his guest at several gatherings in his lavish Waldorf Astoria Hotel penthouse apartment. Parties that ended for me when Dodi broke out a mile-high stash of cocaine; he was rumored to have spent $15,000 a week on the drug. Although I had heard rumors that he owed money all over town, socially he was charming and seemed like a nice guy.

I asked Marla, "Why's Dodi a creep?"

"I was introduced to Dodi at Régine's," Marla said. "Guess it was two months ago. We danced. He was all hands. Very pushy. He didn't care if I wanted to be touched or not."

"Now, Marla," Paul interrupted. "You went back to his suite at the Waldorf afterward, didn't you?"

Marla nodded. "So?"

"*So*, he couldn't have been that bad. Right?"

"A bunch of us went." Marla shrugged, addressing me. "I figured I'd be safe in a crowd. But there were drugs everywhere. Dodi was stoned, acting strange. He grabbed one of the girls. She had to fight him off. And he had these scary men standing around. Bodyguards, I think."

"What'd you do?" I said.

"Got out of there while I could."

The waiter brought menus. Handed them out.

"How about I order for all of us?" Paul said.

Marla, Terry, and I had no problem with that.

We spent the next hour exchanging small talk and sharing our food. I was about to spoon out a portion of Wilson's celebrated lobster mac and cheese when I sensed movement, glanced at the bar, and caught a glimpse of the Goth bartender I'd dated. She was dressed head to toe in black. Her hair was exotically styled and dyed black. She sported thick black eyeliner, black lipstick, black nail polish. An oversized crucifix hung around her neck. She was standing at the service area, mixing drinks. She handed two martinis to a waiter, locked eyes with mine, pinned me with a dagger stare. I wondered if she'd known all along I was there. If she'd spit on my food. I laid down the serving spoon, pushed the lobster mac and cheese away.

We all passed on dessert. I checked the time and stifled a yawn, realizing I was still recovering from last evening and my midmorning sexcapade with Randy, Candy, or Brandy.

Paul paid the check and said he and Terry were headed to the Café Carlyle to catch Bobby Short's last set. Paul asked that we join them. Both Marla and I declined.

We exited the restaurant. Paul had a Town Car waiting. "Sure you two won't join us?"

"Positive," I said.

"Thanks anyway," Marla said.

The Town Car drove away.

"Where do you live?" I asked Marla.

"Eleventh Avenue and Twenty-second Street."

Chelsea. A perilous—especially after dark — high-crime neighborhood. I don't know if it was because I have three sisters that I'm close to, but the silly, chivalrous side of me worried about Marla getting home safely. Although I was heading in the opposite direction, I said, "May I see you home?"

"That would be great," she said.

Our cab took Eleventh Avenue south to Marla's neighborhood, an area just north of Greenwich Village. Chelsea was a sparsely populated, hardscrabble westside district built by railroads and steamship lines.

We drove through Chelsea, passed loitering badasses. Stolen cars were jacked up on milk crates. Homeless men were sprawled out on the sidewalk. A fight broke out in front of a seedy topless bar. Punches were thrown. Stragglers were laughing at the mayhem.

We turned a corner and pulled to a stop in front of Marla's residence, a well-worn, high-rise doorman building. I looked east and saw the infamous Allerton Hotel. I was glad I was armed.

At the time, drug addicts, work-release criminals, and end-of-the-line welfare recipients lived at the Allerton. I was about to ask Marla why the hell she was living in Chelsea, but I figured that her being new to the city, she didn't know any better. Stupid me. I would later discover Marla lived there rent-free, courtesy of a former, wealthy lover.

A uniformed doorman hurried from the building and opened Marla's door. We said how good it was to meet each other. Cheek-kissed good night. As my taxi headed east toward the bright lights and safety of Manhattan's Upper East Side, I turned to look out of the cab's rear window. Saw Marla standing there, watching my taxi drive away with a sad, forlorn look on her face that, for whatever reason, touched my heart.

My cab raced across Twenty-second Street, turned north on Third Avenue. I thought about the fact that even though Marla was indeed a knockout and had been a most pleasant dinner companion, I hadn't sensed any personal connection between us. I didn't expect to ever see her again.

Chapter 9

I WAS AWAKENED THE FOLLOWING morning around 3:30 by the sounds of rapid gunfire. My eyes sprung open. My heart pounded; the reports were close. I lay there telling myself to stay away from the bedroom window, thinking maybe it was a truck backfiring down on Third Avenue. But I knew better. Figured that the shooting was most probably battling Harlem drug gangs; crack use was surging in the city. Widespread violence followed.

I couldn't go back to sleep. I got up, brewed a pot of coffee, and then caught up on some neglected paperwork. Although the modeling and TV commercial business was going well, I'd reluctantly agreed to conduct an off-the-record investigation for a wealthy, cheapskate author that I didn't especially like. Having completed the job, if I wanted to get paid, I needed to mail him an invoice.

For several months the author — I signed a confidentially agreement, so the weasel shall remain nameless — had been stalked and receiving anonymous death threats through the mail. Terrified, he kept cornering me at the bar in Elaine's and begging me to investigate. Even though he'd acquired a slew of enemies, people he betrayed as only an amoral journalist can, the case was relatively easy to solve. I enlisted a couple of ex-cops who helped me stake out the post office where the letters were mailed with inane regularity. We took photographs of suspects and discovered a jilted lover was the culprit. No surprise there. Although the client intended to have his stalker arrested and prosecuted, I convinced him to hold off until I spoke to the guy.

"I checked. He has no criminal record," I told the client. "He's supporting his elderly mother. Emotionally, he's a mess. Let's not be so quick to ruin his life."

I collared the schnook outside the post office soon after, told him who I was. Explained that he would be arrested and prosecuted if he didn't stop with the death threats. But the guy overreacted and gave me attitude. I slapped him around a bit, which did the trick. The death threats stopped. It was no longer necessary to arrest anyone.

Case closed.

But, because I'd foolishly neglected to discuss my fee beforehand, I knew that getting paid by the author could be an issue. When I asked about payment, he told me to send him an invoice.

All paperwork was a dreaded chore for me. I mean, I'd have to figure out the hours worked by each ex-cop. I decided to charge for overtime after eight hours and add a gratuity. The problem being that because of my dyslexia, I still couldn't add, subtract, multiply, or divide. Which would always be a problem in my life.

My telephone rang. I checked the time. Figured it had to be one of my affluent cottontop mentors: Wall Street firm Moore & Schley CEO John McCooey or Tom Counihan, international creative director for the ad agency Campbell-Ewald. Both were lovable reprobates I spoke to most every day. I turned away from the baffling, cheapskate-author invoice, welcoming the interruption. "Hello?"

"Guess who just called, kid?" Paul Derounian said.

"Who?"

"Marla Maples. Kid, she liked you. Wants to know all about you."

Although I knew enough about women to know that I don't know anything about women, I was taken aback. Marla hadn't shown an interest in me. Perhaps that's because women who are interested act disinterested, and women who are disinterested act disinterested? It's all so confusing.

"What's she want to know?"

"She wants a personal reference. She said, 'Why didn't you tell me about Thomas Fitzsimmons? He's so nice. I like him.'" Then Paul said, "I told her, 'What's not to like?'"

Attaboy. Paul always gave me good press and I appreciated it.

"She wants you to call her, kid."

Paul gave me Marla's phone number.

"You gonna call her?"

I thought about it.

"Didn't you like Marla?" Paul said.

"Yeah. I liked her."

"Well, call her. Take her to brunch, a movie."

I heard a phone ring on his end. "I gotta take this call, kid. Promise me you'll call Marla?"

"I'll call her," I promised and hung up.

A wolf pack of predators slouched to a stop and gave me hard looks as I exited a yellow cab in front of Marla's apartment building. I'd phoned Marla yesterday, asked her if she'd like to join me for a stroll through Central Park, then brunch at a Mexican restaurant. She said she'd love to. I told her, "I'll pick you up at your place."

"Did you say you'd pick me up?" Marla said. "You don't want me to meet you somewhere?"

"I'll pick you up at your door. If that's all right with you?"

"Well, a gentleman in New York. *Finally.*"

The predators kept eyeballing me and with good reason: I looked like money. Thanks to an old Navy buddy who worked at Bergdorf Goodman and used his employee discount, I was wearing a Dunhill blue blazer over my .38 Smith & Wesson; a polo shirt, khakis, and Gucci-like loafers. The oversized gold

Rolex on my left wrist was a gift from an old girlfriend who'd paid $30 for it down on Canal Street. I suspected it was a fake.

The harsh blare of car horns came at me from the direction of Eleventh Avenue and a low-flying news helicopter roared thunderously overhead. The predators seemed distracted by the commotion and lost interest in me. They shuffled to the corner and disappeared into the crowd on Eleventh Avenue.

"Ever think of moving out of this area?" I asked Marla as we strolled east on Twenty-second Street. I had suggested we take a taxi to avoid the criminal element. But, because it was a beautiful day, she wanted to walk. "Maybe move to the Upper East Side?"

"Leave all this?" Marla gestured to the spooky, ivy-covered brownstones that lined her street with their battered, overflowing plastic and tin garbage cans edging their properties. "Why would I move?"

I couldn't tell if she was kidding me or not. "The phrase *reeks of urine* comes to mind."

Marla actually hee-hawed. I'd never heard a genuine beauty queen hee-haw before.

"You've never been bothered?" I said, checking out her cowboy hat, bursting halter top, tight jeans, Tony Lama belt, and cowboy boots. "By the gangs? Derelicts?"

"When someone starts acting rude," Marla said, "I look them straight in the eye and tell them they're being rude. Show them I'm not afraid and they stop."

"Really?"

"Really," she said resolutely. "It's all about being one with the universe. I put my faith in God and his love that surrounds all of us."

Good grief.

We walked past the Allerton Hotel with its pimps, hookers, and nodding drug addicts loitering out front. The staticky, boom-box sounds of Latin music emanated from a wide-open window. A gaunt, nearly toothless elderly man swathed in body-oil sodden army fatigues sitting on the hotel stoop called out, "Hey, blondie. Help out a poor old veteran?"

Marla stopped.

Groan.

"How are you today?" she asked the bum and handed him a dollar bill.

"How am *I*?" the derelict shouted, his roach spray breath hitting us like a shotgun blast. "How the hell's it look like I am?"

Several of the Allerton's denizens were suddenly in our faces, dirty hands extended, begging for money. I grabbed Marla by the hand and pulled her along before the situation got out of control. Shouts of "Cheap muthafuckas" followed us as we made our escape.

"I wouldn't make a habit of doing that if I were you," I told her as we crossed Tenth Avenue, one eye over my shoulder.

"It's the Christian thing to do," she said in all seriousness.

"And a good way to get hurt," I said.

"You're angry."

"No. I just don't want to see anything happen to you."

Marla smiled into my eyes. "I like that in a man." She squeezed my hand.

A gentle saltwater breeze caressed us as we strolled east toward the relative safety of midtown. We turned north on crowded Fifth Avenue and I was reminded what it was like to walk the sidewalks of New York with a woman who filled out a halter top and jeans the way Marla Maples did.

Car horns blew. Truckers whistled. Construction workers applauded. Some of the remarks bordered on inappropriate. I was about to slug one foul-mouthed hard hat, but he read my intentions and darted back into a construction site before I could get my hands on him. Marla seemed clueless.

About thirty blocks later, we were walking past Trump Tower. I gazed across the street into the commercial entrance, thinking I might catch a glimpse of Donald.

I'd seen very little of my old wingman during the last ten years. Not that I'd expected to. Since he was now a celebrated real estate tycoon, a married man with three kids while I was single, footloose, and fancy-free. It was the natural order of things. Although I had run into him at parties on billionaire Malcolm Forbes's yacht, *Highlander II*. I'd also spotted him patronizing the FBI-surveilled, Mafia-owned restaurant Da Noi. And I'd see him every so often at Le Club, a trendy New York café society hangout. But he was always in the company of the scumbag Mob lawyer Roy Cohn — the guy made my skin crawl — so I'd only nod a greeting.

I'd once asked Donald why he associated with the likes of Cohn. He'd told me: "Roy gives me great legal advice. And he doesn't charge me a dime. Ever."

Marla and I entered Central Park at the Grand Army Plaza entrance and were tented by the cool shade trees. A dozen sketch artists with varying degrees of talent had set up shop on benches and were hawking their finished wares to tourists. Or offering to sketch someone, while-you-wait, for a fee.

We passed the zoo, a five-and-a-half-acre facility that was stocked with more than two-dozen species, some endangered. Marla slid her arm around my waist as we continued north past the children's zoo, then cut west. She squeezed tight as we dodged inline skaters at the Bandshell. The warmth of her touch sent unanticipated signals to my extremities.

Hand in hand, we continued north until we reached the richly ornamented formal terrace that overlooks the Bethesda Fountain and the lake. The area is considered by many to be the heart of the park. Here is people-watching at its best.

Bethesda Plaza was crowded with tourists. A young, upscale couple pushed the Rolls-Royce of baby carriages through clumps of sweaty homeboys who were breakdancing to music blaring from their portable boom boxes. A dreadlocked drug dealer was making his rounds, threading through the eclectic crowd, muttering, "Smoke. Smoke." Spectators gathered to watch performance artists: jugglers, mimes, and acrobats who were scattered around the fountain. Empty coffee cans or instrument cases were yawning at their feet in anticipation of cash donations. I caught a glimpse of a pickpocket I knew moving through the crowds, instinctively checked for my wallet, then lost sight of him. Rowboats manned by couples drifted lazily on the lake, a mild summer breeze moving them this way and that.

"Thirsty?" I asked Marla.

"Very."

We walked around the east side of the lake to the Loeb Boathouse. We were lucky to find two stools at the end of the outdoor concrete bar overlooking the lake and the Ramble, a thirty-six-acre wild garden.

"Help you?" a bartender said.

Marla ordered white wine. I ordered a beer.

"I love it here," she said as an Italian gondola, powered by an authentic-looking gondolier — striped shirt, porkpie hat — sticked his way across the water, carrying a couple who had a honeymoon look to them.

The bartender served our drinks.

Marla raised her glass in a toast, one eye on the honeymooners. "To lovers."

We clinked glasses.

"So," I said. "You're a Southern belle?"

Marla smiled. Said she was born Marla Ann Maples some ten miles north of Dalton, Georgia, in tiny Cohutta, on October 27, 1963. She spent her formative years in a modest, single-story brick house in Cohutta, then moved into a large, split-level ranch-style house her father had built in a nearby subdivision in Dalton, the so-called carpet capital of the world. It boasted more than 200 manufacturers and 150 factory outlets. Marla claimed that Dalton had more millionaires per capita than any place in the United States. It also enjoyed the highest rate of divorce. She said her own parents, Stan Maples and Ann Locklear Ogletree, divorced when she was sixteen.

Her daddy Stan, a successful builder, suffered a series of reversals in the real estate business that forced him into bankruptcy. A workaholic during the best of times, he spent longer and longer hours away from home, trying to fend off the collapse of his single-family-home-building empire. Ann demanded a divorce. Both Stan and Ann later remarried other people.

Marla had been the star of the girls' basketball team at North Whitfield High School and earned A's in school. She said she still loved to play basketball. I asked her how she got started in beauty pageants.

"It was all my mama's idea." She said her mother enrolled her with a pageant coach down in Dalton. "I always hated the pageants. I did it for Mama. She's never been anywhere, done anything. It was as if she was living out her dreams through me."

Marla said a two-year stint at the University of Georgia, where she dated — among others — football star Herschel Walker, left her more interested in show business than any academic pursuit. That brought her, via Atlanta, to New York City. "It's been six months and I still don't have an acting or model agent."

I couldn't help but wonder what she did for money since her father had financial problems. "I assume you have a job?"

Marla hee-hawed. "Are you gosh-darn crazy?" She looked at me as if I had two heads. "I'll never work." Which I correctly interpreted as "beauty queens don't have to work." Later I would discover that Marla was a modern-day version of Truman Capote's character, Holly Golightly. She lived off "gifts" and "loans" from older men that her mother Ann fixed her up with. Like a very smitten Dr. Jerry Argovitz, president of the Trump-owned New Jersey Generals football team.

The sun moved lower in the western sky. Marla decided she was hungry; Mexican food still sounded good to both of us. We exited the park and hailed a taxi to Rosa Mexicana, located on First Avenue and East Fifty-eighth Street, down the block from Le Club.

There was a thirty-minute wait for a table. I placed my name on the waiting list and managed to find us seats at the small, but busy bar. A bartender put some chips and salsa in front of us.

"Want to try a blue margarita?" I said to Marla.

"I don't usually drink margaritas."

"One can't hurt you."

She thought a moment. "Sure. Why not?"

I ordered two, frozen with salt.

We nibbled on the chips and salsa and checked out the eclectic crowd. Our drinks came. We clinked glasses.

"I have to warn you," Marla said. "Alcohol makes me crazy."

Oh, goodie.

We drank the first two. Ordered two more. And then Marla began laughing hysterically at everything I said. When I'm on, I'm a pretty good comic, but I'm not *that* funny. Marla guffawed at something silly I said, leaned her head on my shoulder, trying to catch her breath. That was when I made a move. Leaned forward. Kissed her softly on the cheek. She stopped laughing. I kissed her on the lips. She kissed me back.

"Mr. Fitzsimmons. Your table is ready," I heard someone say.

"You still hungry?" Marla asked.

"Not really." I shrugged. "Are you?"

She shook her head. "Let's go back to my place."

Now there was a great idea.

I asked for the check, did what I always did when faced with figuring out the gratuity and calculating the total: I didn't even try. I simply overtip. That habit wound up serving me well over the years. I was usually treated like a VIP in every establishment I frequented.

A short cab ride later we burst into Marla's 500-square-foot studio apartment, still flushed from our margarita lunch.

"You're a Marilyn Monroe fan," I said, glancing at several posters Scotch-taped to the walls.

"She's my soulmate," Marla said. "We have a thing, a spiritual connection. Know what I mean?"

Not a clue.

Marla showed me around her studio. Told me that most of the furniture was from her room in her parents' house. She switched on her stereo, put on Willie Nelson and, laughing like two inebriates, we two-stepped around the room. A nuzzle on her ear turned into a kiss, the kiss into a passionate embrace. She squeezed me tight, almost cracking ribs. She was strong. Marla let go and put me in a wristlock.

"Hey." I broke the hold. Pushed her away.

But she rebounded like the basketball player she was and threw an elbow check to my chest that stunned me. Before I knew it, she had me pinned against the wall, laughing maniacally. I was starting to regret ordering her that second margarita.

"Wa-woo-woohoo!" Marla yelled and placed me in a headlock.

"Marla!" I was laughing and squirming at the same time. "What're you doing?"

"Putting you in a Confederate Army headlock," she grunted, applying more pressure. "Yankees are a sucker for it every time."

I twisted and gently flung her away.

"Really?" she said, moving around the room in a half-crouch position, stalking me. "You wanna play rough?" She began dribbling an imaginary basketball. "Let's see you block me," she said and charged, spun around, threw a hip that knocked me aside. I grabbed her, picked her up, and flipped her onto her bed. She lay on her back, giggling like a tickled child. I leaped atop her and tried to pin her. She flipped me over, got on top of me, and began pulling my clothes off. At that point, I realized I'd never met anyone quite like Marla Maples before.

Chapter 10

"My daddy always says I'm gonna kill myself in a car someday," Marla Maples said as we rocketed north along Interstate 75 in Georgia at better than ninety miles per hour, on our way to meet her father. "He says I should've been a race car driver."

It had been about three months since I'd been introduced to Marla at Wilson's restaurant. We'd been joined at the hip ever since. Our nights were a blur of glamorous, star-studded cocktail parties, four-star restaurants, movie premieres, and Broadway plays, where I'd schmooze with potential investors and pitch my movie project to anyone who'd listen. But I was spending money faster than I was earning it. I couldn't keep up the high-rolling life for long. Especially since 99.9 percent of the seemingly interested investors were full of buffalo dung.

"When it comes to money," Malcolm Forbes told me, "few people are for real." Boy, was he right.

Marla floored the accelerator, jerked the wheel to the left, and cleaved through three lanes of horn-blowing, brake-screeching traffic. Next thing I knew we were in the far-left lane, wedged between a four-by-four and a monster sixteen-wheel tractor-trailer that was kissing our rear bumper. The truck driver blasted his air horn with righteous outrage.

"I don't believe you did that!"

Marla hee-hawed. "I scare you?" She powered down her window, flipped the truck driver the bird, and screamed, "Fuck you, asshole!"

Then, to my horror, she opened a purse the size of a mailman's bag, took out a makeup kit and, using the car's rearview mirror, began to apply eyeliner.

"You're tailgating, Marla."

"Oh, relax."

"You're speeding."

"Shut the fuck up."

We'd left New York City's LaGuardia Airport early that morning, flew to Atlanta where, at Marla's insistence, I rented us a racy sports car — a decision I now regretted — for the one-hour drive to her hometown, Dalton.

"Do me a favor and slow down, Marla?" I pointed a shaky finger at the four-by-four in front of us with the Confederate flag and *Death Before Dishonor* bumper sticker. We were so close that I could read the registration tag on the guy's license plate, which was due to expire in two days. "You're riding that guy's ass."

She ceased the makeup application and took her baby blues off the road just long enough to shoot me a look. "I've never had an accident."

"Watch the road!" I said.

The tractor-trailer riding our rear continued to blow its air horn. I could actually feel the heat from his flashing, headlamp-headlights on the back of my neck. I turned and looked. The truck's gleaming chrome grille filled our rear window. I glanced at the speedometer. We were doing 95 miles per hour.

"Guy behind me is really startin' to piss me off!" Marla road-raged. Again, she stuck her hand out the window and flipped him the bird. "Fuck yourself, asshole!"

"Take it easy, Marla."

"Let *him* take it easy."

Marla continued to speed. Tailgate. Fiddle with the radio. And the lunatic behind us continued to crowd us, blow his horn, and flash his headlights. I yanked my seat belt extra-tight. Grabbed fistfuls of the car's leather bucket seat. Propped my feet up on the dashboard. Closed my eyes. Murmured an Act of Contrition — "Bless me, Father, for I have sinned" — and braced for the inevitable impact.

"We're here," Marla singsonged about twenty minutes later. We had stopped on a dirt road in a thickly wooded area. She'd shaved a full twenty minutes off the trip, plus a year off my life.

"Did the propane truck you cut off, the one that jackknifed, did it crash?"

"No." She pulled a brush from the handbag and ran it through her thick blond hair.

"And the kid crossing the road by the Seven-Eleven, on the bike?"

"Aw, the little nigger lost a tad of skin is all." She gestured with the hairbrush toward the woods in front of us. "I told you it's not much." A large, modern mobile home stood in a clearing. A wooden porch bordered the front along with a kaleidoscope of blooming flowers and neatly trimmed foliage. A robust vegetable garden and actual cornfield grew to our right. Across the well-tended lawn, a firewood axe had been left embedded in a tree stump.

We exited the car. I drank in the piney air, closed my eyes, and lost myself in the silence of the surrounding woods. The place had an unmistakable, early American settlers feel to it. I wondered what it would be like to live there. Being a born and bred New Yorker accustomed to twenty-four-hour noise and action, I'd probably go batshit crazy.

Marla, ashamed that her father lived in a mobile home, had been preparing me for this moment for days.

"We had a big house once," she'd said forlornly, repeating the story of her parents' divorce. About her daddy, once a successful builder, falling on hard times. Now he was broke. A simple man with simple tastes, living off the land. The way she described him, I was expecting to meet Jed Clampett.

"There any bears around here?"

"Sure," Marla said. "Black bears. Bobcats too. But they won't bother you."

Yeah, sure. I heard twigs break in the distant woods behind the vegetable garden. Looked and saw the underbrush sway. Something large was moving out there, moving in our direction. Fast.

"That a bear?" I felt for my weapon and remembered, since I wasn't licensed to carry in Georgia, I'd left it home. I scanned the area for anything I could use as a weapon. There was the axe, but I'd never reach it in time. All at once, something sizable and fur-covered crashed out of the woods and disappeared into the cornfield coming our way. What the hell was that?

"Shit," Marla said.

"Shit?"

Marla pointed. A ferocious-looking 125-pound Rottweiler came lumbering out of the cornfield.

"I just hate that dawg," Marla said.

The dog saw us. Growled. Bared its fangs.

Marla grabbed my arm. Scooted behind me, putting me between her and the beast.

"Nice doggie." My voice cracked. "Good dog."

The dog barked, charged.

Marla screamed, "Daddy!"

"Dawg!" a man's voice thundered.

The dog raised a cloud of dust as it skidded to a stop. It turned and pranced happily to the mobile home, stubby tail wagging, and sat on the porch. The screen door swung open and Stan Maples, dressed in blue jeans and a wool Pendleton shirt, strolled out. There was no missing the family resemblance: Marla had inherited Stan's big blue eyes.

"Hey, Daddy."

"Hey, darlin'." Stan's baritone voice was as Southern as a truckload of buttered grits. He gave me the dubious once-over.

"Dawg don't like Yankees." Stan grinned. He seized the canine gargoyle by the collar and chained it to a tree. Only then did Marla rush up and hug her daddy.

"I'm Stan Maples," he said and shook my hand.

I introduced myself.

"How was the trip?" Stan said.

"Trip was just fine, Daddy," Marla said.

I said, *"Your daughter's a maniac, the worst driver I've ever seen."* Only kidding.

I said, "Trip was fine."

"Well, c'mon in," Stan said. "Beer, Thomas?"

"Love one," I said.

"This is Daddy's wife, Deena," Marla said as we stepped into the mobile home. "We call her Baby Woman 'cause she's younger than me."

"Hey, Thomas." Baby Woman looked to be about nineteen years old and pretty in a clean, country girl sort of way. I glanced again at Stan; he had to be in his late forties.

Good for you, Stan.

Marla showed me what there was of the mobile home. It was larger than the average New York City two-bedroom apartment. That's not saying much. There was a small guest bedroom and bathroom. The master bedroom had a king-sized bed and its own hot tub. The large living room was paneled with dark wood. Deer heads and a rack of hunting rifles hung on a wall. The overstuffed chairs and couch were comfortable looking. I loved the potbelly woodburning stove. A small cord of firewood was piled in a corner by the door.

Marla said she needed to freshen up, excused herself, and disappeared into the guest bedroom.

"Nice place you have here," I said as Stan handed me a Dixie beer. I popped it open. Sat on the couch.

"It'll do." He sat on an easy chair and opened a brew for himself. Baby Woman sat on the floor, like an obedient dawg, by his side.

"Marla tells me you used to be a New York cop," Stan said.

I sipped my beer. "For about eleven years."

"She said you worked in Fort Apache. I saw the movie with Paul Newman. Hell of a rough area. Damn if you don't have some stories to tell."

That's when Marla strode into the room.

Stark naked.

I coughed beer through my nose.

"What's the craziest thing you've ever seen as a New York cop, Thomas?" Stan ignored Marla, who moved across the room into the kitchen area, opened the refrigerator, bent over, and poked around inside.

Now, I'd heard plenty of politically incorrect jokes about Southerners sleeping with family members: brothers and sisters, fathers and daughters. And I didn't want to believe that's what I'd stumbled into. Then again, I didn't know what to think.

"Marla," I said.

"What?" Her tone challenging.

"I feel really uncomfortable about this."

"About what?" she deadpanned.

"Please put some clothes on."

"Why? This is the way I am when I'm home."

Baby Woman rolled her eyes.

Stan said, "Ever throw a suspect off a roof like the cops did in the Fort Apache movie? I read somewhere that the movie was based on real events."

"I'm a guest, Marla," I said. "I'm uncomfortable. Please put some clothes on."

"No."

"Ever shoot anyone?" Stan asked. "You know, blow someone's brains out?"

"Put some clothes on, Marla," I said, "or I'm leaving."

"Goddamn it, Marla," Stan thundered. "Get dressed."

"No." She burst into tears. Darted across the room and exploded out the front door. Where the hell was she going?

I got to my feet, quickstepped across the room, looked out of the screen door, and watched as Marla, crying and running like a young deer, disappeared into the woods. The Rottweiler, sitting at full attention, watched her go.

Unfucking-believable.

Speechless, I walked back inside the mobile home, sat back down on the couch, and looked for a reaction of any kind from Stan and Baby Woman.

"Ready for another beer, Thomas?" Stan asked cheerfully. He rocked out of his chair to get me one.

Baby Woman just rolled her eyes.

Chapter 11

What with all the partying, Broadway and concert tickets, dinners at four-star restaurants and gritty pubs, not to mention an emergency loan to a few friends in dire need, money was getting tight. And so, I found myself on a Tuesday evening, sitting at the bar in a Third Avenue pub called Mumbles, waiting to confront two goombahs who were attempting to shake down the owner, thinking about what to do about Marla Maples.

About an hour after Marla had stormed naked from her daddy's mobile home, she returned, her body lashed red by snapping tree branches. She dressed in shorts and a halter — no bra or underwear — and came into the living room, carrying on as if the embarrassing scene had never occurred.

That evening, in bed, when I attempted to discuss the incident and our differing views on modesty, we ended up in a big fight. I wound up sleeping on the couch.

"Ain't nothing, Thomas," Stan told me the following morning. He handed me a cup of coffee. "Marla's high school sweetheart, Jeff? He and Marla used to fight till both of `em were bloody."

Marla walked into the room. "Shut the fuck up, Daddy."

Mumbles's bartender served me a beer. The restaurant, which was a few blocks from my residence, had been founded by an ex-cop I knew, Jimmy Goan, who sold it to the Feldman family. Although the Feldmans had never run a pub before, they knew their stuff when it came to food and they wisely kept the same, popular bartenders.

"I need some help." Micky Feldman, the owner, had phoned me a few days ago. "Some guys are trying to shake me down." Which was not unusual in high-crime New York, where shakedown artists came and went.

"What guys?" I said.

Micky described them. "The big one said his name was Tony. The other one is Sal. No last names."

"How much they want?"

"They said something about five thousand a month—protection money."

"You go to the cops?"

"I will if I have to. But most of my kitchen staff are illegals. You understand."

"Sure. You saying you want me to take care of things?"

"They're scaring the waitresses. Running off customers." Micky paused before he said, "How much?"

Since I was a Mumbles regular and I liked Micky, I told him I didn't want cash. Instead, I'd like to run a house tab. Micky was more than fine with that.

I smelled the stench of overpowering, cheap men's cologne just as the bartender rapped his knuckles on the bar, got my attention, and gestured to the door. Two goombahs— Tony and Sal, I presumed—dressed in black leather jackets like central casting wiseguys, walked in like they owned the joint. They spoke to the girl working the door. She pointed them to me. Showtime.

"Who the fuck're you?" Tony, the larger one, said as they approached. "Where the fuck is Micky?"

Their combined roach spray colognes caused my eyes to water. I broke into a short sneezing fit. "That's nice cologne you two *bathed* in."

"What're you," Sal, the short one said. "A fuckin' comedian?"

"I'm Micky's partner," I said.

"Fuckin' Micky didn't say nothin' about no fuckin' partner," Sal said.

"Let's sit at a table." Preparing for another sneezing fit, I grabbed a handful of bar napkins. Led the way across the dining room to a corner four-top. I sat across from the two punks, my back to a wall.

There are several ways to handle extortionists. Usually, me and a couple of ex-cop associates of mine would grab the thugs and discuss the error of their ways. But since I knew the organized crime figures on Manhattan's Upper East Side and was pretty sure these two bozos weren't "connected," I decided to try a different tack.

It was common knowledge that the local thugs didn't take kindly to outsiders muscling in on their turf. And so, I had phoned a neighborhood racketeer and haberdasher—he owned an upscale men's clothing store—that I was friendly with. A tough-talking throwback to black-and-white gangster films—I'll call him Grayman—and told him what was going on.

"Tony? Sal? Never heard of 'em," Grayman said. The gravel-voiced, five-foot-eight thirty-five-year-old—who reminded everyone of the 1940s actor-gangster George Raft—was prematurely gray and always wore a custom-made gray suit and gray tie. His loan-sharking and gambling operations encompassed Manhattan's entire Upper East Side. "Want I should take care of it?" Grayman said.

"Either you or the cops."

"Fuck the cops." Grayman hung up.

"Now," I said to the two wannabe hoods. "What can I do for you gents?"

"It ain't about what you can do for us." Tony stuck a fat, manicured finger in my face. "It's what we can do for you."

"I'm listening."

"Like we told Mikey, we're gonna provide security for this dump."

Sal said, "Long as we're around, you won't have any problems."

"We don't have problems now."

"Yeah?" Tony said. "Well, things change. What if there's a fight? Your mirrors could get broke. Windows. Customers could get hurt."

"Yeah," Sal said. "And don't forget about roaches. Roaches ain't good for business. You follow?"

"Oh, yeah," I said, wondering why two guys posing as New York City hoods had distinct Midwestern accents.

Tony took out a smoke. Fired it up and took a drag. "Understand, we ain't greedy."

"Yeah." Sal held up a piece of paper with *$5000* written on it. "That's what we told Micky. Cash, of course."

"Of course."

"If that's too much, we can go a bit less." He put the piece of paper away. "For the first month. Capisce?"

"*Capisco.*"

"So," Sal said. "We understand each other?"

"We do."

"Good," Tony said. "Have the cash ready the first of every month." The two pushed back their chairs. Got to their feet. Tony dropped his cigarette, crushed it with his foot, then stuck the finger back in my face. "Don't disappoint us."

The hapless thugs turned, walked the length of the restaurant and out the door. I looked to the bar. Grayman, dressed in a gray sharkskin suit, and I made eye contact. He mouthed the words, "That them?"

I nodded.

Grayman threw back a shot of whiskey and slid off a barstool. Followed the two wannabes out the door, where I knew half-a-dozen authentic goombahs were waiting.

"Phone call," the bartender said, handing me the house phone. "Marla?"

"Hello?"

"I've been attacked," Marla Maples cried.

Chapter 12

A BLUE-AND-white was pulling up in front of Marla's apartment building as I stepped out of a cab. I introduced myself to the two police officers, one male, one female. Showed ID. Told them I was retired out of the old 41st precinct. That I was the one who called 911.

I shared the description Marla had given me of her assailant: Male, black, about forty years old, wearing a filthy faux leather coat, brandishing a broken umbrella, and sitting in a battered wheelchair. We searched the immediate area, giving special attention to the Allerton Hotel. The culprit was nowhere in sight. None of the characters loitering out front of the Allerton would admit to seeing or hearing anything. No surprise there.

Checking doorways and alleys, we made our way back to Marla's apartment building. The doorman announced us. We stepped into an elevator.

Marla opened her front door and rushed into my arms.

"You all right?" I said.

"Thank you for coming," she sniffled, then broke the embrace, stepping aside. "Please come in."

The two cops gawked at her outfit: skintight jeans, red high heels, and revealing brassiere. The female cop took out a memo book and pen. "What happened?"

Marla gestured to the cops to the couch beneath a Marilyn Monroe *Seven Year Itch* movie poster. I sat on a chair beneath Marilyn's *Life* magazine cover poster.

"Well, I declare," Marla said. "I was walking home from evening services at the Marble Collegiate Church. You know, at Fifth Avenue and Twenty-ninth Street? I was walking by the Allerton Hotel, minding my own business, and I said, 'Good evening' to a man in a wheelchair. Would you believe he cursed me? Then hit me with an umbrella." She rubbed her right arm, winced. "He chased me all the way home!"

"In a wheelchair?" the male officer said, eyes on Marla's chest. "He chased you in a wheelchair?"

"My lordy, yes. It was like he was possessed."

After the cops had taken a report, they asked Marla if she wanted to go to the hospital and have her arm x-rayed. She refused medical aid.

From that day on, Marla, claiming she was afraid to return to her Chelsea neighborhood, began spending more and more time at my Normandie Court apartment. Not that my neighborhood was that much safer than Chelsea. Yorkville borders high-crime East Harlem. Regardless, the next thing I knew, Marla had given up her Chelsea studio and moved into my place lock, stock, and barrel.

Saying that Marla made herself at home is an understatement. She jammed her furniture into my second bedroom. Her clothes filled my closets. Her personal grooming articles overwhelmed both of my bathrooms. Other than that, once I'd convinced Marla to adhere to the house rules — always keep the front door locked and, for Christ's sake, do *not* walk around naked, since we have neighbors with binoculars looking in our windows — I've got to admit I didn't mind her company. She was easy to get along with: Forever in a cheerful mood, compliant, always deferring to my wishes. And she made it a point to ingratiate herself to my large circle of lifelong friends. My sisters and friends liked her. The cottontops, Tom Counihan and John McCooey, were smitten. After a while, my doubts about her mental stability began to fade, although her possessiveness and extreme jealousy toward other women — toward *anyone* who monopolized my time — gave me pause. And then there was the curious fact that Marla didn't read newspapers, watch or listen to the news. She was blissfully oblivious to the world around her.

"This is awful," I said one morning, my nose in the *New York Times*. "Nine thousand dead in Mexico City."

"Huh?" Marla, in an exercise leotard, was stretching on my living room floor.

"An earthquake," I said. "Killed nine thousand people and still counting."

"That's terrible." She went back to stretching.

Only when I mentioned that I'd read about Madonna marrying the actor Sean Penn, she perked up. "That reminds me," Marla said. "We have to talk."

"Okay."

"My grandparents are strict Southern Baptists," Marla told me. "They'd simply die if they thought I was living with a man I'm not at least engaged to."

"Engaged?" Sheer terror found its way into my voice. "But I'm not ready to get ma—ma—"

"Married, Thomas. The word is *married*. You can say it if you try. Now say it."

"Ma—ma—ma—ma—"

"You're not funny."

Marla worked on me through the morning, afternoon, and evening. Repeated several times that her grandparents were strict Southern Baptists. Told me that they were demanding to know where she was living and with whom. They were also demanding to know who the man was whose voice was on "her" answering machine.

"It wouldn't be a real engagement, Thomas," Marla cooed the following morning over coffee. "Just for appearances."

"I can't afford a ring, Marla."

"Oh, pshaw!" she said. "I'm sure Tiffany has a layaway plan. If not, there's always Cartier."

"I mean it. I'm just about broke."

Marla smiled. "Any old ring will do."

I sort of understood where she was coming from. Besides, after my two divorces and several quick and passionate love affairs, being engaged again would be no big deal, especially to someone who looked like Marla.

"You do love me, don't you, Thomas?"

I took a moment before saying, "Well, sure. But I told you about my two divorces. I'm not looking to marry anytime soon."

"Then it's settled," she said, unfazed by my lack of enthusiasm. "I'll call my family and tell them we're engaged."

And so we became officially engaged. Then, to keep in the spirit of things, I purchased her a ring: an eighteen-karat gold, two-karat faux-emerald, Irish claddagh ring.

"It's a traditional Irish ring that represents love, loyalty, and friendship," I told Marla as I handed her the gift-wrapped box over a steak dinner at home. I'd broiled us a couple of filet mignons. High-priced dinners in four-star restaurants were quickly becoming a thing of the past. "The Irish use it as a wedding band, engagement ring, or friendship ring—depends on who gifts it and why. If you wear it on your left hand with the point of the heart toward the fingertips, it means you're engaged."

Marla smiled expectantly, tore the wrapping paper off, and flipped open the box. Frowned. "Looks like it came from a Cracker Jack box." She snapped the lid closed and laid the ring aside. She would never wear it.

Chapter 13

MARLA STILL DIDN'T HAVE AN agent. I thought I'd take a chance and walk her into Ford. Granted, she was way too curvy and glamorous for traditional modeling. But maybe they had a gig for her in their thriving TV department. Hey, you never know.

"Would you have a moment, Thomas?" Jerry Ford, the sophisticated, erudite, cofounder of the agency asked as Marla and I walked into the agency's main floor offices.

I told Jerry, "Sure." Then I led Marla up to the second-floor woman's division and introduced her to the head booker, Rusty, asking her to please take good care of Marla. Then I followed Jerry upstairs to the third floor, said hi to the men's division bookers, and followed Jerry into his office.

"I'm afraid it's another stalking." Jerry sat at his untidy desk and directed me to a chair. "More troubling than the last one."

The last stalker had been a doozy. A deluded forty-year-old male, pretending to be a delivery person, had forced his way into a nineteen-year-old model's third-floor tenement apartment. He was down on one knee, begging the frightened Parisian to run away with him — a gleaming meat cleaver in his hand — when I arrived with a policewoman friend in tow. We'd found the model's front door ajar and walked in. Saw the guy brandishing the cleaver, saw the terrified model huddled behind a couch. The policewoman pulled her weapon. The stalker dropped the cleaver and, to make a long story short, was eventually committed to a mental health facility in upstate New York.

"This stalker's a client of ours," Jerry said. "A good client. An art director. Can you believe that?"

"Any previous incidents?"

"Not that I'm aware of."

Jerry handed me a piece of paper with the client/stalker's information.

"Michael Earp?" I said.

"That's what he goes, by." Jerry nodded. "He's stalking Alisa E."

"I don't know her."

"Come to the softball game tonight." Jerry was referring to the inter-modeling agency league Ford belonged to. "Alisa will be there. It will give you a chance to speak to her."

"Sounds good," I said.

"Your friend Marla looks… uh, athletic."

"That she is."

"Bring her. Everyone who shows up gets to play."

"Michael Earp told me he'd kill me," Alisa E. said.

We were sitting on the Heckscher Ballfield bleachers in Central Park—Seventh Avenue and Central Park South from Sixty-first to Sixty-third Streets—our eyes flicking to the game in progress. The blond-haired, blue-eyed white-bread lingerie and bikini model squinted into the late-afternoon sun, lit one Marlboro Light off the stubby, dying embers of another and placed it on trembling lips.

We watched Marla Maples hit a practice line drive down the first base line that could have taken someone's head off. But the guy warming up at base, former Montreal Expos baseball player, model/actor Jack Scalia—who would go on to star as Chris Stamp on *All My Children*—caught the ball with ease.

I turned to Alisa E. "He ever lay hands on you?"

"Just threats," Alisa said, "over the phone."

"What were his words, exactly?"

She inhaled a lungful of smoke, blew it out. "'If I can't have you, bitch, no one can. I'll cut your fucking face up.'" She wiped sweat from her brow. It was 92 degrees and humid. "'Then I'll cut your tits off.'" Her voice cracked. "'I'll slit your fucking throat. You filthy fucking whore.'"

Jesus.

"I was more mad than scared. Told him to go screw himself." Alisa smiled tightly. "That I had friends in the Mafia. Sounds stupid, I know."

"How long you date him?"

"About three months." She looked off. "He's an art director at Dancer Fitzgerald."

"Jerry Ford told me."

"Play ball!" some guy shouted.

Everyone fielded their positions.

Wilhelmina model-actor, Douglas Barr—who would become known for his roles on the ABC TV series *The Fall Guy* and CBS series *Designing Women*—was first up at bat.

"Earp his real last name?" I asked Alisa E.

"Not really," she said. "It's some unpronounceable Slavic name."

"You know his home address?" I asked her. "Date of birth?"

She jotted down the information. Handed it to me. I folded the piece of paper and slipped it into my jeans pocket. Noticed that Marla, who had been standing at the batter's cage, chatting with our attorney friend Paul Derounian, who was playing for Ford, was glaring in our direction.

Marla applauded when Barr grounded out. Then she walked behind the backstop, climbed onto the bleachers. Sat behind us, two seats over. I could tell she was listening.

"I'm going to introduce you to a policewoman friend of mine," I told Alisa. "First thing you have to do is file a complaint. Then we can get you an order of protection; it's a restraining order. Then we'll serve it on Earp at his office, in front of his coworkers."

"You mean, like hand it to him?" she said, panic in her voice. "At work?"

"Exactly."

"He'll go ballistic."

"Maybe at first," I said. "But most guys go away after being served. They're embarrassed. Don't want their coworkers, family, or friends to know."

Alisa shook her head. "He'll kill me. I know he will."

"I won't let that happen."

"What?" She sniggered. "You going to sleep outside my door? Follow me around twenty-four-seven?"

"He violates the restraining order," I said, "he'll be arrested."

"You don't know him."

"Believe me, I know the type."

Alisa E. took one last drag on her cigarette, flicked the butt into the grass. "I've been thinking of going out to LA. See how the business is there."

"That's another way to handle it." I slipped her my business card with my answering service and home number. "Whatever you decide, I'm here for you."

Alisa thanked me, looked over my shoulder, and went pale. "Fuck! There he is."

"Where?"

"Down third base. Behind the outfield. Curly black hair."

Sure enough, a light-skinned male, around thirty years old, wearing a blue, nylon windbreaker — it was way too hot for a windbreaker — was loitering on a path behind left field, looking our way.

Alisa grabbed my arm and squeezed. "Don't let him hurt me." She began to hyperventilate. "Please?"

"Stay put." I patted her hand, got to my feet, stepped down from the bleachers, walked down the third base line. Michael Earp saw me coming. He turned, stuck his right hand in his windbreaker pocket—did he have a gun?—and began strolling south toward West Fifty-ninth Street.

"Hey, Michael," I called out, quickening my pace. "Wait up. I wanna talk to you."

Michael flipped me the bird, walked faster.

I didn't bother to pursue.

Chapter 14

"Stop here," Alisa told the cabdriver.

"I'll walk you in," I said.

Alisa E. grabbed the door handle, stopped a moment to scan the block, looking for her stalker. "I don't see him."

"I'll be right back," I said to Marla.

"Take care, Marla," Alisa said.

"You too," Marla said.

Alisa and I exited the cab. I escorted her through a revolving door, into her doorman building. The doorman glanced in our direction, then went back to reading a newspaper.

"Let me know when you land in LA," I said, reasonably confident that her move to La-La Land would be the answer to her stalking problem.

"Thanks for everything, Thomas." She kissed me on the cheek and disappeared into a waiting elevator.

"White Horse Tavern," I told the driver as I stepped back into the cab.

"I don't understand," Marla said as the cab pulled from the curb. "Why get involved?"

"What do you mean?"

"With Alisa. What're you getting involved for?"

"The girl's being stalked," I said.

"Yeah, but that's not your business."

"Stalkers are everyone's business."

We were on our way to the aforementioned White Horse

Tavern on Hudson Street. Since Ford wound up losing to the Wilhelmina models in a one-run heartbreaker, the winners got to choose where to celebrate, and we losers had to pay the tab. Alisa had declined to join us since she was leaving for LA ASAP.

Marla shook her head. "We drove out of our way just to drop her off?"

"It's not that big a deal."

"It is to me," Marla said. "You have the hots for Alisa or something?"

Who didn't?

"Give it a rest, will you?"

Marla grumbled. "I think you do."

We stopped at a red light.

"What about me, Thomas?" she asked.

"What about you?"

"The Ford TV people said they'd be in touch. I haven't heard from them. I still need an agent. Someone with clout. Not the lowlife bottom-feeders I'm dealing with now." The cab dropped us off at the White Horse.

In bed, later that evening, I stared at the ceiling and thought about the fact that there had been a not-so-subtle change in Marla's attitude toward me since our "engagement." Gone were the cheerful moods. She was no longer so easy to get along with. But I chalked the changes up to the fact that we were not out partying every night, hitting all the hot spots like we used to. I simply couldn't afford it.

Then there was Marla's understandable exasperation at having to deal with low-end agents. Auditioning for cheesecake modeling gigs, low-paying, nonunion industrial films and tits-and-ass bit parts. Fending off drooling sycophants, sidestepping, and fighting off the aggressive ones didn't help her mindset.

"Your problem is you're a star, Marla," I would explain to her whenever she got depressed. "You're not a second lead any more than Marilyn Monroe. There are thousands of parts a year for actresses, but not for stars. That will always be your struggle."

I know this might sound silly, but I began to schedule official Marla Maples days when I'd take the day off to concentrate solely on her personal and professional chores. Those days we might take a casting agent or photographer to lunch — on my tab, of course — or update her résumé and mail her newest headshot to a hundred or more casting agents in New York and LA. Or I'd take her on rounds, cold calls to potential modeling clients, photographers, advertising agencies, etc.

But still, she didn't find acting work.

"I need publicity," Marla told me one day.

She was right. An actor needs PR.

I came up with a plan. Since I wasn't having any luck securing financing for my movie projects, I decided to shoot a promotional trailer.

"I'll write a part for you, Marla. You'll costar. I'll fly my twin brother up from Florida for the shoot. I'll send the tape out. Use it as a demo. If they won't read the script, maybe they'll pop the tape into a VCR. It's a no-brainer. I'll ask Tom Counihan to art-direct the project. He has a ton of experience with industrial films and commercials. I'll hire a press agent. We'll both make the papers."

Marla loved the idea. She called her mother, father, and grandparents in Dalton with the news: She was to costar with me in a demo that would be seen by major Hollywood players. Her family was thrilled. Her mother wanted to fly up to watch the shoot; of course, she couldn't afford it. Marla talked me into purchasing her mother's ticket. Looked like I was finally going to meet Ann Maples.

That day I called Michael Collyer to discuss any legal matters that could arise while planning the demo shoot; things like production company contracts and theatrical union concerns. Finally, I phoned the soon-to-be most influential and polarizing figure in Marla Maples's life: My friend, the East Coast head of publicity at Avco Embassy Pictures.

Chuck Jones.

Chuck Jones quickstepped into the now-defunct Doral Hotel and entered Mormando's Italian restaurant. A devout family man, Chuck had allotted exactly one hour for our meeting. A familiar, if not welcome face in Mormando's, Chuck — a notoriously bad tipper — found a seat at the bar, exchanged a chilly greeting with the starched bartender, Frankie, and ordered a beer. He adjusted his gaudy polyester tie, smoothed down his god-awful maroon-and-white checkered polyester jacket, and looked at himself in the bar's smoky mirror. Although the hair that was disappearing from his head seemed to have taken root in his nose and ears, at forty-three years old, the five-ten former Marine still appeared to be in pretty good shape. Weightlifting three times a week helped, and so did his wife's healthy meal plans.

I had phoned Chuck earlier that day, told him about the demo I was planning to shoot and send to potential investors. Said I'd written a part for a new girlfriend of mine. Marla Maples was to play opposite my twin and me. I asked him to meet us for drinks, so he could meet Marla and discuss the possibility of my hiring him to do our PR.

Although for years Chuck Jones and I spoke almost daily on the phone, and I considered him a true friend—loyal, there for me during good times and bad—I knew little about him. What I did know was that he was a complex mixture of peculiar attitudes.

As I mentioned earlier, Chuck was a family man first and foremost. He was a gentleman. Bright. Aware. A good listener. Generous with his time and money. Yet more than one outraged bartender or waiter had chased me out of restaurants, saying that Chuck, who'd picked up a hefty tab for a group of us, had stiffed them, left no tip. Chuck was even-tempered. A diplomat. Yet he would engage in mortifying disputes with restaurant staff over the quality of his food or size of the portion.

"You're late," he said as I led Marla into Mormando's. "I've got to catch the seven-twenty train."

"Sorry," I said to Chuck.

"It's my fault." Marla stepped out from behind me. "Hello." She stuck out a hand. "I'm Marla Maples."

Chuck's eyes popped. He broke into a silly, bashful grin. "Oh, hi." He shook her hand. "I'm Chuck Jones."

"Nice to make your acquaintance, Chuck."

As usual, I received a genuinely warm greeting from Frankie the bartender, which was the result, I'm sure, of my practice of overtipping. We claimed two barstools. Marla sat between Chuck and me.

"Tell me about this demo you're shooting," Chuck said as Frankie brought Marla a white wine, me a light beer, and Chuck another Heineken.

"Well, I declare!" Marla said as she turned on the Southern charm. She went on to pitch our demo. Did a better job of it than I could have. Two hours and four rounds of drinks later, we were still sitting at the bar. So much for the 7:20 train.

"These are on me," Frankie the bartender said as he set down yet another round of drinks. I shuddered as I watched Marla drain her fourth glass of white wine and start on her fifth. Whenever Marla was overserved, she became mentally irregular: sweet and sexy or argumentative, belligerent, and combative.

"A toast," Chuck said, raising his beer glass. "Thomas's movie project."

Marla and I lifted our glasses.

"And," he added, "to the lovely actress, Marla Maples. May her star shine bright."

"Thank you," Marla gushed.

"Hear, hear," I said as we all clinked glasses.

I took a short pull on my beer and watched as Marla gulped down her wine. She placed the empty glass on the bar. Reeled. Swayed. Then toppled ass-over-teakettle from her barstool. Chuck helped me peel Marla off the deck and balance her on her stool.

"You okay?" I said.

"I think I'm going to throw up."

We rushed Marla to the downstairs ladies' room.

Waited outside.

"She's terrific, Thomas," Chuck said as we listened to Marla heaving her guts up. "Really terrific."

As we left the restaurant, I noticed a familiar face cruising south amid the bustling, rush-hour crowd. His eyes met mine. I nodded. "Hello, Malcolm."

But Malcolm Forbes, one of the richest men in the world, did not acknowledge me. Instead, he spun and hurried off in the opposite direction. I checked the area for his bodyguards. Didn't see them. Odd. Well, maybe not so odd. At the time, the East Fifties along Lexington Avenue was known for gay prostitution.

"Who's that?" Marla said.

"An acquaintance," I said.

"He looked frightened."

He was. Frightened of exposure.

As I mentioned earlier, I had first met Malcolm Forbes, multimillionaire owner and publisher of *Forbes* magazine, a famously rugged individualist and man's man when I was cohosting *Now!* I interviewed him at Timberfield, his forty-acre Far Hills, New Jersey, estate for the show's "Happiest Millionaire" segment. While my production crew was setting up our outdoor interview, along the edge of a large field where Malcolm inflated his hot-air balloons, the man himself, accompanied by a team of bodyguards, came over to greet us. His handshake was abrupt and so was Malcolm. He turned his back on me and spoke to my producer. Feeling slighted, I introduced myself to his security team.

It was a well-known fact that Malcolm disliked the press, but when he heard me telling his security people that I was a novice TV host and an ex–New York City cop, his attitude changed.

"NYPD?" Malcolm said.

"I worked the South Bronx, Fort Apache."

Malcolm smiled warmly and re-shook my hand.

"We won't be ready for about forty-five minutes, Mr. Forbes," my producer said.

"Guess I'll get myself a cup of coffee," Malcolm said.

"I could use one," I said.

Malcolm looked at me for a beat. "C'mon."

Malcolm left his security team with the NBC crew. I accompanied him along a long path that led past red clay tennis courts, a swimming pool, and three guest cottages to his impressive colonial-style residence.

"It was originally a farmhouse," he said as we entered the kitchen. "The oldest section of the house dates back to 1760." He said additions were added in the 1860s, the 1920s, and again in 1961, when he built a bomb shelter.

After some pretty good coffee and small talk, which was all about Malcolm trying to figure out my politics—as I recall, he spoke disparagingly about the Kennedys—he offered to show me around his estate.

I've often wondered why some of the high-powered people I've met over the years have taken a liking to me: from film stars, professional athletes, blue blood trust-fund types, to billionaire businessmen. I believe it's because I'm basically a nice guy. "Zen" is how some people described me. I'm not the competitive sort. I'm pretty good at judging my audience and so I'm circumspect and measured with my opinions. I'm a good listener. Never judge. Once a person realizes that I'm not a threat physically, intellectually, or financially, even the most insecure big shots warm to me. Some solicited my company.

Malcolm led me on a solo tour of his estate. We started in a garage, where he showed off his sixty-eight motorcycles. Next, he showed me his collection of French military paintings and several Fabergé eggs; I think he owned nine. I even got to tour his bomb shelter.

After our TV interview, which included a ride with Malcolm in one of his hot-air balloons, he invited me back the following week to participate in a fifty-bike motorcycle rally. A few months later I got the first of many calls from someone at his office inviting me to a star-studded party on his luxurious yacht, the *Highlander II*, which he kept docked on Manhattan's west side. As I've mentioned, Donald Trump also attended some of these gatherings. We'd usually gravitate toward one another and talk about the old days at Maxwell's Plum, snigger about our mutual ex-girlfriends. But then Donald would move on. He was there to conduct business, make contacts. I was there to have a good time.

One evening, I was shooting eight-ball in a dark, seedy Second Avenue pub with a guy named Jim, an ex-LAPD detective whom I'd only recently met.

"Do any private investigating since leaving the force?" Jim said as he racked the balls. A licensed PI in both New York State and California, Jim was a reformed alcoholic who drank coffee by the gallon and chain-smoked unfiltered cigarettes.

"Occasionally." I chose a warped pool cue. Rubbed a dried-out, crumbling cube of blue chalk on the loose, off-center tip.

"You break," Jim said.

I lined up a shot along the thin, scuffed green felt. Broke. The tip flew off the cue. A solid ball rolled into the corner pocket. I chose another battered stick. Sank one more solid. Then missed a bank shot.

An Irish waitress brought me a pint of Guinness.

"I've got a client will pay a lot for certain information about a guy you know."

"Yeah?" I eyeballed Jim. "How do you know who I know?"

Jim sank a stripe. "I'm an ace detective."

"Who's the client?"

Jim sank another. "Can't say."

"Who's the guy I know?"

Jim missed his next shot. "Malcolm Forbes."

I chalked my cue stick. "What kind of information?"

"Forbes is a closet queen."

I missed my shot. "So?"

It's not that I knew Malcolm that well, but I didn't like where this conversation was going. Fact was that other than the occasional party on his yacht where he introduced me to single women—I was apparently on some approved guest list—I didn't socialize with him. Still, he'd been kind to me and I felt protective. Plus, the cop in me knew something was amiss.

Jim circled the table.

I drank more Guinness.

"My client wants surveillance pictures of him with men. Video, if possible."

"What for?"

"I get paid." Jim shrugged. "I don't ask questions." He sank another one. "I'm told you're friendly with him and his security people. You can get close. It's worth, say, twenty-five thousand?"

I almost dropped my pint of Guinness.

Jim bent and lined up a two-ball combination.

"Dollars? Twenty-five thousand *dollars*?"

Jim made the combo.

I chalked my cue, pretending to consider the offer. Then thought about the fact that I'd met Jim for the first time only a week ago. We'd been introduced in a Second Avenue bar and backgammon club, Knickers, by another ex-cop I knew and didn't especially like; the guy was too slick for my taste.

"So, Jim. Us meeting at Knickers was no coincidence."

Jim's smile revealed yellow cigarette and coffee-stained teeth. "Not really." Jim was ready to shoot when I snatched the cue ball off the table.

Jim straightened. "What?"

"Tell you what I'm gonna do, Jimbo. I'm gonna call Malcolm Forbes, tell him about you and this job offer. Then I'm going to advise him to go to the Manhattan DA."

Jim reared back. "Hold on now—"

"'Cause this has blackmail written all over it."

Without saying another word, Jim placed his cue stick back on the wall rack, turned, and walked out of the pub.

I phoned Malcolm's director of security that very night, told him about the job offer and everything I knew about the ex-LA detective Jim. He was most grateful and suggested I phone Malcolm directly. "He's in the office by eight a.m.," he said. "Need the number?"

"I have it."

"Thomas Fitzsimmons for Mr. Forbes," I told a series of secretaries early the following morning and was placed on hold. Malcolm finally picked up about five minutes later.

"Thomas, glad you called. Party on the boat this weekend. A lot of single women."

"You might have a problem, Malcolm."

"Oh?"

He listened as I recounted my encounter with Jim. "I've already spoken to your security people."

"I appreciate that," he said.

"Want me to follow up? Try to find out who Jim's client is?"

"My people will deal with it."

"Anything I can do?"

"No. Goodbye, Thomas," he said abruptly and hung up.

I never heard from Malcolm Forbes again.

Chapter 15

One week later, two days before our demo shoot, I was at my dining room table, working on last-minute changes to the script, when I heard Marla cry out.

"My God, I can't believe it."

I got to my feet, hurried to Marla's side, saw my twin brother Robert, standing at my front door, the familiar screw-you sneer on his face.

Since I was a kid, people always had the same astonished reaction when they first saw my brother. Although Robert and I think we look quite different, we are in fact identical twins, and yet we have opposite personalities, e.g., I'm a people person. Robert is not.

"I'm Robert, the good-looking one," my twin said as he walked in carrying luggage. "You must be Marla." Gallantly, he took her hand and kissed it. "After knowing me," he said, "you'll throw rocks at him."

Marla giggled. "I know what you look like naked."

Robert's jaw dropped.

"Ahem." My bro and I shook hands. "Welcome, clone."

"You even sound alike," Marla said, wonder in her face and voice. "Is there *anything* different about you two?"

I groaned, knowing what Robert would say.

"Yes," Robert deadpanned. "I wear an extra-large jock."

Later that day we met with half-a-dozen cops and firefighter friends for happy hour at the pub Mumbles. The slightly inebriated group was waiting for us at the bar when we walked in. Gaga over Marla, several of them jumped up and offered her their stools. I bought a round of drinks.

"Mind if I ask you something, Robert?" Marla had to raise her voice to be heard over the din and the jukebox.

Robert picked up his beer. "Shoot."

"Do twins have their own language?"

"Huh?"

"Can twins actually read each other's minds?" Marla sipped her white wine. "If one of you is in an accident, does the other one know? Did you ever swap girlfriends? If one of you is having sex…"

And so on.

A few hours later, after being overserved, I paid the check and said goodbye to my friends. Then Marla, Robert, and I walked back to my apartment. The three of us settled in my living room: A tennis match was on TV.

"I've gotta go give back some beer." Robert belched and headed to the bathroom. A few minutes later, I was about to ask Marla whether we should order takeout food, ask if she was in the mood for pizza, Chinese, or ribs when I noticed she wasn't there.

"Marla?" I called out. "You hungry?"

No answer.

I decided on pizza. Was reaching for the portable phone when I heard loud voices coming from the rear of my apartment. Was that Marla and Robert arguing? I shoved off the couch, making my way to the master bedroom.

What I saw shocked me.

Marla was on top of Robert, grappling with him, trying to kiss his face. Robert was fighting her off, but she had straddled him and pinned him to the bed.

"Hey!" I said.

Marla stopped. Looked at me. Smiled drunkenly. Rolled off of Robert, who sprang to his feet and disappeared into the bathroom. He closed and locked the door.

Marla stretched out, catlike, on the bed. I could read the suggestive look on her gorgeous face: She was hot for a drunken ménage à trois with twin brothers.

That wasn't happening.

Not that I hadn't enjoyed threesomes before — the Holy Grail of recreational sex — but I usually stumbled into those situations, which was typically a roommate thing.

"Take a nap, Marla." I was pulling the covers over her when she made a grab for me. I wrestled her for a moment, forced her to lie back. She was snoring like a drunken sailor within moments.

"It wasn't the wine. I was trying to get your attention," Marla explained the next morning. We were in a taxi, on our way to LaGuardia Airport to pick up her mother, Ann. Some sort of Pakistani rock music was playing on the taxi's radio.

"Attacking my brother got my attention, all right."

"Well, I had to do something," she said. "You're not fucking me." She poked my leg. "Who are you fucking?"

"Don't start," I said.

But start she did. Rattled off the names of beautiful women who I had been associated with, asking me point-blank if I'd had sex with fellow acting class students like Emmy Award–winning film and TV star, Sela Ward, and model-actress Susanne Gregard, who had only just married Dodi Fayed. Marla also grilled me about some of the infamous women I knew: Miss South Carolina, model, actress, Donna Rice, who became the subject of a scandal as former senator and presidential candidate Gary Hart's "friend." And Rita Jenrette, aka Princess Rita Boncompagni Ludovisi of Italy, who as you know I'd worked on a low-budget horror movie with.

"I've never been involved with any of them," I told Marla. But I could tell she didn't believe me.

"If you're not sleeping with me," Marla said time and again, "you're sleeping with someone else."

But the fact was, as beautiful as she was, after our initial "honeymoon" I'd lost interest in Marla sexually. I mean, it's challenging to feel passion for someone you're always butting heads with. And, since our "engagement," Marla had become opinionated, domineering, and sexually aggressive. Traits I found, as an alpha male, to be libido killers. Then there was the first and only time I performed cunnilingus on Marla.

I was working it, doing my best. But there were no moans or groans of pleasure. No shivers or shudders of delight. Wondering what the problem was, I stopped and looked up. Saw that Marla was reading a *Cosmopolitan* magazine.

"What?" she said.

I gave up.

For once there was no traffic to speak of, so our taxi made it to LaGuardia in less than fifteen minutes. The driver dropped us off at Delta arrivals. Marla threw the vehicle's door open and practically sprinted into baggage claim. I paid the driver.

"What's the hurry?" I said, catching up.

Marla was poised at the bottom of the down escalator, anxious eyes on the crowd of arriving passengers floating down from the main concourse. I checked my watch.

"They just got to the gate. It'll be ten or fifteen minutes, at least."

Marla shook her head. "Mama's always one of the first off."

"She's in coach," I said by way of explanation. Which we all know meant that first class deplaned first, then business class, and then the long line of coach passengers.

"Mama always gets upgraded to first class."

"How she manage that?"

"That's just Mama." Marla pointed. "There she is!"

Sure enough, a raven-haired beauty, accompanied by a fawning silver-fox airline pilot, was stepping onto the escalator. Ann saw us, smiled, and waved.

"That's your mother?" I was incredulous. I mean, no one has a mother who looks like that. Where Marla was a white-bread beauty, Ann could easily pass for a glamorous Greek or Italian film star.

Marla and Ann wrapped their arms around each other.

"Mama—" Marla turned to include me. "This is my fiancé, Thomas."

"I'm very pleased to meet you, Ann."

Ann graced me with a smile, a warm hug, and cheek kiss. "Nice to finally meet my handsome future son-in-law." She turned to the pilot, batted her eyes, and introduced Marla and me. "Thank you so much, Captain."

"Call me James." The captain handed me Ann's carry-on luggage. "Don't forget. Dinner next Saturday?"

"I'm looking forward to it, James," Ann said.

James tipped his cap and walked off.

Ann handed me her checked baggage stubs. "Be a darlin,' Thomas, and fetch my luggage?"

The next morning, Saturday at 5:00, my twin brother, Marla, Tom Counihan, David Broadnax, four other actors, a ten-man production crew, and I met on the set: the now-shuttered Uzi's restaurant. (Ann Maples did not join us. She never got out of bed before noon.)

Our lawyer friend Paul Derounian and his friend, Miss Hawaiian Tropic Terry English, arrived to watch and assist any way they could. The acting teacher, Bob McAndrew, was also on hand as a dialogue coach. Chuck Jones came with a photographer from the *New York Post*. We set up for the first scene and began shooting by 6:30.

I'd written a scene in which Marla's character, a sexy blond bombshell, had information on a killer my twin and I were hunting. While we were questioning her in the restaurant, the killer showed up and opened fire. Naturally, we returned fire, killing the perp.

We recorded using three-quarter-inch tape, did four takes per setup, and shot fifteen pages in two days. We ended it Sunday at 4:00 p.m. Then the entire crew, all fifteen of us headed, to P.J. Clarke's for a wrap party. We sat at a round table in the back room. Most of us ordered their legendry burgers. My favorite waiter, Aldo, bought us two rounds of drinks—that's thirty drinks. Although Tom Counihan picked up the entire check, it was his wife who scrutinized the bill and signed the credit card receipt.

"Thomas." Aldo grabbed me as our party headed out the door. "That bitch stiffed me." He showed me the receipt. Sure enough, Tom's wife had written zero as a tip.

More flabbergasted than embarrassed—I mean, why would anyone stiff a waiter, especially one who'd given us thirty free drinks—I pulled out my wallet and handed over $200.

My brother took a taxi to the airport and headed back to Florida.

Considering that I wrote the vignettes, produced, directed, costarred, and didn't have the faintest idea what the heck I was doing, the finished product turned out pretty well. My twin, Robert, was a natural actor, especially when playing the heavy. Marla was a dream to work with. She looked simply beautiful in the black cocktail dress her mother had chosen for her.

It took a week to edit the tape and lay down the soundtrack. With much celebration and fanfare, I sent the finished product to potential investors and—thanks to attorneys Michael Collyer, Paul Derounian, and Wall Street honcho John McCooey—to a few Hollywood big shots.

And again, we waited.

Ann camped out in my second bedroom that week. She was cheerful, willing to chip in, do dishes, make beds, clean up after her Marla-boo. And I soon discovered that, like her daughter, modest she was not. Her robes and dressing gowns were always falling off her shoulders or flapping open as if buffeted by gale-force winds. It was the first time, but not the last, I'd enjoy that wonderful cleavage.

I'd never been visited by the mother of a woman I was shacking up with before. I must admit, I felt uneasy about it at first. But Ann seemed to have no problem with our living arrangement. Although she did ask me on several occasions, "When are you going to get Marla a real engagement ring?"

But soon Marla was bickering with Ann, picking fights. I couldn't understand why. One night while we were lying in bed, I asked Marla what the problem was. She broke down and, to my surprise, described a jealous, sibling-like rivalry that had existed between her and her mother since childhood.

"I was closer to my daddy." Marla closed her eyes in painful memory. "Mama could never handle that. She was mean to him. Always wanted more; money, clothes, a bigger house, more expensive car. Nothing he did was ever enough. Sometimes I think she divorced him just to break me and Daddy up, to hurt me." A tear rolled down her face. "I've never forgiven her for that."

Marla drew a deep sigh. "After the divorce, she wanted to control my life. She was after me constantly about my weight, hair, makeup. How I dressed. Who my high school friends were. She made sure I dated boys whose parents had money. But the worst thing was Mama dating my classmates."

"Dating?" I said. "Dating-dating?"

"I'd be in the front seat of a car, kissing my boyfriend. Mama would be in the back seat, making it with one of our classmates."

Scary stuff.

A few nights later, Marla and I were in bed and there was a knock on our bedroom door. Ann, her robe flapping open, entered, made a beeline to the bed, pulled back the covers, and jumped in beside me. I was in the middle.

Now, I'm no prude, and as I mentioned earlier, I've stumbled into threesomes before. But a mother-daughter combination was just too weird.

Ann's shower-clean scent filled my senses. I could feel the warmth of her silky-smooth, semi-naked body next to mine. She threw a shapely tan leg possessively over my stomach. Dragged a long, polished nail through the hair on my chest.

I froze. My heart thumped. Blood flushed my face and other places. My eyes stayed riveted on the TV. *The Honeymooners* "Chef of the Future" episode was on. Ralph and Norton were shooting their miracle kitchen appliance TV commercial and Ralph, frozen from stage fright, was saying, "*Hamana-hamana-hamana-hamana.*"

I knew how he felt.

Marla and Ann exchanged a brief, stabbing glare.

Marla growled that growl.

Ann rose from bed, left the room, and closed the door behind her. Marla broke into tears. We never spoke of the incident.

A few days later I was sitting on my couch, reading a horrific story in the *Daily News* about a young girl, Jennifer Levin, who was brutally raped and murdered the evening before in Central Park, when Marla sat beside me.

"This poor girl," I said and showed her the front-page story. "She was killed at Eighty-third Street. Behind the museum. That's only about ten blocks away."

Marla pushed the *News* away and produced the *Post*, which was open to the paper's gossip column, Page Six. The *Post* had published a production photo of my brother, Marla, Terry English, and me along with a story about my screenplay and demo.

Chuck Jones had come through.

The story, dated August 27, 1986, quoted an enthusiastic Dodi Fayed, who'd viewed my demo, as saying he was buying my whole movie deal. 'It's [*Blue Gemini*] a wonderful idea. It would be very expensive to find an actor and then create his twin by special effects."

The reporter wrote that Fayed said he would budget the film at about $6.5 million—$20 million today—for filming next year. To say that I was ecstatic, rapturous, lottery-winning happy would be a major understatement.

"We did it, Marla!" I whooped. "We did it!"

I paced my apartment, Dodi's words percolating. I read and reread the article several times. "I've gotta call Chuck Jones," I said. But Marla had tears in her leading-lady eyes.

"I know what you're thinking." I was trying to have some fun. "The wealth and fame will change me." I fought to keep a straight face, gathering my future Academy Award–winning thoughts. "Not a chance." I raised my right hand as if to take an oath. "When I'm a big star, I'll *never* forget you and all the other little people that made me what I am today."

"You asshole!" Marla snatched back the newspaper, stabbing a manicured finger at our photo. "I look fat!" Ann came strolling into the room and placed a consoling arm around her weeping daughter. And the accusing look Ann gave me said that she also thought Marla looked fat and that I was somehow responsible.

I examined the newspaper photo again. I thought Marla looked beautiful. But rather than argue with my volatile leading lady and her wacko stage mother, I grabbed a cup of coffee, dropped into a chair, and called Chuck Jones. Then sat there, wondering when Dodi Fayed would call.

"That's it?" Marla said after a while.

"Huh?"

"You just going to sit there?"

"What do you want me to do?"

Marla stormed from the room.

Ann followed her.

"I'm fat!" I heard Marla shriek.

Ann said something. Marla said something back.

I heard a commotion. Something crashed to the floor. I double-timed it to my bedroom. Saw Marla shove Ann into a wall. Then haul off and punch her.

Chapter 16

MARLA AND I ESCORTED ANN to the airport a few days later. As we sat at the gate and Ann charmed an older, male gate agent into a first-class upgrade, I purchased a newspaper and read about the arrest of a neighbor, one Robert Chambers, in the death of Jennifer Levin. Dubbed the "Preppy Killer" by the press, Chambers confessed to my friend, First Grade Homicide Detective Mike Sheehan, to meeting Levin in one of our local haunts, Dorian's Red Hand, walking her into Central Park, killing her, but said it was during rough, consensual sex. There was another article, *How Jennifer Courted Death*, where Chambers's attorneys attacked the victim's reputation, claiming that Levin had sexually assaulted their client, who they portrayed as a Kennedyesque preppy altar boy with a promising future.

"Let's get out of town," I said to Marla after Ann had taken off. We were sitting in a cab in bumper-to-bumper traffic on our way back to Manhattan. "I mean, what else're we gonna do: Sit around and wait for Dodi Fayed to call?"

"Why don't you call him?" Marla said. "Or better yet, call his new wife. Susanne Gregard's your pal, right?"

"Give it a rest, can't you?"

Marla was quiet for a moment. "Where should we go?"

"How about Atlantic City?"

"I love casinos."

I thought for a moment about calling Donald Trump, asking if he could get me a good deal at one of his two casinos. But since we hadn't socialized in years, I decided it was not appropriate.

"I'll call Paul Derounian," I said. Paul was an Atlantic City regular and registered high roller. "Ask him where to stay."

When we got home, I phoned Paul, who invited himself and a date along, saying he wanted to help me celebrate the success of *Blue Gemini*. Paul made reservations for four at Resorts Casino.

My plan was for us to see some shows, hang out on the beach and boardwalk, sip cocktails, and catch the sunsets. Marla had other ideas.

She loved to gamble.

"I need money, Thomas," Marla told me. It was around 6:00 p.m. and we'd just settled in our high-roller suite (thanks to Paul) overlooking the ocean. Marla had changed into a very flattering sundress. I put on a blue blazer. Khakis. Boat shoes. "For what?"

"Blackjack," Marla said. "I love to play blackjack."

"I don't gamble," I said cheerfully, looking forward to happy hour with Paul and his date. "That's one vice I was spared, thank God."

"Are you serious?" Marla said.

I looked at her. "What?"

"What's the sense of staying in a casino if we don't gamble?"

"There's entertainment. The beach—"

Exasperated, she plopped down on the bed and explained to me that whenever she'd been to Vegas — which was often — her dates always gave her money to gamble: a couple of thousand, at least.

"I don't have that kind of money," I said.

"Or you're just cheap." Marla made a disgusted face. "I should have known with that stupid engagement ring you gave me."

That pissed me off. After all, I'd been supporting Marla, paying all her bills since she moved in with me. She contributed nothing, nada, zilch. Did I mention we ate takeout most nights? I hired a housekeeper to clean the apartment and do our laundry.

"I don't have money for gambling," I said. "Period."

That evening Marla, after a few drinks, berated and embarrassed me in front of Paul and his date. Called me cheap. Announced that we were no longer having sex. Said that I had to be fucking someone else. That our problems were all my fault.

Rather than argue with a drunk and angry female, I left Marla at a blackjack table and returned to our room. The next day I cut the weekend short, rented a car, and drove us back to the city.

Come Monday morning, Dodi Fayed still hadn't contacted me. I placed calls to his Manhattan hotel, office, left messages with his assistant. Sat by the phone and waited.

A most welcome booking came in from Ford a few days later. I was to fly into Miami, shoot a German tobacco ad for Lux cigarettes. (I'd already shot print ads for Old Gold, Kent, and Newport, just to name a few.)

"The booking is for three days," I told Marla. "But I'm going to visit my parents afterward. I'll be gone about a week."

"I want to go," Marla said. "I want to meet your parents; you've met mine. Besides, I need a vacation."

"You can come," I said, "if you behave yourself. No emotional meltdowns. No getting drunk. No nudity in front of my parents."

Marla promised to be on her best behavior.

I flew into Miami, shot a series of ads, then rented a car and picked up Marla at the Fort Lauderdale International Airport. We drove to my parents' condo in Deerfield Beach. Arrived about three in the afternoon.

I introduced Marla to my mother, Madeline. Then I led her to a back bedroom, said a quick hello to my father, who was bedridden due to a devastating stroke. I remained in the sickroom while Marla joined Madeline on the condo terrace.

We all know how difficult it is watching parents age and deteriorate. Growing up, my police lieutenant father had been a strong, strapping, domineering authority figure. Not a violent guy by nature, but not averse to kicking ass when my brother and I screwed up. Which was often. Not that I held any grudges. I understood him by then. Raising five kids on a civil service salary was a tremendous challenge. But we always had a roof over our heads, clothes to wear, and never went to bed hungry.

Now the emaciated authority figure I once looked up to and feared couldn't even talk. Not that we would've known what to say to each other. We'd never bonded. I don't recall ever hearing him utter a single "attaboy." Not after I'd been honorably discharged from the Navy, joined the NYPD, or landed the WNBC *Now!* show. His seeming indifference caused me great sadness. My father acknowledged me with a nod and fell asleep.

I grabbed myself a beer and joined Marla and my mother on the terrace. They were sipping hot tea, nibbling on cheese and crackers. Kids were frolicking in the condo's community swimming pool. I sat down, piled some cheese on a cracker, and popped it in my mouth. Chewed and inhaled the clean, 80-degree Florida air. Marla excused herself, said she had to use the bathroom.

"What are you doing with this one?" Madeline said as soon as we heard the bathroom door close. "What happened to the last one?"

"Constance? We divorced. Remember?"

"Not that one. The other one."

"Which other one?"

"Don't be a wiseguy."

I couldn't help but smile. Wondered if my father knew that he'd married a good woman; the best, as far as my siblings and I were concerned. Or had he taken her old-fashioned values of loyalty, devotion, and benevolence for granted. I sipped my beer.

"Where'd you find this one?" Madeline said.

"Marla, mom. Her name's Marla." I ate another cheese and cracker. "So, what do you think of her?"

My mother shook her head. "She's going to commit suicide someday."

"What?" I was shocked, to say the least. I mean, I knew Marla could come off as a ditz with her spirituality nonsense and that she was nervous about meeting my mother; most women would be. But what could she have said or done to give that impression?

"Why do you say that?"

"I'm an old woman," my mother said. "I just know."

We stayed with my parents that night. Checked into a Fort Lauderdale motel the next day. Spent that week visiting my retired cop and firefighter friends. We'd go to the beach in packs, spend the days in the sun, drank margaritas, played backgammon, volleyball, Kadima. Nights we'd meet at the various seafood restaurants or attend BBQs and house parties. It was at one of those house parties that I peeked into a bedroom and saw Marla snorting cocaine.

She didn't know I'd seen her. And I didn't mention it at the time. There was no reason to. I'd never seen her snort coke before. It wasn't a problem, as far as I knew. And, because of my background, I knew she'd never do it in front of me.

We were driving to dinner the following night. I'd picked up another couple, a retired firefighter named Sean, and his wife. We were heading north on North Ocean Boulevard, a narrow two-lane road, when Sean fired up a joint and passed it to me. Now, I'm not a big pot smoker, but I wasn't averse to the drug. And we were on vacation. I took a drag. Marla became outraged. Lectured me about the evils of pot.

"Oh, so pot's no good for me," I said, "but you can snort cocaine?"

"I've never snorted cocaine."

"Liar," I said. "I saw you last night."

Marla hauled off. Punched me in the face.

I lost control of the car. Veered into the oncoming lane. A southbound minivan rounded the corner. Came at me head-on.

"Look out!" Sean yelled.

I wrestled the steering wheel. Stepped on the gas. Shot back across the road to the northbound lane. The minivan clipped the driver's-side rearview mirror as it sped by.

"Holy shit!" Sean said. "That was close."

I saw red. Pulled off the road. Parked on a grass shoulder. My heart felt like it would burst from my chest. My hands trembled. I threw open my door. Strode around to the passenger side. Yanked Marla's door opened. Grabbed her by the hair. Dragged her from the car. Threw her into a drainage ditch. Got back into the car. Drove away.

A few minutes later Sean said, "I'm not feeling comfortable with this."

"You see what she did?" I snapped.

"We saw," Sean's wife said. "She's one psycho bitch, but you can't just leave her."

I heaved a sigh, then slowed and made a U-turn.

A whimpering and thoroughly wet and disheveled Marla was waiting for us at the side of the road. I pulled up. She got back in the vehicle. We never spoke of the incident.

But I cut the vacation short.

"You're gonna have to move into the second bedroom," I told Marla when we'd returned to my Manhattan apartment. Marla freaked. Panicked. I could see her mind work. She had nowhere else to go. No money. No prospects.

"I'm not kicking you out," I said. "I still love you, but we're going to be friends."

"Friends?" Marla shrieked.

"Pals."

She paced my living room. "No sex?"

"No sex."

"What are you, a fucking queer? A faggot?" Marla raged, arms flailing. "Any man doesn't want to fuck me is a faggot."

"Calm down, Marla," I said.

But Marla didn't calm down. It was the first time I witnessed her slap herself across the face: once, twice, three times. Spittle flew from her mouth. Blood trickled from her nose. Frankly, I was horrified. My heart broke for this disturbed young woman. "I'm not kicking you out," I assured her. "I swear."

Marla slapped herself again.

"Stop," I shouted.

But Marla didn't stop. She let out a primordial scream. Dashed across the room and ran her head into my living room wall. Knocked herself unconscious.

Chapter 17

It took several weeks, but once Marla realized that I was not kicking her out of my apartment, that I still included her in my life — squiring her to business and social activities, as well as financially supporting her —there were no more psychotic meltdowns.

Soon Marla started dating. Making friends of her own. Living her own life. She decided she needed her own apartment, as I knew she would. How she planned to pay rent I had no idea. But Paul Derounian found her a roommate situation with an Eastern Airlines flight attendant on East Eightieth Street. Paul and Chuck Jones helped her move.

I didn't see much of Marla in the months after she moved out. But knowing she could always count on me to protect her, she would mention her ex-cop boyfriend to anyone who caused her concern: handsy casting directors, leering photographers, the occasional aggressive dinner date. And how did she reciprocate?

"She's running you down," Paul told me after I'd struck out with a couple of models at a cocktail party. I had been having a dry spell lately. More women than usual were spurning my advances, giving me the cold shoulder. Honestly, I didn't think much of it. I mean, everyone experiences a slump on occasion. Right?

"Who's running me down?"

"Marla," Paul said.

"Why would she do that?"

"She's jealous."

I shook my head. "We're friends. I'm having a dry spell. That's all."

"That redhead you were just talking to?"

"Tina," I said.

"I know for a fact she had the hots for you. Until Marla spoke to her."

Come to think of it, I did remember Marla speaking to Tina. "What's Marla saying?"

He shrugged. "Start paying attention."

And so, I did. Discovered that Paul was right. Marla was proprietary, running off any woman who showed an interest in me. I never did find out what BS she told them. But she was maddeningly successful. That is until Joni S. came into my life.

I had just finished watching the TV news about how the Preppy Killer, Robert Chambers, had pled guilty to manslaughter in the first degree in the death of Jennifer Levin and was sentenced to serve five to fifteen years in prison. Had started watching a follow-up story about the horrifying *Challenger* space shuttle explosion that occurred seventy-three seconds into its flight and killed all seven crew members, when my phone rang.

"I need you to talk to a lady for me," Murray "Don't Worry" Richman, the attorney who had handled my first divorce from the New Hampshire beauty queen, said. "You'll like her. She's a knockout. Spent her youth winning bikini contests from Key West to Daytona Beach."

"This a paying gig?" I said.

"Since when does Sir Galahad get paid for helping a damsel in distress?"

"Bite me, Murray."

Murray laughed. "Her name's Joni S. Got a pen?"

I wrote down Joni's number. "What's the problem?"

"The usual," he said and hung up.

I met Joni S. at the bar in Mumbles the following evening. She *was* a knockout: Crystal Gayle–length raven hair, curvaceous, great legs, and a fifty-teeth wide smile. As I ordered Joni a wine, me a beer, Marla strolled in, spotted us, and came our way.

Awkward.

"Hiya, Fitzy," Marla said cheerfully as she sat beside Joni. Then volunteered that she was waiting for a guy she was dating. John something or other was a model and owned the Beach Bum tanning salon down on Eighty-sixth Street. Although I was predictably angry with her for sabotaging my social life, I didn't hold grudges. As the bartender set down our drinks, I introduced the two glamour girls.

"So nice to meet you." Marla was all smiles and Southern charm.

"Yeah, yeah," Joni said dismissively. She turned her back to Marla. Said to me, "We need to talk in private."

"We'll get a table." I picked up our drinks. "You'll excuse us, Marla?"

"S—sure," Marla stammered.

We sat at a table in back.

"I've got a problem," Joni said without preamble. Told me she'd fallen for a New York City restauranteur while he was on vacation in her hometown of Fort Lauderdale. Joni said she'd just won a Sunday bikini contest at a raucous Intracoastal bar called Bootleggers when Carlo sent a bottle of expensive champagne to her table—not an unusual occurrence, since she routinely won bikini contests and guys were always sending her champagne.

"I didn't believe in the love-at-first-sight thing," Joni said. "It never happened to me before." After only a month, Carlo told her he loved her, wanted to spend his life with her, and asked her to move to New York City with him. Joni quit her bookkeeping day job, packed her bikinis—she had over 100—and moved into an upscale doorman apartment building on Manhattan's Upper East Side.

"Stupid thing to do," Joni said. "Guy turned out to be a chauvinist pig." She fidgeted in her chair, tugging down her mini.

"Old-world Eye-talian. From Genoa, like the salami?" Joni said from day one they butted heads. That she couldn't take the constant conflict and moved out of his place and into a horrendous, but temporary living situation.

"I'm afraid," she said.

"Of?"

Joni drank some wine. "Two days ago, I embarrassed Carlo in his restaurant in front of his customers and employees."

"How?"

"I'd left a Movado watch at his apartment. Went to his restaurant to pick it up. He said something stupid. I grabbed him by his tie, pulled him across the bar. There was a big scene."

I sipped my beer. Glanced toward the bar. Didn't see Marla. "Where's the restaurant?"

"Seventy-fourth and York."

"Da Noi?"

"You know it?"

"Your ex wouldn't be Carlo Vaccarezza?"

Joni's jaw dropped.

According to the New York newspapers, Carlo Vaccarezza once worked for John Gotti: mobster, murderer, extortionist and boss of the Gambino Mafia crime family. as a driver-bodyguard. The papers reported that the feds claimed that Da Noi was a Mob-operated money laundering operation, and that Gotti was the actual owner. Carlo was a front man.

"You know Carlo?"

I nodded. "I've met him. I know the chef better, Raffaele Esposito."

"I love Ralphy," Joni said.

A contact at the FBI had warned me to stay out of Da Noi, that it was under surveillance, so I stopped frequenting the place.

"Call me stupid," Joni said, "but I had no idea that Carlo was in the Mafia. I even had dinner with John Gotti. I had no idea who he was."

"Has Carlo contacted you?" I said. "Threatened you in any way?"

"No," Joni said. "Call it intuition. I'm afraid he'll come after me."

"Best way to handle a guy like Carlo is let him know we're friends. He has a problem with you, he'll have a problem with me." I checked the time. "If you've got no plans, let's go have dinner at Da Noi."

"Wait," Joni said, suspicious.

"No strings attached. Promise."

"Then why stick your neck out for me?"

I shrugged. "Someone has to do it."

Joni and I walked into Da Noi around 8:30.

The upscale Italian eatery was crowded as always. The usual piano player, I forget his name, was playing something from the American songbook. We squeezed into a slot standing at the smallish bar and ordered two glasses of red wine. I glanced into the dining room. Sure enough, John Gotti himself was sitting at a table with two male associates. To his right was a blond bombshell, his *goomah* (married man's girlfriend) Lisa Gastineau, ex-wife of former New York Jet Mark Gastineau.

A familiar blondish comb-over, on the other side of the dining room, caught my attention. I careened my neck to get a better look. Saw my old pal, Donald Trump, sitting at a table with one of his attorneys, Jay Goldberg. I didn't think anything of it at first: Donald and Gotti in the same restaurant. But then I recalled that a former Da Noi waiter once told me that Gotti and Donald used to meet in private in the restaurant's tiny downstairs party room.

"You're in construction," I once said to Donald. "How do you deal with organized crime shakedowns?"

"We have no choice," Donald said. "We pay the freight. Pass the expense on to the customers."

Da Noi's bartender set down our drinks. Joni and I toasted. The piano player crooned Jerry Vale's "Pretend You Don't See Her."

I said to Joni, "You mentioned your apartment situation isn't working out?"

"Yeah." She made a face. "I'm staying with a nutcase I met at work."

"What kind of work?"

"Bookkeeping for a fashion designer, Charivari." She sipped her wine. "The bitch does drugs. Brings strange guys home. I'm afraid to sleep at night. If you hear of an available apartment, even something temporary, let me know?"

"Will do."

"Joni." Carlo, oozing charm, was suddenly there.

"Carlo," Joni said. "Meet my friend Thomas."

"Yes. Of course. Thomas." We shook hands. "I haven't seen you in a while."

"I've been on the coast," I lied.

"Will you be joining us for dinner?" Carlo asked.

"We just came for drinks," Joni said.

"I'm glad you came." Carlo stroked Joni's back, an intimate gesture that surprised me. What surprised me more was that Joni didn't object. Carlo whispered in Joni's ear. She nodded.

"Excuse us a moment, Thomas?" Carlo took Joni's hand, led her over to the piano bar. I drank some wine, one eye on Joni and Carlo. I glanced around, got a look at myself in the bar mirror. Adjusted my black silk knit tie and realized that an attractive brunette at the other end of the bar was giving me the eye. I checked for a wedding ring, didn't see one. I smiled and was about to make my move when a guy in a blue blazer sidled up beside her. He said something to the lady. She laughed and began flirting with him. Oh, well.

I sipped my red wine. Couldn't help but overhear a couple of older businessmen to my left discussing some sort of an explosion at a nuclear power station somewhere in Ukraine: Chernobyl. I heard hearty laughter, glanced to the dining room, saw the gossip columnist Cindy Adams with her comedian husband, Joey Adams. That's when John Gotti stood up. He bent to whisper something into Lisa Gastineau's ear, then headed downstairs, I assumed, to the men's room. Suddenly Donald was on his feet. He tossed his napkin on the table, nodded to his lawyer, and followed Gotti.

I thought about what my contact at the FBI had told me. Wondered if the restaurant was still under surveillance. Whether it was bugged.

Ten minutes later, Joni was still talking amiably to Carlo. The piano player was singing "Al Di Là." A barstool opened up. I sat. Was about to order another glass of wine when Joni slipped in beside me. "Carlo wants to buy us dinner."

I glanced at the dining room. Carlo was helping a busboy clear a four-top. The same table Donald and his attorney, who was nowhere to be seen, had been sitting at. Just then Donald emerged from downstairs. Beelined it out the restaurant's service-entrance side door, where I knew his limo would be waiting.

"Up to you," I said to Joni. "You hungry?"

Joni glanced at her now-empty wineglass. Glanced at Carlo just as John Gotti returned to his seat. Carlo said something to Gotti. Gotti looked to the bar, smiled, and waved for Joni and me to join them.

"Let's get the hell out of here," Joni said.

"Good idea," I said.

Chapter 18

"Tommy Fitz," an amused male voice said.

"Who's this?"

"Guess."

It was sometime in November 1987 when I got that call. My father had died back in July and I was still dealing with the loss. Wishing that our relationship had been different. Thinking that maybe there was something I could have done, should have done to change things. But time had run out. I was feeling guilty about that, in no mood to play games with some nitwit on the phone.

"You get two guesses," the caller said.

I was about to hang up, but the voice sounded familiar. "C'mon. Who is this?"

The guy laughed.

The reception wasn't good, so I pressed the phone closer to my ear and suddenly recognized the voice. I couldn't remember the last time I'd spoken to Donald Trump on the phone.

"How's it going, Donald?"

"Great. You can't believe how great. Things are greater than great..."

As Donald prattled on about how great everything was, I speculated why, after all these years, he'd reach out. I mean, besides the occasional sightings at Le Club, at various functions—like parties on Malcolm Forbes's yacht, the evening I spotted him in Da Noi—we hadn't communicated in years. Not that I had a problem with that. People move on. Lose touch.

While I was mostly single, playing the field, Donald had settled down. Married. Had kids. Became a high-profile, multimillionaire developer who was constantly in the news. Just the year before he'd made nationwide headlines by saving Central Park's all-but abandoned—$12 million boondoggle—Wollman ice-skating rink. Accomplishing in three months, under budget and for no profit, what the city couldn't achieve in six years.

"But enough about me," Donald was saying. "The reason I called, I'm sitting here in my custom, Trump-edition Cadillac limousine with a friend of yours. Can you believe it? Cadillac made a special-edition Trump limousine for me. And they gave me two custom convertible Allantés. Painted them in my favorite color. Gold."

"Tell him it's me." I heard a familiar female voice's laughter in the background. "It's me, Fitzy."

"Know who that is?"

Now everything made sense. "Marla Maples."

"You're right," Donald said. "Marla Maples."

A lot had happened in the last eight months besides my father's passing. For one thing, Joni S.'s living situation became intolerable. Still anxious about her ex, Carlo, I allowed her to move into my second bedroom, albeit temporarily. But Carlo never did contact her. Eventually, the feds locked up John Gotti, seized Da Noi, and Carlo fled to Florida, where he would own and race thoroughbred horses. Although Joni no longer needed my protection, we got along so well that we became inseparable: platonic BFFs.

As wildly popular as she was, Joni slept in her own bed every night and never brought a guy home. She paid rent and her share of expenses, which was just as well since my finances had taken a turn for the worse. Not that I was the only one.

Back on Monday, October 19—"Black Monday"—stock markets around the world crashed and as a result, the US markets were volatile. Advertisers cut back. TV commercials and modeling gigs were almost nonexistent.

At the time I wasn't too concerned. I'd struggled before. And my financial issues were petty compared to someone like a Donald Trump. Every day the business press was trumpeting the fact that he, as well as other fat cats, were being forced into bankruptcy.

On the upside, I was dating a couple of lusty wenches, thanks to my new roommate and BFF Joni, who was always fixing me up; she was the best and only wingwoman I ever had.

I hadn't seen much of Marla. But we spoke on the phone often, and I knew that she was pursuing her dreams of becoming an actress. The press agent Chuck Jones had become her full-time agent, manager, confidant, and was aggressively promoting her career. Submitting her for film and TV auditions. Making sure that she was seen in all the right places, whereby design (I'd learn later) she'd frequently run into Donald Trump.

I saw my potential movie investor, Dodi Fayed, one last time. He invited me to yet another party at his penthouse suite at the Waldorf Astoria. There were several boldfaced names and a couple of celebrity drug dealers in attendance. But I couldn't keep my eyes off the lovely Denise Brown, who I hadn't seen since my Studio 54 days. She and her younger sister Nicole were enjoying cocktails on the suite's enormous outdoor terrace overlooking Central Park, chatting with O.J. Simpson.

To my regret, I spent so much time talking with Dodi about investing in my film project, that when I later searched the crowd for Denise, she, Nicole and O.J. were gone. Although Dodi never did invest, he arranged for me to meet another potential investor, Adnan (AK) Khashoggi, his uncle and at the time one of the richest men in the world. (He would one day sell his 282-foot yacht, *Nabila*, to Donald, who would name it *Trump Princess*.)

I met with Khashoggi at his Manhattan residence in the Olympic Towers on Fifth Avenue, across from St. Patrick's

Cathedral. An exotically beautiful domestic escorted me into a vast home office, past two steely-eyed bodyguards, and directed me to sit in a chair in front of a large desk, across from the slight, unimpressive Saudi Arabian billionaire. AK, dressed in a *thobe*, a traditional Arab robe, was on the phone, speaking Arabic.

I sat for a few moments in uncomfortable silence, checking out the over-the-top furnishings in the palatial room, noticing that AK was nervously twisting one end of his thick, black mustache. Another exotic beauty entered the office, laid some paperwork on his desk, and left. Khashoggi finished the phone call, looked across the desk at me, sat forward, and folded his small hands.

I smiled expectantly.

AK did not smile back. "How do you know my nephew, Dodi?"

Right to the point. No introduction. No pleasantries.

"I know Dodi socially," I said.

"Ah," AK sneered. "You're one of his party friends?"

"No. Not exactly," I said. "I'm a former police officer. Now I'm a writer." I gestured with an expensive, leather folder that contained my movie proposal, shooting schedule, budget, sample script. "I've written this movie about twin cops—"

AK's raised hand silenced me. He looked to the door and called out, "Muhammad?" A thirtysomething Arab guy in a custom-made gray business suit strode into the room.

"Muhammad, my nephew, will assist you," AK said dismissively. He picked up his phone and turned his back.

"This way," Muhammad said.

I didn't like being snubbed. But I kept my cool, got to my feet, followed Muhammad from the office and into a small conference room. He gestured to a seat.

"I am Muhammad." He offered his hand.

"Thomas," I said as we shook.

"May I see what you have?"

I handed him my proposal.

Muhammad flipped through the pages. Focused on the budget. Then said AK wasn't interested. That he didn't invest in movies. Never had.

"So why did Dodi set up this meeting?" I said.

"Who can say what my cousin will do," Muhammad said, "or why." He handed me back my proposal. "Perhaps he was thinking, since he is a relative, that in a way AK is in the film business."

Whatever that meant.

"So," Donald was saying over the phone. "I want to invite you to my book party for *The Art of the Deal*. Did you know I wrote a book? The party's tonight. At Trump Tower. You've heard about it, right? The whole city's talking about it. It's in all the newspapers, the party of the decade."

"Sure." I did a mental eye roll, thinking that people don't change. Donald was still the same show-off he'd been when we first met in Maxwell's Plum. Only this time he was showing off for Marla.

"It's the most sought-after party invitation ever," Donald said. "I get dozens of calls every day begging for tickets. Everyone who's anyone will be there. Can you come?"

"Love to." I wanted to ask if I could bring Joni, but I knew what Donald wanted. "You want me to bring Marla?"

"That would be great. Great. Really great."

"Listen to me, Donald," I said. "Marla can't hear us, right?"

"Right."

"She's like flypaper. You're not going to have a fling and walk away. Be careful."

Donald laughed. "Thanks, Tom. See you tonight at the party."

"You never told me you were friends with Donald Trump," Marla said as she high-heeled out of her East Eightieth Street apartment building. I held the yellow cab's door open. Marla stepped in. I slipped off my black, Canali tuxedo jacket and got in on the other side.

"Trump Tower," I said to the cabdriver.

I shot my gold and black onyx cuff links. Made sure they were securely fastened. "Depends on what you mean by 'friends'." I glanced at Marla. She was an absolute knockout in a little black cocktail dress and six-inch heels.

"I knew him a long time ago," I said. "I run into him occasionally in the city. I mean, he doesn't send me Christmas cards. Didn't invite me to his wedding." I gazed at a large group of camera-laden Asian tourists strolling west. A screaming ambulance was suddenly kissing our bumper. Marla and I stuck our fingers in our ears. The cabbie did his best to move to the right. The ambulance jumped the sidewalk, raced by.

"How'd you wind up in Donald's limo today?" I said.

Marla was checking her makeup in a compact mirror.

"I was walking up Fifth Avenue," she said. "He came out of the Pierre Hotel. Saw me. He said, 'I know you.'" She touched up her lips. "He said he's been looking all over for me."

The cab turned onto Fifth Avenue into heavy traffic.

"*Does* he know you?"

"My lordy, yes." She closed the compact, slipped it into her clutch purse. Marla told me she'd initially been introduced to Donald in Atlantic City by dentist Dr. Jerry Argovitz, president of the Trump-owned New Jersey Generals football team. Soon after arriving in New York, she was reintroduced to Donald by American financier and sports promoter Theodore "Teddy" Forstmann at the US Open tennis championship.

"So, it was just a coincidence?" I said. "Running into him at the Pierre?"

Marla shook her head. "I knew he'd be there."

I reached for my wallet and took out cab fare. "How'd you know?"

"Chuck Jones."

That made sense. As a press agent, Chuck would have easy access to a celebrity's published social calendar. And Donald, media whore that he'd always been, wanted everyone to know what events he was attending.

What I didn't know at the time was that Marla was actually stalking Donald. Be it an opening night on Broadway, charity fundraiser, sporting event, Marla was there. But she had difficulty attracting the workalcoholic tycoon's attention, could not penetrate his deep entourage of business associates, hangers-on, lackeys, and his ever-diligent wife, Ivana.

I later learned that Marla even staked out Trump Tower. She could be found at all hours loitering around the sixty-eight-story, bronze-colored building's gilded residential entrance. Whenever a limo stopped to discharge passengers, she'd spring into action and strut past the car: sweater tight, skirt short, heels high. But she never did catch a glimpse of Donald.

Marla glanced out the yellow cab's window and informed me, "I saw Donald at the Rainbow Room last week." She said that she'd caught his eye and slipped him her phone number right under Ivana's nose. "When I got into his limo, Donald said he'd lost my number. That it had mysteriously disappeared from his suit jacket pocket. That he'd been looking for me ever since."

I fidgeted with my tie and wondered what Marla's game plan was. I mean, this whole Trump fixation was breaking news to me. And Donald was very married.

Marla turned toward me, posed. "How do I look?"

"Gorgeous," I said. "So, you were waiting for Donald outside the Pierre?"

"For over an hour."

"Why?"

Marla looked at me like I had two heads. "He's rich. Not just a millionaire, a billionaire. He knows *everyone*. Besides…" She batted her eyes and winked. "I can tell he likes me."

Klieg lights were sweeping the night sky, Hollywood-style, in front of Trump Tower. Police barricades held back groupies who gawked at the celebrities who were being photographed and interviewed on a red carpet. The line of limos waiting to drop off backed up traffic. We were forced to exit the cab on the north side of Fifty-seventh Street. We had a tough time negotiating the crowd.

A team of blue-suited security guards greeted us and checked our names off a list. We stepped into the disco-pulsing, six-story blue marble atrium. Twenty violinists serenaded arriving guests. There had to be a thousand people in formal wear. Champagne was being passed around by circulating white-jacketed waiters. A parade of women waving red sparklers wheeled in a giant cake replica of Trump Tower. Hundreds of red balloons floated down from the sixth-story atrium and bounced onto the gyrating crowd.

We were directed to a serpentine receiving line, where Donald stood with Ivana on one side, Random House honcho Si Newhouse and Donald's coauthor Tony Schwartz on the other. Steven Spielberg was on the line in front of us. Supermodel Cheryl Tiegs, who was once married to a successful feature-film director friend of mine, Stan Dragoti, was behind us.

We inched forward. And for the first time, I got a look at Donald's head of security: a brawny, former college linebacker, Matt Calamari. He and two other beefy guys were standing behind Donald, all muscle and menace.

"Let's skip the receiving line," I said.

"No." Marla dug her fingernails into my hand. "Stay with me." I grabbed two glasses of champagne from a passing waiter. Handed one to Marla.

Half a glass of champagne later, Stephen Spielberg shook Donald's hand, hugged Ivana, and moved on.

"Here we go." Marla broke into her brightest beauty pageant smile. We shook hands with Donald's coauthor, then Si Newhouse. Donald saw us and winked at Marla.

"Tommy Fitz." Donald shook my hand. "Thank you for coming." I congratulated him on the book and then made a show of introducing him to Marla.

"So nice to meet you, Marla," Donald said and blushed boyishly. "Thank you for coming."

We moved on to Ivana.

"Ivana," I said. "We met a few times in the old days at Maxwell's Plum. I'm Thomas Fitzsimmons."

"Of course, Thomas," Ivana said politely. I doubted she remembered me. "How nice to see you again."

"This is Marla Maples."

"Wonderful party," Marla said. She and Ivana exchanged sincere smiles and handshakes. Ivana thanked us for coming. We moved on.

Another blue-suited security guard directed us toward the rear of the atrium. We exchanged our empty glasses of champagne for full ones. Checked out the crowd.

The boxing promoter Don King was holding court in a floor-length mink coat. Marla and I chatted briefly with Phyllis George, Barbara Walters, and then gossip columnist Liz Smith; a really good dame.

At a makeshift podium, there was a call to attention and borscht belt comedian Jackie Mason—the last time I'd seen him was at the Lion's Head pub, when he was bugging my ex-wife Constance—introduced Donald and Ivana with the words, "Here comes the king and queen."

Donald stepped up to the podium. Spoke about how great the party was, how great Trump Tower was, how successful *The Art of the Deal* was, selling 54,000 copies in one week. He stated he would donate his share of the book's bound-to-be-enormous profits to various charities.

"Gotta hand it to Donald," I said to Marla. "He certainly knows how to throw a party."

After Donald's speech, Marla and I negotiated our way to the escalators. Finding a relatively quiet spot on the second floor, we checked out the throng below.

I said hello to a Mid-City Gym acquaintance, actor Michael Douglas, while Marla fought off the advances of an admirer of hers: Charles Evans, the producer of the Academy Award–

winning film *Tootsie*. We watched as Donald and his bodyguards worked the room. He rode the atrium escalators up to the sixth floor, looked around, and rode down again, scanning the crowd at each floor; obviously searching for someone. I saw the Trump security guard speak into a radio. Donald looked in our direction and spotted Marla. His face lit up.

"I told you he likes me," Marla said.

Donald stepped off the escalator and was making his way to us when Ivana touched his arm, stopping him. She introduced her husband to a prosperous-looking older couple.

"Time to go," Marla said.

"Really?"

"Really."

We slipped out of Trump Tower without saying a word.

The following morning, I sent a magnificent basket of wine and roses to Donald's office, congratulating him again on his book, and thanking him for the invitation to the party. I signed the thank-you card from Marla Maples and Thomas Fitzsimmons. About an hour later, I received a phone call from Donald's executive assistant, Norma Foerderer, asking me to stop by his office later that day.

It was hard to believe that the Trump Tower atrium was the scene of last night's festivities. The place was immaculate, the pink marble floors and walls gleaming.

I walked over to the elevator bank and approached a blue-suited security guard.

"Thomas Fitzsimmons to see Donald Trump."

The guard looked me over, checked a list, then picked up a phone and dialed. A moment later, he gestured for me to enter a private elevator. "Press the executive office's button."

I stepped inside, pressed the button, and the door swished closed. I looked at myself in the floor-to-ceiling mirrors: A fresh haircut; blue cashmere Dunhill suit, black-knit silk tie, Gucci-like loafers, $30 knockoff Rolex wristwatch. I decided that there was nothing to give away the fact that I had less than a thousand dollars in my bank account. If only my father and the nuns at St. Barnabas could see me now.

I stepped off the elevator, turned right, and pushed through glass doors. I announced myself to an anchorwoman-pretty brunette receptionist. A moment later, Norma Foerderer, an attractive woman in her fifties, greeted me and escorted me into the inner sanctum.

Donald sprang up from his chair. "You're just in time." He came around his enormous desk. Shook my hand. Gestured me to a chair. "You look great," he said. "Great. Really great."

"Thanks." The first thing I noticed was the spectacular view, which was hard to appreciate because the office was packed with sports memorabilia and overflowing with congratulatory flower arrangements. The wine and roses Marla and I had sent was prominently displayed atop his cluttered desk. I checked out the many magazine covers featuring Donald that hung on the walls: *Time*, *GQ*, *Esquire*, *Playboy*.

"No one's doing better than you." I pointed to the array of magazine covers. "Love those *Playboy* covers."

"You want something to drink?"

"Nothing. Thanks."

"So," Donald said. "How long have you known Marla Maples?"

"Since before she was a virgin." Only kidding. I said, "Long enough to know she's no one-night stand. Not like what we're used to."

"You dated her?"

"Sort of," I hedged. "We're really just friends."

"Mr. Trump?" Matt was standing in the doorway. "Excuse me for interrupting."

"C'mon in," Donald said.

Matt stepped into the room. He glanced at me, then back at Donald.

"You can talk in front of Tommy Fitz."

"There's another one downstairs." Matt grinned. "Really gorgeous this time."

"Can you believe it?" Donald said to me. "I've got groupies. They show up here all day long wanting to meet Trump." He leaned forward, shouted, "Norma?"

Norma walked into the room.

"Has Catherine Oxenberg called today?" (At the time Oxenberg, daughter of Princess Elizabeth of Yugoslavia, was a heartthrob and one of the stars of the nighttime soap *Dynasty*.)

Norma sighed. "No, Donald."

"I can't believe it. She calls here ten times a day looking for a date. Right, Norma?"

"Well, she calls—"

"Victoria Principal," Donald said. "She's another one. Right, Norma?"

"Yes, Donald." Norma dropped a stack of papers on Donald's desk and left the room. I pinched my nose to stifle a sneeze, cursed the roomful of fragrant flowers, and wondered why Donald was telling me all this. Did he want me to report back to Marla how popular he was?

Matt said, "What should I do about the groupie?"

Donald grinned. "Get her contact info; you never know." He looked at me. "I don't know what I'd do without Matt."

"Just doing my job, boss." Matt turned to leave.

"Matt?"

Matt stopped. "Yes, sir?"

"You'd do anything for me, right, Matt?"

"Yes, Mr. Trump."

"You'd kill for me, right, Matt?"

Matt glanced at me, then back at Donald.

"Matt?"

"Yes, Mr. Trump."

"You'd kill for me, Matt?"

"Yes, boss."
"You're sure you'd kill for me?"
"Yes, Mr. Trump. I'd kill for you."

Chapter 19

I WAS SITTING IN MY apartment, sipping coffee, reading an article in the February 6, 1988 *New York Times* about a serial rapist, Tommie Lee Andrews, becoming the first American ever convicted in a case involving DNA evidence. I remember thinking that unless the ACLU found a way to discredit science, the criminal justice system was about to change and for the better.

I finished that article, turned to the Arts & Leisure section, and saw a story about the life and times of deceased, celebrity makeup artist Way Bandy.

"Way Bandy died."

"Who?" Joni said, slipping on the jacket of her short and sexy business suit, on her way to work. We had just finished our usual morning coffee klatch, caught up on the latest gossip at "21", Four Seasons, Elaine's, etc.

"The makeup artist," I said. "I think you met him with me once." I explained to Joni that during the 1970s the Alabama native was the most famous and highest paid makeup artist in the fashion industry. "Way was a real gentleman," I said. "I didn't even know he was sick."

"Bummer," Joni said and high-heeled out the door.

I'd first met Way Bandy at the renowned photographer Francesco Scavullo's eastside studio. If memory serves me correctly, Scavullo was photographing the actress-model Rene Russo for the cover of *Cosmopolitan* magazine. Way was, of course, doing her makeup. As was my routine, I'd made a cold call, flimflammed my way into Scavullo's studio: A new Ford model asking for someone to look over my modeling portfolio in the hopes of being booked for a future gig. Understand that making money as a model never did come easy for me. I knew I had a good boy-next-door look, but I was far from being a star and had to work harder than anyone else to book jobs. Which I did.

While most models in those days wore a uniform of jeans and cowboy boots, I wore business suits when on go-sees or making cold calls. As a result, the photo studio receptionist, assistants, and even the photographers sometimes thought I was an ad agency executive or potential client.

There were over four hundred working photographers listed on the Ford agency go-see list. I schlepped my portfolio to around ten studios a day. Saw every photographer on that list at least a dozen times. Some liked my chutzpah, thought me a mensch, and hired me. Others thought me a schmuck, a putz, resented my ad agency ruse, and began to turn me away at the door. Oy vey.

Although the distracted and slight-of-stature Scavullo did take the time to glance at my portfolio, he suggested I show the photos to Way.

"Way is better at spotting new talent than I am."

My meeting with Way took no more than fifteen minutes. He looked at my pictures, was warm, friendly, and encouraging, attitudes rarely encountered in the modeling world. He wrote down the names of several A-list photographers that he said I should visit and to feel free to say he sent me.

After that, I'd run into Way and Scavullo at Studio 54, Régine's, and other nightclubs. And, of course, I worked with him on several photo shoots and TV commercials. As a matter of fact, Way was the poor schnook who had to deal with Cheryl Tiegs at a Cover Girl commercial I booked.

I'd been hired to play Cheryl's significant other in the national network spot, which we filmed in an industrial, sparsely populated section of the lower West Side. I think it was the second day of a three-day shoot that Cheryl showed up late, smelling of booze. She was a mess, in full diva mode.

"I'll have to use Spackle on her face," Way said to me as we waited outside a studio lavatory for Cheryl to finish puking. Then Way turned to one of the female production people entering the bathroom and said, "Please, please, please don't give her any blow."

The usual one-hour makeup job took over two. When it was finally time to shoot, Cheryl repeatedly flubbed her one and only line: "I like the look." I lost count of how many takes we did.

We wrapped after three days of filming. I said my goodbyes to the ad agency people, director, and crew. Exited the lower West Side studio. Stepped out into heavy rain, wondering how the hell I was going to find a cab in that desolate area.

"Thomas," Way called out to me. He and Cheryl were getting into a limo the client had provided her.

"C'mon, Thomas. We'll drop you off."

I pulled my jacket up over my head and made a dash for the limo.

"What are you doing?" I heard Cheryl say to Way. "Who told you to invite *him* into my limo?"

"It's raining," Way stammered. "Is it a problem?"

"Yeah," Cheryl said. "It's a problem. But you've already invited him."

Now, understand that I didn't take Cheryl's addlebrained behavior personally. Although I'd met her a few times when she was married to my friend, director Stan Dragoti, she didn't know me or anything about me. As a matter of fact, even though we were a couple during the three-day shoot, she never spoke to me or acknowledged my existence in any way. Regardless, I wasn't getting into that limo. I thanked Way for the offer and walked up to Tenth Avenue in the pouring rain.

My home telephone rang. I closed the *Times*, got to my feet, walked across the room, and picked up a portable. "Hello?"

"My name's Harrigan," a gruff voice said. "Michael J. Harrigan, attorney-at-law."

"Yeah?"

"I'm trying to reach Thomas Fitzsimmons."

"You've reached him," I said.

"I need to find a missing person." Harrigan said. "I need someone to help me find her. Someone who can keep his mouth shut."

"You practice law in New York?"

"Los Angeles."

"How'd you get my name?"

"Steven Ross."

Ross, the founder, CEO, president, and chairman of Warner Communications, was a super-nice guy who I'd partied with occasionally over the years. He'd once hired me to investigate a kickback scheme at MTV, a company he owned. But the gig was cut short when the subject of the investigation abruptly resigned and fled the country. Last year I'd reached out to Steve about investing in my movie. He graciously passed my proposal onto one of Warner's film subsidiaries, but I'd yet to hear back from anyone.

"Go on," I said.

"Where shall I begin?"

I reached for a pad and pen. "Subject's name."

"Pamela Watt. Originally from somewhere in Pennsylvania. She married, then divorced a golden boy Canadian hockey player. They were together for five years, had two kids, lived in New Jersey."

"Where's the hockey player now?"

"Back in Canada," Harrigan said. "Read somewhere that he remarried and coaches high school hockey—not that I know for sure. He hasn't returned any of my calls."

"What about Pamela? Age? Description?"

"Now she's around thirty-two, five-nine, brown eyes and hair. She was a model in the old days. Supposed to have been a real beauty. Got older, left the big time and wound up with an obscure New York City modeling agency called Dee Edwards. That's the last time my client saw her."

"Got a date of birth? Social Security number? Last known address?"

"No." Harrigan paused. "What about your fee?"

"First off," I said, "I'm not a licensed private investigator. I'm a security consultant. I hire investigators. Supervise the job, write the reports. I get two-fifty an hour. The investigators get one-fifty an hour, plus expenses."

"Can you do better on the price?"

"You want cheap detectives, counselor," I said, "try the Yellow Pages."

I heard the flick of a cigarette lighter, then Harrigan puffing away. "I suppose you want a retainer."

"A certified check for ten thousand, along with a letter of agreement that authorizes me to act on your behalf. Once the retainer is used up, I'll notify you and you'll inform me whether your client wishes to go further."

"Who said anything about a client?"

I didn't dignify that with a response. "Any other questions?"

"What type of expenses should I anticipate?"

"Depends. Where did she divorce the hockey player?"

"We don't know."

"If she got a quickie divorce outside of New York State, say in Reno, then remarried and changed her name, that would complicate things. I might have to travel or hire investigators in other states. With your approval, of course."

"What about the model agent as a lead?"

"Dee Edwards closed years ago."

"How do you know that?"

"It's why I get the big bucks, counselor." I wasn't about to share the fact that at the time my primary source of income, modest as it may have been, was still modeling.

"So," Harrigan said. "Sounds like you're the right man for the job."

"Depends," I said, "on why your client wants to find Pamela?"

"Does that matter?"

"To me, it does."

"I'll get back to you." Harrigan hung up.

Shit.

I didn't expect to hear from the LA attorney again.

FedEx was at my door at ten o'clock the following morning. Inside the envelope was the signed agreement from Harrigan and a certified check in the amount of $10,000. I picked up my phone and called an ex-cop/private detective I worked with in the past.

"Yeah?" James T. said groggily.

"Wake up, rat's ass."

"Oh," he said. "It's you."

I picked up the Harrigan check and examined it. "Looks like I've got a paying client. A lawyer from LA."

"A lawyer? Get the money up front."

"I'm way ahead of you."

"What kinda case?"

"Missing person," I said. "Do me a favor and check out Michael J. Harrigan, a lawyer in LA." I recited the information on the lawyer's letterhead. "I want to know what kind of law he practices. Who his clients are."

"I'll get right on it."

I hung up. Thought about how to go about locating Pamela Watt. Since the modeling world was a small one, I phoned Rusty, the head booker at the women's division of Ford. Told her I was trying to find an ex-model, gave her Pamela's name. Rusty said she did indeed remember Pamela, but didn't say much else—no comment good or bad. But she connected me to a guy named Bill in Ford's billing department. Within five minutes, Bill gave me Pamela's last known address in Oyster Bay, Long Island.

"We sent her a residual check to that address a few years ago," Bill said. "She cashed it."

I headed for the main branch of the New York public library and searched the Oyster Bay phone books. Found a residential listing for an Anthony Watt; the address matched the one Ford had given me. Then I researched the latest US census.

"I located Pamela," I told the lawyer Harrigan the following day. It was 9:01 a.m., LA time.

"Where is she?" Harrigan said.

"Not so fast," I said. "You never did tell me why your client wants to find her."

"You receive my check?"

"I haven't cashed it yet."

I heard Harrigan puffing on a cigarette. "My client was involved with Pamela once. Now he's having some marital problems. All he can think about is her, his great lost love."

I sort of knew where the guy was coming from. I'd once tried to rekindle an old flame. Put a lot of time and effort into it. Learned that, after we'd enjoyed a second honeymoon, our old issues were new again.

"When it comes to lost loves," I said, "they say you can't go back."

"Maybe you and I can't," Harrigan said. "Rich people do whatever the hell they want. Now, where's Pamela?"

"Oyster Bay, Long Island." I gave him the address. "The last US census indicated that six people are living there. Four adults and Pamela's two children. There're two phones listed. One to Anthony Watt, Pamela's father, I assume. Another to a Robert Winston. I checked the local marriage records. She's married to Winston."

"I'll call the client and get back to you." Harrigan hung up.

I dialed James T. "Get anything?"

"Harrigan's an entertainment attorney. His main client is King World. They produce and syndicate TV shows for CBS. Roger King is chairman of the board."

"I'll bet he's our actual client," I said.

"Good chance," James T. said. "We're talking big bucks here."

My call-waiting beeped. "Hold." I flashed to the next line. "Speak."

"The client wants more," Harrigan said.

"Like?"

"Everything. Is she happy? Are she and her husband financially set? Is the husband a good guy or a bad guy? He wants pictures."

"Pictures?"

"Of Pamela."

I thought about that. "Look, we don't peek in bedroom windows."

"No. Nothing like that. He wants to know what she looks like these days, that's all. If she's fat and ugly, believe me, that will be the end of it."

I hung up with Harrigan, flashed back to James T. "Pack your camera. I'll pick you up in an hour."

"Shit," James T. said as I drove a rental car down Pamela Watt Winston's tree-lined street. "Can't see the house." The residence was set back off a winding, thickly settled residential country road, on a deadman's curve and not visible from any vantage point.

"Why does the client want to know so much about this broad, anyway?" James was dressed in black. "You said she's married, right?" He reached into a camera bag and snapped a telephoto lens onto a Nikon. A sixteen-wheeler whizzed around the curve, going in the opposite direction. The turbulence rocked the rental.

"They used to date."

"This better not turn out to be a stalking." James pulled on a black watch cap. "I could lose my PI license."

I slowed the car, aware that in upscale Oyster Bay, diligent residents would soon notice our strange vehicle and call the police. Not that that would be much of a problem. I just didn't want to go through the hassle of explaining myself.

"I'll drop you," I said. "Find a place to wait."

I pulled a U-turn. Hit the gas. Sped by Pamela's property, passed an old colonial, then a split-level ranch, and eased down on the brakes. James opened the car door. Stepped out and disappeared into the thicket. I punched the accelerator and raced away. Slowed at a curve. Stopped. Threw the steering wheel to the left. Backed into a narrow clearing. Inched into some foliage, where I had a clear view of the line of trees and bushes forming a perimeter around Pamela's house.

I used binoculars, looking for James T. I saw him moving quickly across several vast lawns. He stopped, looking, I assumed, for signs of dogs. I lost sight of him as he crawled down a small ravine, across two more front yards. I caught a fleeting glimpse of him as he rolled onto Pamela's property. I set down the binoculars. Settled back. Killed the engine. This was gonna take a while.

I reached to the back seat and grabbed a business magazine I'd purchased on the way to pick up James. Flipped to the article that profiled Roger King.

As James T. mentioned earlier, Roger King was chairman of the board of King World Productions, the leading distributor of television syndicated programming in the country, including such iconic series as *Little Rascals, Wheel of Fortune, Jeopardy!, The Oprah Winfrey Show,* and *Inside Edition* He had a reputation as a party animal and threw lavish industry parties. He was also known for giving newcomers in the industry a helping hand.

"Now that is interesting," I said to myself as I closed the magazine. What with me looking for investors for my movie, Roger King might be a good person to know.

About thirty minutes later a late-model Lexus rolled down Pamela's driveway. A woman was behind the wheel. She made a left and sped away. Just then James stepped from the bushes. He saw me, gave me a thumbs-up sign, and hurried my way.

Chapter 20

"PAMELA WAS A COKE whore with a heavy booze problem," I told the attorney Harrigan. "Locked up for DUI in '80, again in '82. Got some heavy credit card debt. Her husband, Robert, is a personal trainer at a local health club. He calls himself Gino and claims to be a former bounty hunter; we couldn't verify that."

"I'm looking at his picture now," Harrigan said, referring to James T.'s photos I'd FedExed him. "Looks like a thug."

"He is," I said. "With a bad temper. Cops have been called to the house for domestic disputes several times. No arrests. Sources tell us Gino's a player. Been dipping his wick in his client pool. They were separated for a while. Pamela took him back."

Pamela listed her current occupation as a fit model for Ann Taylor on East Fifty-seventh Street. She commuted into the city five days a week on the Long Island Railroad. Following evening cocktails at the upscale St. Regis Hotel's King Cole Bar, she caught the 7:03 train to Oyster Bay.

"She's still a beautiful woman," Harrigan said, again referring to the photos. "Very beautiful."

"What's Roger King gonna do with all this info?"

Harrigan stammered. "Who?"

"Save it, counselor."

I heard Harrigan light a smoke. "If anything, he'll probably arrange to bump into her, most probably at the King Cole Bar. You know, 'Fancy meeting you here. How've you been?' Etcetera. Etcetera. Etcetera."

"He better not stalk her," I said.

"Fax me your final invoice," Harrigan said. "I'll get a check cut by the end of the week and we're square. You did a great job, Fitzsimmons."

"Thanks," I said. "By the way, I hope this isn't out of line, but I've written a screenplay, an action-adventure about twin New York City cops. Any chance I can send it to you? Maybe you can show it to your client?"

"Sure," Harrigan said. "Send it along. I'll take a look. If I like it, I'll pass it on to Roger's production company. No promises."

"Thanks," I said. "I appreciate it."

"Any time."

"You need anything else on this coast, be sure to call."

"Count on it," Harrigan said.

I couldn't help but feel uneasy after hanging up with Harrigan. I walked into my kitchen and poured myself a third cup of morning coffee, thinking, What if I'd inadvertently aided and abetted a stalker? James T. could lose his PI license. We could both be prosecuted, sued civilly, or both. But the worst-case scenario would be Roger King physically harming Pamela.

I decided that I needed to know a lot more about our client. And not just what was in the public record or what I'd read in the press. I needed a personal reference. And so, I grabbed my Rolodex. Flipped through the cards, searching for showbiz contacts who might very well know Roger King. First card I pulled was Larry Hagman, the star of *Dallas*. Then Carroll O'Connor of Archie Bunker fame. Merv Adelson, TV and movie mogul and husband of Barbara Walters. And, of course, Steve Ross. I was about to start by calling my dear friend Larry Hagman — aka the "Mad Monk of Malibu" — when my phone rang.

"Hello?"

"Brunch. Sunday at the Grand Hyatt?" Donald Trump said. "Bring a date. Oh, and pick up Marla?"

I opened my calendar and saw that I was free. Figured I'd ask Joni to come along. "What time?"

"Around twelve-thirty," Donald said. "And don't forget about Monday the twenty-seventh."

"Monday?" I checked my calendar, flipped forward to the 27th. It was blank. "What's the twenty-seventh?"

"You kidding?" Donald said. "The heavyweight championship of the world title fight in AC. Tyson vs. Spinks? I forget to tell you? It will be the greatest fight of all time. Tickets are impossible. Dozens of celebrities are calling me, begging for tickets."

It wasn't lost on me that, as I mentioned earlier, I hadn't heard from Donald for eight or nine years, and yet now I was apparently on his speed dial. His go-to best buddy and wingman. All since he met Marla Maples.

"It'll be the richest fight in boxing history," Donald was saying. "Jack Nicholson will be there. So will Sylvester Stallone, Sean Penn, Madonna, Warren Beatty, Oprah Winfrey, Billy Crystal, George Steinbrenner, Chuck Norris—"

"I'd love to go," I said. "I happen to know Tyson."

"Yeah? Me too. See you Sunday."

"Oh, hey, before you go, you ever do business with a guy named Roger King?"

"Roger King," Donald said. "A great guy. He's with CBS. Supported my television city project. You know about that?"

"I think I remember reading about it," I said. "Over at the old Penn Central railroad yard?"

"That's it. I planned a series of residential towers. Seventy-six-hundred apartments. A one-hundred-and-fifty-story headquarters for a major network; NBC, CBS, whoever. Eighteen-hundred square feet of studio space. But the city fought me tooth and nail. It was a war to the death. I wound up selling my interest to investors from Hong Kong and mainland China."

"Is Roger King a stable guy?"

"Why you asking?"

Since I didn't wish to sound like a gossip, and King's love life was none of Donald's business, I said, "I'm planning on sending him a screenplay I've written. See if he's interested."

"You wrote a screenplay?" Donald said.

That was the very first time I told him about my writing. "I did," I said. "Been sending it to production companies."

"Maybe I can help you with that," Donald said. "I know some people. Marvin Davis over at Paramount."

"Dodi Fayed verbally committed to the project," I said, "but I have my doubts."

Donald snickered. "Dodi's a member of the lucky-sperm club. Never did a day's work in his life. He's not for real."

"But Roger King is?"

Donald hesitated. "Yes. He is. But he's got a booze problem. I've heard he can be violent; not that I ever witnessed it. I've heard he's been arrested a couple of times for drunk driving. Bar fights. Fighting cops. Least that's what I heard."

Great, I said to myself. Just great.

"Thanks for the information," I said.

"Anytime," Donald said. "See you at brunch Sunday."

"Sunday," I said and hung up.

I spent a sleepless night, agonizing over Pamela Watt Winston and Roger King. I tossed, turned, and punched pillows. Every conceivable worst-case scenario played relentlessly in my mind. By morning I'd convinced myself that Roger King was most probably a combination stalker-rapist-serial killer.

I phoned Harrigan. "I wanna talk to the client."

"Why?"

"I've got skin in the game, counselor," I said. "I need to be convinced he won't stalk Pamela."

"No reason to," Harrigan said. "He called Pamela at work. They're meeting for drinks at the King Cole Bar today at five-thirty."

"No way," I said.

"Way," Harrigan said.

I felt a sense of relief after hanging up with him. But after an intense cardio workout, followed by a session punching the heavy bag, I had to admit that I was still troubled—call me paranoid. But after totally misreading the Buddy Jacobson-Jack Tupper-Melanie Cain love-triangle murder, I felt justified. I decided to be at the bar when King met Pamela, see how things went.

It was relatively quiet when I arrived at the fabled, wood-paneled King Cole Bar in the St. Regis Hotel, the place where the Bloody Mary — known as a "red snapper" — was invented. Several groups of shopping-bag-laden tourists were scattered around cushy lounge chairs, drinking fancy, expensive cocktails. Two businessmen, lone drinkers, were seated at the bar, hovering over large, straight-up martinis under the watchful eyes of the fairy-tale king, knights, musicians, and assorted minions in Maxfield Parrish's celebrated thirty-foot-wide mural that hung over the bar since 1935.

I decided against sitting in the bar area. Instead, I claimed a seat in the extended lobby by a large window, where I could keep an eye on clogged Fifty-fifth Street, as well as the hotel lobby and entrance. I settled back in the chair, casting a watchful eye on the activity outside. A few minutes later, one of the most incredibly beautiful women I'd ever seen strode by the hotel. I sat forward, careened my neck to get a better look. Quickly lost sight of her. But then spotted a thin stream of smoke coming from a darkened doorway across the way. I stood, moving to the next window to get a better look.

A figure clad in a black leather jacket stepped from the doorway, a cigarette dangling from his lips, angry eyes sweeping to Madison Avenue and then back to the hotel.

I wasn't sure, but from this angle, the guy looked an awful lot like the photos I'd seen of Pamela's husband, Gino. Same muscular frame and greased-back hair. Instincts told me that if the guy was, in fact, Gino, there was going to be trouble.

Shit.

A line of limos picking up and dropping off inched past the St. Regis as Gino proceeded to smoke, pace, and bop in and out of the doorway, his eyes flicking every few seconds toward Madison Avenue.

A black Bentley pulled up. The driver, Roger King — he looked exactly like his photos in the press — exited. King smiled broadly, glad-handed the valet, handed over his keys — they obviously knew him — and entered the hotel. I looked at Gino; he didn't react. I'd bet that he had no idea what the six-four Roger King looked like.

King, looking every bit the mogul he was, walked casually into the lobby, turned left, and entered the King Cole Bar. I looked across the street just in time to see Gino, eyes riveted on Madison Avenue, straighten and become alert as a guard dog. He pitched his cigarette to the curb. Zipped back into the darkened doorway. Common sense told me that Pamela Watt Winston was coming down the street.

My adrenaline started pumping. I moved to a richly upholstered couch that was located alongside the bar entrance, pretending to be reading one of those glossy travel magazines left lying around. Pamela high-heeled into the lobby and headed my way. I peered over the top of the magazine as she neared. She was wearing a short, clingy dress that revealed a sinful amount of cleavage and shapely dancer's legs. Pamela caught me gawking. Made eye contact. She nailed me with a sultry look that I felt in my toes. Then she smiled a quick little smile and sashayed into the bar, my eyes trailing in her wake. Wow. I now understood King's fascination.

I lost sight of Pamela, looked to the lobby, and saw Gino come barreling in, his chest heaving, eyes everywhere. I glanced back to the bar and saw Pamela and King locked in an all-out embrace.

"You look fantastic," I heard King gush.

"So do you," Pamela gushed right back.

I hoped Gino hadn't seen what I'd just seen.

But he had.

Pamela's husband came storming across the lobby, murder in his eyes. His black leather jacket flew open as he passed me. Was that a weapon or a beeper clipped to his belt? If he really did once work as a bounty hunter, he might very well be packing a gun.

Gino paused for a second outside the bar. He stuck his head in. Looked around, then stepped inside. "Pamela!"

I pulled my .38 from my ankle holster. Placed it in my right hip pocket. The last thing I wanted to do was get involved in yet another crazy-ass love triangle, especially one I'd helped create. But if Gino started shooting, I'd have no choice.

King and Pamela were standing off to my left when I walked into the unfolding cringe-worthy scene. Gino was screaming something about Pamela being a bitch, slut, whore, etc. She looked terrified. But Roger King had a condescending smirk on his face; he was either one cool customer or crazy.

"You're comin' with me," Gino snarled.

"No," she said, "I'm not."

Gino made a grab for Pamela.

She pulled away. "Take your hands offa me."

"Back off, bucko," King said.

Gino shoved King.

King shoved Gino.

Gino threw a punch. Missed.

King slapped Gino. Hard.

Pamela screamed. The tourists scattered.

"Take it outside!" the bartender shouted.

But the two men charged each other like rodeo bulls. Tumbled across a coffee table, obliterated several people's drinks, and crashed onto the carpeted floor, punching, gouging, biting, and cursing each other.

"Gino. Stop!" Pamela screamed. "Someone help!"

Not me, lady. I backpedaled just as the manager, bartender, and two waiters moved in to break them up.

Chapter 21

CALL ME DENSE, BUT I honestly didn't know that anything, other than flirting, was going on between Donald and Marla until that Sunday brunch at the Grand Hyatt.

Joni, not a real big fan of Marla's, had declined Donald's invitation at the last minute; just as well. I considered bringing along Miss Alabama, but decided against it. I knew to be careful who I brought around a pseudo-celebrity like Donald. I hailed a cab and collected Marla at her place on East Eightieth Street.

As we headed west, I reached into my suit jacket pocket and handed her the Anita Baker *Rapture* CD that she'd asked to borrow.

"Thanks." Marla slipped the CD into her purse. "Donald's never heard Anita Baker before."

The cab turned south onto sunny, Sunday-morning quiet Lexington Avenue. "Great outfit, by the way," I said, approving of Marla's short, formfitting sundress and heels.

"Thank you," Marla said. "I like your tie."

We entered the hotel on East Forty-second Street. Rode the escalator to the second floor.

"See you inside," Marla said and headed to the powder room. I walked into the restaurant and was directed to Donald's table.

A waiter approached. I ordered a spicy Bloody Mary. Donald ordered a virgin Mary and a Chardonnay for Marla. As the waiter moved off, I thought about telling Donald that he was right about Roger King, that the guy did indeed have a violent temper, but thought better of it. My comment would require an explanation. Like I said earlier, King's love life was none of Donald's business.

It had taken the bartender, manager, two waiters, and two burly security guards to break up the Gino-Roger King brawl at the King Cole Bar. Since Roger King was a well-regarded, wealthy regular, Gino was the one who was escorted, kicking and screaming, out of the bar and to the street. Pamela, slowly calming down after her fit of hysteria, stayed behind with King.

I noticed a stir in the Grand Hyatt restaurant. Everyone turned to look. Marla Maples, every bit the blonde bombshell, was cat-walking across the room. Donald and I shot to our feet. I helped Marla with her chair, sat her between Donald and me. The room settled into a huddled, whispering, gossipy buzz.

"Been talking about me, boys?" Marla did an excellent, sexy Mae West. "Or are you just happy to see me?"

It was then that I saw the look on Donald's face: the full-on blush and awestruck leer. I could almost hear his dental fillings melt, feel the lustful, pulsing hormones crisscrossing the table.

I said, *For Chrissake, why don't you two get a room.* Only kidding. I picked up my menu, glanced at it, and said, "Shall we order?"

But Donald, eyes on Marla, couldn't even speak.

I knew at that moment that my old pal was toast.

I could tell that Marla Maples knew it too.

The morning of June 26, 1988, I cabbed it alone to the East Sixty-third Street heliport. Since brunch at the Grand Hyatt, Donald had taken to picking up Marla at her residence in his limo — a somewhat reckless act for a married man, in my opinion, given his high profile. I paid the cabdriver, stepped out of the vehicle into the tiny, trailer-like terminal building, and saw a glossy black Trump chopper at the ready. I set my valise on the floor and took a seat. Smoothed the folds from my suit pants. I checked the time. Donald and Marla were late. I picked up a recent copy of *Sports Illustrated* and read about tomorrow's Mike Tyson vs. Michael Spinks heavyweight title fight.

I'd originally met Mike Tyson through my childhood friend Steve Lott, who was Mike's roommate and part of his management team. We'd hang out at Steve and Mike's Second Avenue apartment or go out to dinner. We even triple-dated on occasion. Thanks to Steve, I'd already attended several of Mike's early fights, where I became acquainted with his entourage. It was apparent to us all that Mike would one day be the heavyweight champion of the world.

I flipped the page. Stopped at the next article: BUDDY JACOBSON, HORSE TRAINER AND CONVICTED KILLER, DIES AT 58. There was a photo of Buddy alongside a photo of his victim, my pal Jack Tupper, and a photo of the beautiful Melanie Cane. Apparently, bone cancer had claimed Buddy's life. Good riddance.

The Trump limo rolled down the narrow concrete ramp that led to the heliport and came to an abrupt stop. I got to my feet, shouldered my valise, and stepped outside just as the limo's rear door flew open.

"I can't believe it," Donald said as he stepped out. "I've never been late for anything in my fucking life."

"It's not my fault, Donald," Marla pleaded.

But Donald huffed and puffed across the tarmac and stepped into the helicopter. I almost called bullshit on that — he was frequently late — but kept my mouth shut.

We walked across the tarmac and climbed into the chopper. Marla took a seat alongside the brooding Donald. The chopper engines started. We lifted off, banked over the East River, gained altitude, then flew south over the Fifty-ninth Street Bridge.

We touched down about forty minutes later on the Trump Castle Hotel's landing pad in Atlantic City. Stephen Hyde, CEO of the Trump casinos, along with Donald's Atlantic City director of security, Lynwood Smith, and bodyguard Big Jim Fair, greeted us.

Donald told us he'd call later to plan a prefight dinner, then he went off with Hyde and his security team to attend to business. Since at the time Donald's wife Ivana was CEO of the Castle, we couldn't stay there. A concierge hustled us into a waiting limo, transported Marla and me to Donald's other hotel, the Trump Plaza on the boardwalk.

Once in my room, I loosened my tie, lay back on the bed, phoned my pal Steve Lott and told him I was in AC for tomorrow's fight and arranged to meet him downstairs in the Trump Plaza lobby later that afternoon.

"I'll take you to Mike's sparring session," Steve said. "Then we'll go back to his dressing room and hang out."

"Bring your handball gloves?" Steve said, as always, when we shook hands in the hotel lobby. We'd first met playing handball at the Bronx's Orchard Beach when we were about thirteen years old.

"I'll spot you ten points," I said. "Tie one hand behind my back. Play lefty. Blindfolded."

Steve laughed, then launched into a rapid-fire repertoire of god-awful jokes — he always told the worst jokes — as he led me across the lobby to an escalator. We walked past several security guards into a large, private banquet room where a full-fledged boxing ring had been erected. I saw Tyson, in gloves and protective headgear, cage-lion pacing the ring.

"Who's Mike sparring with?" I said.

"Greg Page," Steve said.

"I hear he's the next Ali," I said.

"Never happen," Steve said.

Tyson looked our way. I waved. Tyson didn't wave back.

Steve led me to a ringside seat. I looked around, saw some guys I knew: Bert Sugar, editor and publisher of *The Ring* magazine; Kevin Rooney, Tyson's trainer; his cornerman Matt Baranski, and Robin Givens, Tyson's new wife. I'd never met Givens.

As I settled into my seat, I noticed that, unlike other sparing sessions I'd attended, the room was church-quiet. No one was talking. All eyes were on the ring.

Tyson was still pacing and, even with the headgear, I could tell he was angry. Greg Page was leaning casually on the ropes across the ring, staring the champ down.

The ring bell rang. The two fighters moved into the center of the ring. Long story short: Page proceeded to pummel Tyson. Sticking and moving. Landing punches at will. Tyson was swinging at air. Page kept pouring it on. A visibly frustrated Tyson charged Page, tied him up, then knocked him into the ropes. An embarrassing wrestling match ensued.

"Let's get out of here," Steve said disgustedly.

"What was that all about?" I said as we exited the banquet room, stepping aside to allow boxing promoter Don King and his entourage to enter.

"Him," Steve grouched, gesturing to Don King. I followed my friend down the escalator, across the lobby, and out the hotel's front doors. The sun was out. Even with the chill, AC's famous boardwalk and beach were crowded with sun worshipers and families with small children. Steve and I walked across the boardwalk, leaned against a metal railing, and looked out at the Atlantic Ocean.

"What's up with Don King?" I said.

"He's distracting Mike. Filling his head with a lot of racist baloney," Steve said. "'Whitey's the devil. Whitey's enslaving you. Whitey doesn't care about you.'"

"Why?" I said. "What's in it for him?"

"He wants to be Mike's manager."

We did not go back to Mike's dressing room after the sparring session that day.

"What the hell's keeping Marla?" Donald said the following evening as we walked into Roberto's Ristorante in Trump Plaza and sat at a table. We were scheduled to attend a star-studded, prefight press conference and cocktail party, which started in about an hour.

A waiter approached. I ordered a dry martini, up, lemon twist.

Marla, wearing a short, tight cocktail dress and heels, strode in a few minutes later, accompanied by three fawning businessmen. I got to my feet and Donald introduced me to the aforementioned Stephen Hyde, CEO Trump Casinos, along with Mark Grossinger Etess, president and COO of the under-construction Trump Taj Mahal casino hotel, and Jonathan Benanav, executive vice president of the Trump Plaza casino hotel. I knew instantly that I would become fast friends with all three of those guys.

"We're in a hurry," Donald told our waiter.

We all ordered and as conversations progressed, I realized from the eye contact, arm touches, and giggles that Marla was quite familiar with Donald's three senior executives. I guess he had no problem with that.

"Tommy Fitz," Donald said. "Tell everyone what you told me."

"I saw Tyson sparring with Greg Page." I sipped my martini "The champ didn't look good."

"Tyson's distracted," Etess said. "He's not training hard enough. It's driving Kevin Rooney [his trainer] crazy."

"Don King have anything to do with it?" I said.

"Him and Robin Givens," Etess said.

"Gold digger," Donald said. "She's beautiful. A real operator—and before anyone asks: No, I never had an affair with Robin Givens." Donald smiled at Marla. "I mean, a man would have to be crazy to piss off Mike Tyson. Am I right?"

No argument there.

After dinner, we attended the cocktail hour and press conference in one of the large banquet rooms. Donald left Marla and me on our own and took off with Hyde, Etess, and Benanav to schmooze with guests. We headed to the buffet, chose some desserts, and sat at a table with Jack Nicholson, John McEnroe and his then-wife, Tatum O'Neal. And there was Warren Beatty, Billy Crystal, Madonna and husband Sean Penn. Oprah Winfrey and Richie Pryor were sitting at adjoining tables. I'd later discover that Donald had invited the celebrities and had given them free ringside tickets, along with paying for their transportation and overnight accommodations.

As we finished our dessert, I noticed the press surreptitiously checking out Marla. Reporters and their cameramen were gesturing toward us, whispering to each other. I suspected that they suspected who she was.

As we all know, the main event was a nonevent. Tyson knocked out Spinks before most people were in their seats. Donald, Marla, and I were about to make our way to Tyson's dressing room to congratulate him, when the press swarmed us, taking rapid-fire photos.

Chapter 22

A LOT CHANGED DURING THE months following the Tyson fight. Because of the tabloid press's growing suspicions, Chuck Jones and I helped to move Marla out of her East Eightieth Street apartment and into a place on East Sixty-eighth. That apartment was owned by Jillian L., a lady friend of mine. During the months that followed, we moved Marla, under cover of darkness, in and out of several other short-term rentals. Donald finally stepped up to the plate and stashed her in one of his hotels, the St. Moritz on Central Park South.

The modeling and TV commercial business slowed down even more and so to earn extra money, I signed on with a former FBI guy I knew. William L. had once bodyguarded the likes of Henry Kissinger and now ran his own security company. Since, thanks to Chuck Jones, I'd already been part of a team that bodyguarded Goldie Hawn and Kurt Russell, William L. assigned me to guard Geena Davis, who was in town to promote *The Accidental Tourist*, or maybe it was *Beetlejuice*? I can't remember which.

Anyway, Geena—a beautiful and talented actress—was accompanied by a doofy-looking guy during the two-day press junket. The PDA was off the charts with Geena and the Doof acting like horny teenagers, climbing all over one another, trading tongue-darting lip-locks in elevators, limos—basically, at every opportunity. Everyone involved with the press junket was put off by the couple's cringeworthy conduct. I was happy when the assignment was over.

"Don't assign me to Geena Davis and her horndog boyfriend again," I told William L. "You do and I swear I'll throw a bucket of cold water on them."

I began to get calls from acquaintances who knew of my past and present relationship with Marla, inviting me to movie and Broadway premieres and assorted charity functions, all requesting that I bring Marla. A cartoon light bulb lit over my head. Common sense told me that my sudden popularity was because of Marla's increasingly visible association with Donald; word was slowly getting out.

Donald also began to invite me to more and more social functions, both in the city and AC, which almost always included Marla. He and I dined alone on occasion, usually upstairs at "21". We attended a Broadway play. Cindy Adams would report in her column that Donald had attended with a "male staffer." But I was usually part of an entourage.

One evening I was heading home after attending the Directors Guild of America DGA film awards, with Donald, sans Marla. After dropping him off at Trump Tower, his driver drove me uptown to Elaine's. I needed a nightcap after spending the evening dodging slobbering advances from a very beautiful but totally inebriated actress, Kathleen Turner. Not that I was the only one she flirted with that night. She was all over Donald at first, but he managed to fend off her advances by enlisting the help of her long-suffering husband, Jay Weiss.

"You see that," Donald kept saying to me after Kathleen moved onto her next target. "You see that? Was she coming on to me, or what?"

I caught Donald laughing about twenty minutes later when he saw Kathleen interrupt a conversation I was having with Mid-City Gym acquaintance, actor Michael Douglas. She edged Michael aside and began flirting with me. Convinced that the ultra-hot and erotic *Body Heat* actress was simply smashed and not serious — after all, her husband was there — I played along. Which turned out not to be a good idea. As the evening wore on and I tried to break away, Kathleen became aggressive, obnoxious, a total bore. Donald was the one who rescued me when he announced we had to leave.

"Can you believe Kathleen Turner?" I said as we stepped into his limo.

"Hey," Donald said. "She came on to me first."

I guess it had to be around 1:00 a.m. when Donald's limo dropped me off and I walked into a bustling Elaine's. I looked through the crowd at the tables. Saw a few of the usual boldfaced names. Al Pacino was sitting at table seven with Diane Keaton and another couple. Miramax honcho Harvey Weinstein was sitting at table eight with *Godfather* author Mario Puzo. An assortment of organized crime figures were at table ten. A group of local and federal cops were at table six. Elaine herself was at table four, kibitzing with the actors Michael Caine, Roger Moore, and two ladies.

I squeezed through a clot of revelers, bellied up to the bar, and stood alongside a guy I knew from the hood, Pulitzer Prize–winning reporter Mike McAlary.

I bought him a drink.

After some small talk, McAlary said, "What's up with your ex, Marla Maples?"

"She's doing great," I said.

"Reporters are getting wind of what's going on."

"What's going on?"

McAlary smirked.

"Okay. What reporters?"

"For one, Bill O'Reilly."

I had read recently that O'Reilly had been hired by King World—my former client Roger King—to replace David Frost as host of the tabloid-gossip TV program *Inside Edition*. New to King World, he'd most definitely be looking to break a juicy love-triangle story.

"Tell your pal Trump, if he doesn't want his wife—hell, the whole world to know what's going on—he should be more discreet."

A finger stuck me in the back and a voice said, "Stick 'em up." I turned around and saw Larry "J.R." Hagman along with his wife, Maj, standing behind me.

"Larry, Maj," I said. "Buy you a drink?"

"We just finished dinner; food still sucks here," Hagman said as we shook hands. I hugged and kissed Maj. The Hagmans were one of my all-time favorite couples.

"Where you off to?" I said.

"We're on the way home," Hagman said. Home in Manhattan being a sprawling Trump Parc condominium on Central Park South.

"Lunch tomorrow?" Hagman asked.

"Mumbles?" I said. "Noon?"

A few months earlier, Hagman told me he was being blackmailed.

"Can't believe it," he groused. "The guy's a friend of mine. A good friend."

It was early evening and we were sitting in my living room watching a sporting event on TV. Joni was out as usual, gallivanting around. I couldn't wait for Hagman to get a load of her.

"This guy, Albert F., asked me to invest in a start-up," Larry informed me. "But the business plan made no sense. I told him I wasn't interested. Then he asked for a personal loan. When I said no, he threatened to tell my wife about an affair I had." Hagman lit a joint he'd brought along, took a hit. "I don't know what to do." He offered the joint. I waved it off. He blew out the smoke.

"Go to the cops?" I said.

Hagman shook his head. "Not a chance." He took another hit. "I thought about paying him off—" He blew out the smoke. "But if I give in, he'd never stop." Hagman looked off, took a moment. "I thought about having him killed."

I almost burst out laughing. The antithesis of J. R. Ewing, the amoral, greedy, scheming oil tycoon he played on *Dallas*, Hagman was the most lovable, nonviolent, peaceful guy I knew. I didn't believe for a second that he was capable of harming another human being. But then again, I've been wrong about people before.

"There's one other alternative," I offered.

"Yeah?"

"You can defuse the whole situation if you tell your wife."

Hagman choked on the marijuana smoke.

Hagman walked into Mumbles sans his wife the next day. We sat at a table by a floor-to-ceiling window with a view of Third Avenue.

"I've been meaning to ask," I ventured as we looked at menus. "How *did* you handle the blackmailer?"

"Took your advice," Hagman said. "Told my wife."

"Ouch," I said. "How'd that go?"

"As expected," he said. "If Maj had a gun in her hand, she would have shot me."

"And the blackmailer? Albert F., wasn't it?"

Hagman nodded. "I took care of him."

"Do I want to hear this?"

Hagman leaned over the table, used the menu to shield his mouth, and lowered his voice. Just for a minute, I was looking into the evil that was J.R. Ewing.

"I found a guy," Hagman said. "A contract killer, the real deal. Put one-hundred-thousand dollars in an escrow account. Told him, the day I die of *natural causes*, Albert F. dies. Then I told Albert F. what I'd done." Hagman sat back, flashed the malicious J.R. grin. "You should have seen his face."

My jaw dropped. Was Hagman kidding me? Putting me on? He *was* famous for his wicked sense of humor. But there was something in his demeanor, something in his eyes.

Just then my roomie, Joni, dressed in a clingy red dress that accentuated her eye-popping figure and shapely legs, came strutting into Mumbles. She saw me. Waved. I waved her over.

"You coming or going?" I said as she approached.

"Going to La Côte Basque for cocktails."

Hagman and I got to our feet.

"Say hello to Larry Hagman."

Hagman gave Joni the once-over. "Hello, darlin'," he said in his best Texas twang. He bowed, took hold of Joni's hand, and kissed it. "A pleasure. An extreme pleasure."

"Yes, it is," Joni said, a twinkle in her eyes.

Hagman smiled.

Joni smiled.

Oh, boy.

"Join us for a drink?" Hagman, not waiting for an answer, ushered her into the chair alongside him.

"Just one," Joni said.

I signaled our waiter.

"So, Larry," Joni said. "Who's richer: Larry Hagman or J.R. Ewing?"

"Depends," Hagman said, "on what you consider rich."

"Can Larry Hagman afford to buy Joni a Rolex?"

"A whole truckload." Hagman smiled.

Joni smiled back. "I like that in a man."

Chapter 23

A FEW DAYS LATER, there was a message from Marla on my answering machine. She said she and Donald were having a few people over the following evening, a sort of housewarming for her at the St. Moritz and asked that I attend. I called her back, said I'd be there. Asked Joni if she'd like to join me.

"Will Marla be there?" Joni inquired.

"It's her party."

"I'll pass."

My favorite St. Moritz doorman, Nicholas "Nick" Turturro, brother of the award-winning actor and producer, John Turturro, said a cheerful hello as he opened my cab door. Nick would go on to become an award-winning actor best known for his roles on the television series *NYPD Blue* and *Blue Bloods*.

"Anyone here yet?" I asked Nick.

"Whadda mean?" Nick said.

"Upstairs at Marla's. Donald's having a few people over."

"Yeah? First I heard of it. But something's going on." He gestured to half-a-dozen paparazzi loitering on the corner.

"A celebrity checking in?" I said.

Nick shook his head. "I woulda heard," he said and rushed to help a lady get a cab.

I stepped out of the stream of pedestrian traffic, glanced at a group of mollycoddled children as they exited a sleek limo and entered the art deco Rumpelmayer's tea and pastry café. I checked the time, not wanting to be the first one at Marla and Donald's party.

I decided to grab a quick drink in the hotel's lobby bar when a camera flash caught my attention. Bill O'Reilly had just stepped out of the rear of a yellow cab. O'Reilly waved to the shutterbugs, entered the hotel, and walked across the lobby.

I wondered what the TV-tabloid journalist was doing at the St. Moritz—snooping, like McAlary said? Or was it a coincidence? I mean, the St. Moritz *was* a bustling hotel that hosted corporate events and had several outstanding restaurants and cafés.

I lost sight of O'Reilly, bellied up to the lobby bar, ordered a beer. Twenty minutes later, I paid the check, stepped across the lobby and into a waiting elevator. Got off on the fourth floor. Knocked on Marla's door. No answer. I rang the bell. Knocked again. Put my ear to the door.

"Who is it?" Marla said.

"It's me."

"Oh… ah… hold on a sec, Fitzy," Marla said, sounding flustered. "I just got out of the shower."

"Am I too early?" I said. "Should I come back later?"

"No," Marla said. "Gimme a minute."

I waited. Paced the hall. Checked myself in a floor-to-ceiling mirror. Adjusted my Hermès tie. Pulled out a pocket comb, pulled a Fonzie, and put the comb away.

"Coming," Marla called out.

The lock clicked off.

Marla pulled the door open.

I stepped inside.

"Hiya, Fitzy."

"Why's it so dark?" I said. "Put some lights on."

"Sure."

All at once, the lights flashed on.

"Surprise!" a gang of people yelled.

I almost had a heart attack. They got me good and they knew it.

"Happy birthday, you old geezer," someone called out. Everyone laughed. Someone stuck a cold bottle of beer in my hand.

I glanced around the suite. There must have been over fifty smiling faces. My mother, three beautiful sisters: Maureen, Patricia, and Carol. My twin brother, Joni, Chuck Jones, Paul Derounian, Michael Collyer, Tom Counihan, John McCooey were front and center. Guys I'd been to kindergarten, grammar, and high school with were in attendance. Navy buddy Dominick Porco and his wife Janie Elder were there, as well as cops, ex-cops, and firefighter friends. My booker from Ford and several models from Ford, Wilhelmina, Elite, and Zoli were also in attendance.

After hugging and kissing my mother and sisters, I waded into the crowd, shook hands with the guys, hugged and air-kissed the ladies, and endured the enthusiastic back slaps, birthday toasts, and a chorus of congratulations, you old fart. Formally attired waiters were circulating with trays of hors d'oeuvres and flutes of Dom Pérignon champagne.

I wound up with my mother, brother, and sisters, and had pictures taken under a large *Happy 40th Birthday* banner that was strung across a wall.

"My God," my mother said. "I can't believe that you two are forty years old." My twin and I exchanged fist pumps.

Forty years old. I'd been mulling over that landmark birthday for weeks. Concluded that, although life had thrown me some curveballs, I'd been truly blessed.

"Where's this big shot who's throwing the party?" my mother said. "What's his name again?"

"Trump, Mother." I put my arms around her. "Donald Trump."

"Kind of name is that?" my mother said just as several of my childhood friends, fixtures at our Woodlawn home, came over to pay their respects to her.

"Happy birthday, Fitzy." Marla grabbed my empty beer and stuck another cold one in my hand. I gave her a big, heartfelt hug.

"Thank you for doing all this."

"Thank Donald," she said self-effacingly. "He's paying the bill."

Of course, Donald was paying, but he had no idea when my birthday was and even if he did, he wouldn't think to throw a party. This get-together was all Marla's doing and I knew it. "Where *is* Donald?"

"He just called." Marla took my hand and led me to the window facing Central Park South. She gestured down to the street, at the milling paparazzi. "He was outside a few minutes ago. Saw the paparazzi and left. He didn't even get out of the limo."

Someone called out, "Telephone for Marla."

"Who is it?" she asked.

"A friend of Fitzy's wants to bring a guest."

"I'll take it." I walked across the room and accepted the phone. "Who's this?"

"Thomas! It's me, Shannon M."

Shannon was a dear friend. A stunning thirty-year old Irishwoman who worked in the business-affairs office at the A-list talent agency William Morris. "Hey, Shannon."

"They surprise you?"

"Big-time. You coming?"

"I'm in the lobby. But I've got a William Morris client with me. Can I bring him along? I think you know him."

I held my breath. "Yeah?"

"Bill O'Reilly."

So, I wasn't paranoid. O'Reilly *was* there, snooping. "Look, Shannon, this is just close family and friends. O'Reilly wouldn't feel comfortable."

"Sure he would," Shannon said. "He's Irish like us. What's one more at a party?"

"You're not hearing me, Shannon," I said. "I love ya and you're most welcome, but don't bring O'Reilly. I won't let him through the front door."

Chapter 24

I WAS CONTACTED BY A purchasing agent from the Trump-owned, Plaza Hotel on Central Park South. Seems one of their food suppliers needed help. The hardworking Russian immigrant—I think his name was Boris— owner of a Meatpacking District wholesale slaughterhouse, was being extorted by a local gang. At the time the Meatpacking District was a center for drug dealing, transsexual prostitution, and the mayhem that went with it. After speaking to Boris, I suggested he go to the police. But Boris, who wished to hire me to deal with the extortionist, associated the NYPD with his homeland's KGB.

I accepted the well-paying gig. Staked out the place for a few days. Took some photos of the gang. Unlike the bungling, phony goombahs trying to muscle in on Mumbles, I could tell these mutts were the real deal. I recognized several of them as associates of the notorious Hell's Kitchen gang known as the Westies. This was over my head.

With great difficulty, I persuaded the very reluctant Boris to speak to a contact of mine who worked in the NYPD's OCCB (Organized Crime Control Bureau). Convinced him that renowned Detective Sergeant Joe Coffey, who specialized in jailing the Westies, was not the KGB. Boris paid me for my time and the NYPD took over. I don't recall the details, whether anyone was ever arrested or not, but I know that the Westies never bothered Boris again.

Later that week, I was table-hopping at Elaine's when Elaine summoned me to her table and introduced me to an aspiring

British fashion designer. The stunning young blond woman was the daughter of another Elaine's regular.

"Thomas," Elaine said. "Meet Blondie."

Blondie stuck her hand out and smiled into my eyes. "My name is Catherine." Her smoky, deep voice was alluring, her accent a tad cockney. She reminded me of Miss Moneypenny, an enigmatic character in the James Bond novels and films.

"Lovely to meet you," I mimicked. "May I call you Moneypenny?"

Catherine had a hearty laugh. "By all means."

"Do me a favor," Elaine said. "Blondie doesn't belong here with us old farts. Take her out. She likes jazz."

"It would be my pleasure," I said.

"Now!" Elaine said.

I escorted Moneypenny out the door, into a cab, heading for the West Village. The cab dropped us at Bleecker and Thompson Streets. We took in a set at Kenny's Castaways, moved onto the Village Vanguard, then the Blue Note. Then we headed uptown to P.J. Clarke's for a nightcap.

It had to be around 2:30 a.m. when I ordered Bushmills, neat, from Dennis the bartender. Moneypenny ordered her seventh—or was it her eighth?—Beefeater and tonic. Rocky Graziano, the former world middleweight champ and infamous cheapskate, was two stools down with his usual entourage. As was ritual, I bought the champ a drink.

The more Moneypenny drank, the more affectionate she became. I wasn't complaining. When her hand slipped from my arm to my thigh, to my crotch, I knew it was time to leave. We finished our drinks. Dennis handed me the tab. I glanced at the total. Laid down some bills. Overtipped as usual. Walked out the door and into an altercation.

"Faggot!" A man sitting in the passenger's seat of an idling, black D-series Ram pickup truck threw a beer can at an attractive brunette woman walking east on Fifty-fifth Street. The brunette ducked. The can exploded against Clarke's brick wall.

"Cocksucker!" another man yelled from the pickup's driver's side. The brunette stuck up her middle finger. The pickup screeched to the curb. The doors flew open. Three drunk, burly good ol' boys armed with baseball bats and wearing black muscle T-shirts piled out.

"We're gonna teach you a lesson, beaner," the fattest of the trio said.

"You're making a mistake," the brunette said. She was one cool customer, swinging her shoulder purse in front like a lariat. "A big mistake."

The rednecks broke into riotous laughter.

The brunette kicked off her heels and stepped into a boxer's stance. "C'mon, *pendejo*. One at a time."

I said to Moneypenny, "Look at this shit."

Moneypenny belched a squall of Beefeater and cigarettes. "Let's go."

"I can't."

"For bloody Chrissake, why not?"

"Can't let them hurt that lady."

"Lady?" Moneypenny squinted at the brunette. "That's a tranny."

"Huh?"

"A cross-dresser, you eejit."

It took a moment for me to focus. Moneypenny was right. The brunette was an Hispanic man in woman's clothing. I glanced at the pickup truck: Tennessee license plates.

"Don't arse around, Thomas," Moneypenny said with some urgency. She took my hand and tried to pull me away. "You said you're not a copper anymore."

Believe me, I didn't want to "arse around." Since I knew when I left my apartment that I'd be drinking, I was unarmed. So how to handle three drunk thugs with baseball bats? I looked down deserted Third Avenue. The 19th police precinct was located eight blocks south. I prayed a cop car would come cruising north.

"All right," Moneypenny said. "If you're trying to impress me, you've succeeded. You're bloody-well brave." She placed a bejeweled hand by my arm. "Now, are you going to take me back to your flat and fuck me properly, or bugger around here?" She squeezed my left buttock and whispered in my ear, "I haven't had sex for over a year."

I felt my breath catch. "You're killing me."

"Yee-aay-eee," one of the rednecks hollered.

The three men, practice-swinging their bats, advanced on the victim. The guy snatched up his high heels and tried to make a run for it. But the rednecks spread out, cutting off his escape. I knew I should mind my business. Drag the hot and horny Moneypenny back to my place; that is what I lived for. Knew that I'd be a complete eejit to arse around and bugger off here.

"Help!" the victim screamed. "Police!"

I saw one of those heavy, metal-wire NYC sanitation trash baskets on the corner. Figured I could use it as a weapon. "Why don't you go back inside?" I took out my wallet and handed Moneypenny cash. "Order a drink. Play the jukebox. I'll only be a moment. Tell Dennis I'll have another Bushmills. Neat."

Moneypenny snatched the money. Said, "You're a blummin' knobhead, you are," and disappeared inside Clarke's. That was when the fat redneck charged. The victim sidestepped. But the fat guy knocked him against Clarke's brick wall, then jabbed his bat into the guy's midsection, doubling him over.

I'd seen enough. I grabbed the trash basket, dumped out the contents, was about to fling it at the rednecks, when someone yelled, "Hold it!" I looked toward the voice. Saw the gun first, some sort of automatic, then a guy stepped from behind a car: the Grayman. The Upper East Side racketeer stepped onto the sidewalk, his gun hand unwavering.

Grayman acknowledged me with a nod. Then said, "Drop the bats, you shitkicking assholes, or I'll drop you."

The rednecks regarded him. "You a queer-loving Jew-boy," the fat one said, "or you a faggot too?"

I groaned. Grayman wouldn't hesitate to shoot. I heard Clarke's door open, glanced to my rear. Rocky Graziano was standing there.

"Hello, Grayman," Rocky croaked.

"Champ," Grayman said, eyes on the rednecks.

Was the champ backing us up?

"One last time," the Grayman said. "Drop the fucking bats."

"I'd do as he says," Rocky said, "if I were you."

I held my breath.

They dropped the bats.

"Now, get the fuck out of here." Grayman gestured with the gun. "Go back to hillbilly land. And I mean *now*." Reluctantly, the three piled into their truck, cursing us and our ancestors every step of the way. The fat guy revved his engine. "Faggots!" he hollered one last time. Threw a beer can that exploded on the concrete sidewalk. The truck, tires screaming, peeled away. Rocky stepped back into Clarke's.

I hurried to help the victim to his feet. "You okay?"

The guy nodded. "Thanks."

"Don't thank me," I said. "Thank him." I gestured to the racketeer.

But Grayman was gone.

Chapter 25

My mother died suddenly. Her death shattered me. I felt gutted. Emotionally adrift. I would feel that way for a very long time. The well-attended funeral service for Madeline Theresa Cimino Fitzsimmons was especially sad. Not only because she was much loved, but unlike my father, who'd been bedridden with a stroke for years before dying, my mother had never been sick a day in her life.

My brother, three sisters, and I took turns greeting visitors at Hodder's funeral home on McLean Avenue in Yorkers. You'd think that we were giving away free beer, judging by the way the viewing room filled up. Danny Boy's Pub—now Danny Mac's—was conveniently located on the other side of the parking lot, and it was apparent that a few of the mourners had gotten a head start mourning.

I was sitting in a pew with my older sister Maureen, keeping her octogenarian, nearly deaf mother-in-law, Nora Dowd (from Belfast), company. On my right was a former Eastern Airlines flight attendant I was having a fling with. The brunette beauty suffered from low self-esteem, along with a booze and kleptomania problem. What could be more fun than that?

"DO YOU NEED ANYTHING, NORA?" my sister said into Nora's ear.

"That man?" Nora said with a thick Irish brogue, pointing a knurled finger across the room. "That man. Over there. That man who just walked in."

Maureen's eyes searched the crowd and she saw Marla and Donald. "YES, NORA. WHAT ABOUT THAT MAN?"

Nora said, "He looks like Donald Trump."

"YES," Maureen said. "THAT IS DONALD TRUMP."

The whole room turned to look.

Donald was like a deer in headlights.

All at once, Marla was swallowed up by my extended family and friends whom she'd befriended when she and I were dating—many had attended my fortieth birthday party. I hustled over to Donald. Introduced him to my brother and sisters. He offered his condolences. Normally I would think that Marla was the sole reason that Donald attended my mother's services. As with my fortieth birthday party, she'd most likely come up with the idea. But I wasn't as confident this time. That's because, in my opinion, Donald had changed during the past five months.

I'd been home, brewing a pot of coffee when *Special News Bulletin* flashed across my TV screen. "This just in," a talking head said. "Five people, including three high-level executives of Donald J. Trump's three casinos in Atlantic City, were killed today when their helicopter crashed in pine woodlands on the Garden State Parkway near Forked River, New Jersey. Among those killed were Stephen Hyde, CEO Trump Casinos; Mark Grossinger Etess, president and COO of the Trump Taj Mahal casino hotel; and Jonathan Benanav, executive vice president of the Trump Plaza casino hotel."

The change in Donald was subtle in the beginning. First thing I noticed was that he and Marla weren't arguing as much. Donald had become less confrontational. Dare I say a tad more introspective? We'd be out for one of those "We're in a hurry" dinners at "21" or Le Cirque, and he'd blurt out things like, "Life is short." "Life is unpredictable." "If you're not happy with your life, make yourself happy."

There was the time we traveled to AC for the Rolling Stones concert. That morning, Donald, his brother Robert, Marla, Joni, and I toured the Taj Mahal construction site, which was over budget and behind schedule. Joni and I hung back with Donald's security while Marla, Donald, and Robert entered the massive, half-finished structure and began an inspection. At one point, Donald, to my surprise, put his arm around Marla and hugged her. The gangs of construction workers—laborers, equipment operators, ironworkers, etc.—went ballistic. Whistling, applauding, and shouting, "Way to go, Mr. Trump!"

Marla beamed. Donald gestured a thumbs-up, basking in the admiration and attention. Later that day, we attended a press conference for the Rolling Stones concert that Donald had booked into the AC Convention Center, next to Trump Plaza. The media event was jammed, the entertainment press out in full force. But the band sent word that they wouldn't make an appearance while Donald was in the room. And they refused to even take a photo with him unless they were paid $5000 per photo, in cash, up front.

"Can you believe this?" Donald said to me. But instead of going on the offensive, brashly lashing out at Mick Jagger and the other Brits, he became quiet, circumspect. Perhaps it was the culmination of all the enormous pressures in his life that this inconsequential slight affected him, but I thought I saw tears welling in his eyes. I couldn't remember ever seeing Donald vulnerable before.

We left the press conference. But we did attend the concert that evening. Saw the show with Robert and his wife Blaine, Marla, and Joni. We all enjoyed it. But we didn't go backstage afterward as we usually did with other A-list acts.

It was close to Christmas when the more sensitive Donald called me at home and said to me, "I'm going to fly down to Dalton, make a quick stop, pick Marla up. Take her to Aspen for Christmas vacation. What do you think?"

I think you're out of your freaking mind.

"Didn't you tell me that Ivana and your kids will be in Aspen?"

"Yeah, but I've rented a place for Marla out of town. There's no chance of them running into each other."

Famous last words.

"I think you're taking a big gamble."

"Life is short," Donald said.

I first learned about the New Year's Eve Marla-Ivana confrontation at Bonnie's Restaurant on Aspen Mountain from Chuck Jones. He told me that, instead of renting Marla a place outside of Aspen, Donald had sequestered her close by in a penthouse at the Brand Building, a luxurious condo overlooking Aspen Mountain: a mere two-minute drive, or five-minute walk from the Little Nell, where the Trump family was staying.

From what Chuck told me, I concluded that, with her guru and spiritual advisor Kim at her side, Marla had stalked Ivana, who'd inadvertently stumbled upon evidence of her affair with Donald. Ivana had already confronted Kim, asking who Moolah — mispronouncing Marla — was. Marla, aware that Ivana was hunting her, went on the offensive and orchestrated the very public clash that ended with Ivana ordering Moolah to "Stay away from my husband!"

"How you gonna handle the PR?" I asked Chuck.

"No one really knows who Marla is," Chuck said. "But if anyone asks, I'll deny she was in Aspen. Say she was home in Dalton."

"Can you get away with that?"

"It's a nonstory," Chuck said. "No one cares."

It seemed that, at first, Chuck was right.

Despite dozens of witnesses and the presence of paparazzi who always staked out Bonnie's, a celebrity hangout, the incident found no traction in the press.

Donald also opined that the Aspen debacle was no big deal. "It was great," he said. "Really great. Having two beautiful women fighting over me. Besides, Ivana has to get used to other women if we're going to have an open marriage."

"Are you saying," I was incredulous, "that Ivana agreed to an open marriage?"

"Not yet," he admitted. "But she will."

Donald, stuck on stupid.

It was over a month later when *Daily News* gossip columnist and Trump family friend and confidante, Liz Smith, broke the bombshell story.

EXCLUSIVE! LOVE ON THE ROCKS read the February 11 *Daily News* headline. Ivana was quoted as saying that she was "devastated that Donald was betraying her." Smith went on to report, "The marriage of Ivana and Donald Trump seems to be on the rocks, and inside sources say lawyers are already at work trying to divide the complex Trump holdings."

New York Post's gossip columnist Cindy Adams's story on February 12 identified an enigmatic actress-model Marla Ann Maples as the other woman, which triggered a gossip tsunami. Chuck Jones was besieged with phone calls, all asking to interview Marla. Donald encouraged her to go into hiding. Which she did.

And the media frenzy began in earnest.

"Cover for me?" Donald said over the phone the morning the *Post* story broke. Since Ivana had changed the locks on their penthouse apartment and locked Donald out, he was calling from 63J, his father's Trump Tower apartment a few floors below.

I was in my bathroom, standing in front of a mirror, practicing sniffling and sneezing on cue, on my way to an audition for a Dristan—or was it a Comtrex?— cold-medication TV commercial.

"What do you need?" I said.

"Tell everyone you're still dating Marla?"

"Wait a minute." I sneezed. "Didn't you want Ivana to find out about Marla? I mean, why else would you take her to Aspen?"

"I don't know what I want."

"Meaning, what?"

"I may reconcile with Ivana."

"Does Marla know?"

"No," Donald said. "And don't tell her."

Here we go again.

Guys cover for each other, sure, but Marla was also a friend of mine. I asked Donald precisely what he expected me to do.

"I'll have Chuck Jones set up an interview with the papers this afternoon," Donald said. "Maybe a TV network."

Spreading the word that I was still dating Marla was one thing. But lying to the press? And on national TV? Donald had some pair asking me, or anyone, for a favor like that. But he *had* been a most generous friend. I felt that I owed him.

"Marla onboard with this?" I said.

"Sure," Donald said. "Well?"

I took a moment before I said, "No problem."

I don't recall how many tabloids, TV, magazine, in-person, and telephone interviews I did during the next few weeks, or the media outlets involved. That's because they were *all* involved. Soon the media overwhelmed me. My phone rang constantly. I couldn't so much as go to a restaurant or run errands in my neighborhood without being approached by reporters. I became paranoid, started exiting and entering my building through the loading dock or garage, one eye always looking over my shoulder. I found myself thinking, Why the hell had I gotten involved in this?

The New York tabloids published front-page Trump divorce stories for twelve days straight. Articles would appear in every major newspaper, magazine, and all TV networks in the United States, across Europe, the Middle East, and even down under in Australia.

Marla, still in hiding, called me up after watching one of my TV interviews, furious that I was still saying we were dating. Marla said that they, meaning her mother Ann and guru Kim, wanted her relationship with Donald out in the open—not surprising after what happened in Aspen, but still, it was the first I'd heard of it.

"I'm only doing what Donald asked me to do," I said. "He told me you were in the loop."

"He's a liar."

"Look, if you want me to stop," I said, "I'll stop. No more interviews."

"That's what I want," Marla said. "Besides, looks to us like you're enjoying the attention too much anyway."

Honestly, I was stung. Although, when I thought about it, I had to admit that Marla had a point. I mean, who was I? A nobody ex-cop and struggling actor/model/writer thrust into the middle of what would soon become the biggest tabloid divorce in the last fifty years. Suddenly I was a somebody, now known as a close friend and confidant of billionaire Donald J. Trump. My picture was in the papers, my interviews ran on network TV. Old friends and new acquaintances were coming out of the woodwork, some complimentary, some critical, a few asking for access to Donald. To be frank, I'd have to say that yes, I was enjoying the notoriety. But what I didn't know at the time was that the media's interest in Marla was about to ramp up, become even more fierce, and the pressure on me more intense. Especially after I snuck Marla and Kim out of the Hilton—Donald scrambled to move her out of the St. Moritz—and hid them at a friend of mine's empty summer house out in Southampton, New York. The press's inability to locate Marla whipped them into a frenzy. On the phone, in person, through intermediaries, members of the tabloid press hounded me — the *National Enquirer* offered me $100,000 — all asking the same question: Where is Marla Maples?

Chapter 26

"You know where Marla is?" Donald asked me. He'd just returned from visiting Ivana in Palm Beach. "She's disappeared."

No surprise there. I mean, the papers had chronicled Donald's trips to Mar-a-Lago, speculating that, even though they'd slept in separate beds, (according to the *New York Post*) reconciliation was imminent. Then Donald told reporters that he still loved Ivana and what a great institution a good marriage was. He then repeated for the umpteenth time that he and Marla were just friends. Marla was beyond furious.

"You know where she is?" Donald repeated.

I lowered the volume on my stereo as Kenny Rogers whined *You picked a fine time to leave me, Lucille.* "Not a clue," I lied. Actually, Marla and Kim, using "borrowed" passports, had flown down to Guatemala, where Kim had a college friend working with the Peace Corps. But Marla had sworn me to secrecy under penalty of dismemberment and/or death.

"I can't believe she'd pull this now." Donald went on to rant about his deteriorating business situation. The fact that the soon-to-open Taj Mahal was turning out to be a financial boondoggle, what with cost overruns and scheduling issues.

"Hell," he said. "There's still no water on the upper floors. The electrical is half finished and I've a soft opening coming up. Marla picked a fine time to pull a disappearing act."

"What did you expect?" I said. "You've been screwing her around for weeks. And didn't you tell me you had a dozen Marlas waiting in the wings?"

"Just help me find her, Tom?" Donald asked.

"I'll try."

Donald phoned me three more times that day. Six times the day after and the day after that. Then, out of frustration and in hopes of flushing Marla out, under the guise of his alter ego, phony-baloney press agent "John Barron," he called the press.

DONALD DUMPS MARLA: GEORGIA PEACH IN TEARS AFTER TRUMP'S FAREWELL PHONE CALL, read the *New York Post*'s March 22, front-page headline. The Cindy Adams story was ridiculously self-serving, with quotes like " [Marla] told him [John Barron] that she's never been in love like this before. She said she had never been attracted to anyone more than Trump." Donald had no idea that Marla wouldn't see the New York papers until she returned to the United States three weeks later.

Then Liz Smith got into the act.

MARLA HID IN TRUMP TOWER, the March 23 *New York Daily News* front-page headline read. Liz reported that Marla had spent five-and-a-half weeks living in apartment 63C, across the hall from Fred Trump Sr.'s apartment, while Ivana occupied the Trump penthouse. Donald vehemently denied the story. Told the press: "What kind of man would I be if I was sneaking Marla in and out of Trump Tower? What kind of man would I be?"

What kind of man, indeed.

I declined an invitation to the April 5 Taj Mahal soft opening after Trump's AC security guys warned me ahead of time that Donald was on a foul-mouthed rampage, dressing down his new senior executive staff —with good reason. Apparently, many of the Taj's shops were not open. The roof leaked. Room keys didn't work. And there was no running water on the top floors. Turned out that every one of the A-list celebrities who Donald boasted were attending were no-shows. Many of the slot machines were inoperable, as were the changemaking machines used to feed slots and the "count room" was in turmoil.

Turned out it was lucky I skipped the opening, because my agent arranged for me to audition for a TV pilot with a casting agent—*The Karate Kid, Pope of Greenwich Village, Dirty Dancing, Beverly Hills Cop II, Miami Vice*— Bonnie Timmermann, first thing that Monday morning. But instead of reading for a part, the appointment at her Park Avenue office turned out to be more of an uncomfortable meet and greet. I don't recall specifically what Bonnie said to me, but I got the distinct impression that if I wanted to work in one of her projects, I'd have to sleep with her. Not that that was unusual: straight and gay casting couches were a fact of life in the biz.

Sometime later I was at home, about to leave to meet Joni at the Four Seasons for cocktails, when my phone rang. I picked up, ready to curse out whichever member of the press was bugging me. "What!?"

"Hiya, Fitzy."

"You back?"

"In Dalton," Marla said. "Donald's been driving my daddy and mama crazy."

"They're not the only ones," I said. "You see the newspapers?"

"Not the New York papers," Marla said. "What's been going on?"

I spent the next half hour filling her in. Quoted excerpts from some of the tabloids. Told her about the Taj Mahal opening debacle. That Ivana was challenging the prenuptial agreement. Marla's emotions ran the gamut from outrage to amusement. When I read her the "Donald Dumps Marla" story, she burst out laughing.

"God," Marla said. "He's such a liar."

"You gonna call him?"

"Maybe," she said. "Maybe not."

That's when she informed me that Diane Sawyer, co-anchor of ABC's *Primetime* had called her parents several times, wanting her to do an interview.

"You going to do it?" I said.

"I'm thinking about it."

I made a party of it. Supplied the food and booze. Joni invited six lovely, eligible ladies to our apartment. I was like a kid in a candy store. With Sade singing in the background, I worked the room, oozing charm. Served drinks and snacks with plans of luring at least one of our guests into my bed before the evening was through.

"Everyone find a seat," Joni announced. She switched off the music and used the remote to turn on the TV. Marla's *Primetime* interview started at 10:00.

"Anyone need anything?" I said as our guests settled in, squeezed onto the couch. Some sat on the floor facing the TV. A leggy redhead, a Julliard graduate and fledgling concert violinist from Ireland, sat on my easy chair. I liked redheads.

The program music started. Intros were made.

Marla's segment began.

"Why did you decide to talk?" Diane Sawyer asked right off the bat.

I thought Marla looked beautiful but nervous. She handled herself pretty well. She said that most of the tabloid stories, especially the "Best Sex I Ever Had," were totally fabricated. Said she had nothing to do with breaking up Donald's marriage, which was bullshit. Said that Donald had never given her any money—double bullshit. I thought Sawyer would ask Marla the obvious follow-up question, how she paid her bills, but she didn't. Marla did a good job of covering for Donald, referring to him several times as a married man trying his best to honor his family. Whatever that meant.

"Do you love him?" Sawyer asked.

"I do love him," Marla said.

My guests let out a chorus of "whoops!" and hollers.

"Gold digger!" the redhead shouted.

"Slut!" a blonde chimed in.

"Home-wrecker," a brunette spat out.

As the segment ended, Joni said, "Let's go," and switched off the TV.

All the ladies got to their feet.

"Go?" I said. "Go where?"

"Magique," the redhead said.

"There's a troupe of Chippendale's dancers," the blonde said, "performing tonight."

"Male strippers?" I said, crestfallen. "You're going to watch male strippers?"

"You should come with us, lad," the redhead said.

"It'll be fun," the brunette said.

"I'll pass," I said.

Before I knew it, Joni had led the ladies out the door, leaving me alone. I brooded for a few minutes. Thought about heading down to Elaine's; there was usually action there. But I wasn't in the mood. It was time for a cold shower.

Chapter 27

A FEW MONTHS LATER, Marla, Donald, Joni, and I were in the Trump limo, on our way to dinner at Lutèce. Donald was talking on the car phone, arguing with bankers and lawyers. When we arrived, Donald told us to go on inside, order him a diet soda, and that he'd be right in.

"Donald's pissing me off," Marla told me after the owner, André Soltner and his wife Simone, greeted us effusively, showed us to our table, and a waiter took our drink order.

"You've gotta lighten up," I told her. "Read the papers. He's going down the tubes." I placed my napkin on my lap. "Not only could he go broke, but from what I read, he could be in debt for hundreds of millions. Especially if Ivana gets the one-hundred million she's asking for. I wouldn't be surprised if he wound up sleeping in my extra bedroom."

"My room?" Joni said. "No way. He gets the couch."

A waiter served our drinks.

Marla said, "You really think that's possible?"

"Donald sleeping on my couch?"

"Going broke."

"Sure," I said. "But there's broke, and there's billionaire broke. Knowing Donald, he'd find a way to come back."

"But what if he couldn't?" Marla asked. "What if he really lost everything?"

"Well, listen to you," Joni said. "Miss Glass Half-full."

"It's not just that." Marla lowered her voice. "I'm thinking about taking a gig representing No Excuses jeans."

I'd never heard of No Excuses jeans but I said, "That's great."

"Donald wants a third of my fee."

That info underscored Donald's dire financial situation. I mean, a few years ago he was on top of the world, claiming a $3 billion fortune. Now he was hustling his mistress.

A waiter laid menus on the table.

Donald walked in, sat, placed a napkin on his lap, and picked up a menu.

"What?" Marla said.

Donald scowled. "Ivana's filing for divorce tomorrow morning. Once the banks find out, I could be ruined."

A few weeks later I, along with Chuck Jones, escorted Marla to the Four Seasons restaurant for a No Excuses jeans press conference. Marla announced that she was thrilled and proud to represent the jeans company and that she would donate part of her $500,000 fee, which Chuck had negotiated, to some obscure charity, the Better World Society.

To me, Marla came off like a ditz as she spoke of her concerns for the environment, something she obviously knew little about. Not that the press cared one way or the other. All they asked were stupid questions about her relationship with Donald.

"Does Donald ever moan, 'Oh, Ivana'?" one of the reporters asked. Chuck Jones cut the press conference short. We were on our way out of the Four Seasons, fending off reporters asking even stupider questions than before, when I spotted a shifty-eyed guy in a rumpled suit coming our way. I stepped in front of Marla to block him. But the guy deftly sidestepped me, reached under my left arm, and handed Marla a blue folder.

"You've been served," the guy said and walked away.

Cameras clicked. Video whirled.

Marla smiled for the media. Handed me the folder.

I opened it up. She had just been served a subpoena to give a deposition in the divorce case of *Trump v. Trump*.

I used a Four Seasons pay phone to call Donald, informed him about the subpoena, something I'd kick myself in the ass for later. Because Donald panicked and hired Marla a lawyer. Then refused to pay him when, in the end, it turned out Marla didn't testify. He told the lawyer to collect his fee from Marla. Then Donald told Marla that, even though he was the one who hired the lawyer, it wasn't his problem.

"If I were you," Donald said while the three of us were in his limo, on the way to dinner at the Palm, "I wouldn't pay." That was the very first time I saw Marla slug Donald. She leaped on him and struck with a flurry of lefts and rights.

"Watch my hair," Donald giggled as he covered up.

Which only made Marla angrier. "You dick!" she screamed.

I grabbed her by the waist and, as I pulled her away, she threw a kick that caught Donald on the shoulder.

"Hey, no kicking." Donald slapped her leg.

I never would know if the lawyer got paid.

During that week, Donald's business and personal problems went from horrific to catastrophic. But instead of defending himself and attacking his legion of critics as was usual, Donald, chronically high-profile, laid low. He told me over the phone that he was bothered by the fact that the members of the press who'd helped to build his Midas touch reputation were the same ones taking delight in tearing him down. "I thought they were my friends."

A few weeks later, it was Donald's turn to cheer me up. I was down in the dumps because I'd just attended the funeral service of Jillian L.'s cousin, CAA booking agent Bobby Brooks. Brooks had finally read my screenplay, watched the promotional tape, and was interested in helping me get it produced. But Brooks had been killed, along with Grammy-winning blues-rock guitarist Stevie Ray Vaughan, in a Wisconsin helicopter crash. I mused that, when it came to the movie business, if I didn't have bad luck, I'd have no luck at all.

"I wish I were you," Donald said, his way of cheering me up. We were in his father's sixty-third-floor Trump Tower apartment. Marla was in the kitchen unpacking two Carnegie Deli Reubens and a salad for herself that was just delivered. I could almost see the aroma of mouthwatering corned beef fog the apartment.

"You get all the women you want," Donald continued.

"I wish."

"You've no responsibilities."

"Not even a cat or a plant," Marla chimed in.

"You have no net worth to speak of. But you live large."

"Well," I said, "I'm sort of a savant."

Marla giggled.

"If my casinos and hotels tank," Donald said, "thousands will be out of work. I mean it. Thousands. I don't know if I can live with that."

"He's scaring me," Marla said after Donald had eaten a mile-high Reuben and a pile of fries and, saying his stomach was upset (duh), he went to lie down.

"How?" I said, picking at my Reuben.

Marla ate some salad. "He's not sleeping."

"He never could sleep like regular people."

"He eats nothing but shit." She used her fork to point to the platter of heart-attack food. "His cholesterol is well over four hundred."

"He's always eaten shit."

"Now his creditors are taking everything from him."

"The economy sucks," I said. "He's not the only one having problems."

"They want to put him on a spending allowance."

"That's a laugh."

"Right?" Marla nodded. "Four-hundred-and-fifty-thousand dollars a month."

"That's all?" I said sarcastically. "Wait, I'll break out the violins."

Marla ignored me. "His next book, *Surviving at the Top*?"
"What about it?"
"He says it might as well be his obituary."
"He's just being dramatic," I said.
"It's like he's given up. He's talking about killing himself."
"When? What exactly did he say?"
She shook her head and began to cry.

But within days, Donald was back to his old combative self. Waging war on his creditors, lawyers, Ivana and, unfortunately, Marla, who he eventually blamed for his financial situation and the breakup of his marriage.

"He's lashing out at everyone around him," Marla informed me.

"At least he's not talking about suicide anymore," I said. "Right?"

"Still, I'm not going to stick around for any more abuse."

She took off for LA two days later.

And before I knew it, she was dating. There were photos of her in the gossip columns and tabloids with other successful, desirable men. But this time Donald didn't call me in a panic and ask me to help patch things up. Instead, he did what Marla was doing and threw himself into the singles scene.

Elite Model Management owner John Casablancas invited Donald to one of his revolving-door model parties at a Sutton Place penthouse. Beside a dozen or so models, the only other guest was financial manager and future pedophile and sex trafficker, Jeffery Epstein, a nodding acquaintance who we both recognized from various Manhattan hot spots and model parties.

Interestingly enough, Casablancas had been courting me for months, asking for an introduction to Donald. At the time, his model agency was struggling, and he was looking for investors. The problem for me was, although I liked John, I knew that he'd offer his stable of beautiful models to Donald as an incentive.

Silly as it may sound, I wasn't about to facilitate Donald cheating on and hurting Marla. But John had sidestepped me, approached Donald in Atlantic City, pitched him on investing in Elite, and they became fast friends.

Casablancas rushed to greet Donald and me as we entered the large penthouse with breathtaking East River views. He instructed a waiter to fetch us drinks and introduced us to his female guests. After an hour Donald and I cut two likely prospects from the fawning group. We said our thanks and goodbyes to Casablancas, and escorted Jade and Collette downstairs to Donald's waiting limo.

Donald wanted to show the city to Collette. I wanted to ply the svelte, feline Jade with alcohol and get her back to my apartment. And so, I asked Donald to drop us off at Neary's, an old-world upscale Irish pub a few blocks north.

As usual, the garrulous and gracious owner, Jimmy Neary, greeted us at the door and found us stools at the crowded bar. A starched, bow-tied charming old bartender served us drinks.

"To your success in the modeling business, Jade," I toasted with a Jameson, neat. "You can't miss with that face," I said, meaning it. The girl was cover-girl material. Period. We drank our drinks, glanced around, and checked out the moneyed, somewhat geriatric crowd. I pointed out a few notables.

"There's Maureen O'Hara," I said. "She's my all-time favorite movie star." The still stunning sixty something redhead was dining at a table with the mystery author Mary Higgins Clark.

"Who?" Jade said.

"Maureen O'Hara. She starred in *The Quiet Man. Miracle on Thirty-fourth Street.*"

Jade shook her head.

Kathie Lee and Frank Gifford were at their usual table. The governor of New York State was sitting at a corner table. The governor of New Jersey was sitting across the room in the opposite corner.

"And that's John Glenn at the end of the bar."

"Him?" Jade said. "He's a movie star too?"

"He used to be an astronaut."

"That old guy?"

Jimmy asked us if we wouldn't mind moving down a few stools to allow another couple space at the bar beside us.

We gladly complied.

"So, Jade," I said after we'd settled on our new seats. "How do you like New York?"

"It's different." She set her wineglass on the bar. Folded her hands primly on her lap. Smiled and made dead-on eye contact; a man could get lost in those big green eyes.

"How so?"

Before long I realized that I'd made a mistake. Jade was not a ready, willing, and able hot-to-trot party girl. She'd been milking cows on her family's dairy farm in Belleville, Kansas—wherever that was—a mere two months ago. And she was young. And innocent. And maybe a little frightened.

I switched from horndog to big brother. I mean, Jade was so beautiful, so unprepared and alone that I knew she had a hard road ahead of her. And I didn't want to see her wind up like another innocent I had met and partied with years ago at Studio 54. Eighteen-year-old Gia Carangi, who became a top model practically overnight, had fallen in with bad company. She drank and drugged her way out of the business within four years. Died from substance abuse at age twenty-six.

Jade and I wound up talking for two hours. She asked questions about the modeling world. I told her everything I knew and I knew plenty. When we came to the subject of the casting couch, I said, "Trust your instincts. Anyone makes you uncomfortable, you tell Johnny Casablancas. He's a top agent. He'll take care of things." I ordered a third Jameson. Jade was still working on her first wine.

"As a matter of fact…" I reached for my wallet, opened it, and handed Jade a PBA (NYPD Police Benevolent Association) union card. Pointed out that I'd signed it and that my phone number was written below my signature.

"Anyone ever makes you uncomfortable, show them that card. Tell them we're close friends. All the sleazy photographers and casting agents know who I am." I drank some whiskey. "You can call me at that number even before calling Casablancas. You understand? I don't care what time it is. Call me and I'll come and get you wherever you are." Just then Neary's front door opened and Grayman walked in, scanned the crowd, and headed my way.

"Fitzy," Grayman said. "Just the guy I wanted to see."

I introduced Grayman to Jade. He said a polite hello and got down to business.

"I want you to do me a favor," Grayman said.

"If I can."

"You know how many light bulbs a casino like Trump Plaza goes through a month? And the Taj Mahal? *Fugetaboutit*. You have any idea?"

"No. But I think you're about to tell me."

"Plenty."

"Let me stop you right there," I said. "I don't work for Donald. Never have. I don't get involved in his business."

"An introduction to Trump. It's worth ten large."

"He has directors of purchasing that handle buying for the casino. I could introduce you to them. My pleasure."

Grayman shook his head. "I wanna deal with the boss." He ordered a glass of red wine. "I have to remind you: You owe me for that thing."

I wondered if he was referring to the fact he'd done me a favor by "discouraging" the two wannabe hoods that tried to shake down Mumbles. Or the night he'd intervened with the bat-wielding rednecks outside of P.J. Clarke's.

"I'll see what I can do," I lied. There was no way in hell I'd walk a racketeer into Donald's office. Grayman offered to buy us a drink, but we declined. It was getting late. And I was planning on escorting Jade home to the Upper East Side tenement before I swung by Elaine's for a nightcap.

I had just paid the tab when Jimmy Neary approached.

"Someone wants to meet you," Jimmy said.

When I saw who it was, I jumped to my feet.

"I wanted to meet you," Maureen O'Hara said with a lilting Irish brogue, "because I heard your last name was Fitzsimmons, and I'm actually a FitzSimons." She offered her hand along with a dazzling smile. I wanted to hug her, but controlled myself.

"It's FitzSimons on my grandfather's birth certificate," I said. "It was Fitzsimmons on his marriage certificate. I think they changed the spelling at Ellis Island."

"You *think*?" The smile left her face.

"Now, Maureen," Neary said. "Take it easy."

It was suddenly apparent that the former movie star had had a few cocktails.

"Will you listen to him?" she said to Neary. To me, she said, "*You* need to make certain what your family name is."

I shrugged, having no idea what her problem was. "What difference does it make after all these years?"

"What difference?" She smirked. "The difference is: If you're a FitzSimons, you're my cousin. If you're a Fitzsimmons, you're a piece of British garbage."

Chapter 28

About a week later, I was in my apartment, eating lunch when I received a hysterical call from Jade. She said she'd been booked for a modeling gig and the photographer had tried to rape her.

"What's his name?"

"Alan B."

I knew Alan well and assumed that, since Alan routinely rented his studio to other photographers, she had to be referring to someone else. "You mean," I said, "You're at Alan B.'s Fifth Avenue studio, now?"

"Yes," she said. "I brought the phone into the lavatory. He's right outside the door. Trying to get in."

"Who is?"

"Alan B.," she said.

I gotta admit, I found that hard to believe. "I'll be there in twenty minutes."

"Fitz." The five-ten, three-hundred-pound fashion photographer, Alan B., offered the usual hardy handshake and a big smile when he opened the Fifth Avenue studio's steel-framed front door. "What're you doing here?"

I stepped inside, looked around. The studio was like a second home. I'd been there for dozens of modeling gigs, all sorts of planned and impromptu parties, and on occasion just to hang out after hours. The usual cute studio receptionist was busy at her desk. In the main studio, the backdrops were in place. Strobe lights were on standby. A large-format 4" by 5" camera was mounted on a tripod. A young photo assistant was down on one knee, fidgeting with a strobe unit pack. Everything seemed normal.

"Came to pick up Jade," I said, noticing that Alan had sterile gauze wrapped around his left hand. "Happened to your hand?"

"It's nothing," he said. "An accident. Look, we're in the middle of a shoot. Can you come back later?"

"Where's Jade?"

The smile slipped from Alan's face. "Changing."

I walked across the studio floor. Entered the dressing room. Saw that the black phone cord was snaked under the lavatory door. "Jade." I knocked. "It's me."

Jade opened the door a crack, peeked out and stepped aside, allowing me to enter.

"You okay?"

She shook her head. Placed the phone down on the toilet tank. Her face was blotchy, green eyes red and swollen from crying. I leaned back on the sink. "Tell me what happened."

Jade retied the silk robe she was wearing tightly around her. She said that while she was changing outfits, Alan walked into the dressing room and said inappropriate things. Said that if she wanted to work for him in the future, she had to "take care" of him.

"I thought he was joking at first. But he wasn't. I showed him the card you gave me. Told him you were my friend."

"And?"

"He laughed. Told me you were *his* friend." She said that's when Alan grabbed her breasts and tried to pull her robe off. "He tried to rape me," she said. "I tried to scream, but he put his hand over my mouth. I bit his hand. Told him I'd call the police. He said no one would believe me. But he backed off. That's when I ran in here and locked myself in."

I'd seen my share of sexual predators over the years. Richie G. and I arrested rapists, child molesters, and spousal abusers. But we'd also dealt with females with an agenda. We'd witnessed an angry woman whip her bare torso with a wire hanger, raise bloody welts, and tell us that her husband had beaten her. The thought crossed my mind that I didn't know Jade well.

I'd known Alan B. for at least five years. He'd been one of my earliest clients and was partially responsible for my modeling success. I'd never witnessed him misbehave with any of the models. The Alan B I knew was a gentleman. Although, I knew that the most prolific predators were wolves in sheep's clothing; well liked, charismatic, and beyond reproach. I had to admit that I had no idea what Alan B. was like behind closed doors.

"What do you want to do?" I said.

"Please help me get out of here."

I waited outside while Jade changed. I could see Alan in his office, speaking on the phone, adjusting the gauze on his hand—Jade said that she'd bitten his hand.

"I'm ready," Jade said. She was dressed in jeans and a sweatshirt, with a black faux-fur-lined jacket draped over her arm. We headed for the door.

"Jade?" Alan hung up the phone and hurried to intercept us. "Jade. Where are you going? We're not done here."

"She's not feeling well, Alan," I said without looking at him. "Call John Casablancas and book a replacement."

We left the studio, walked to the elevator. "Sorry you had to go through that."

"So, you believe me?" Jade said.

I didn't hesitate. "I do."

She asked me to hold her purse while she slipped her jacket on. We stepped onto the empty elevator. I pressed L.

I struggled with what to do next. If Jade decided to go to the police and file a complaint, Alan would be arrested. His life ruined. I considered that maybe his attacking Jade was an isolated incident. Maybe he'd never done anything like that before. That he'd never do it again. But the cop in me knew better. Being a predator was a lifestyle. Apparently, Alan was just better than most at concealing his aberrant behavior.

"I'll take you to the police station if you want to report what happened."

"They won't believe me," she said.

"Yeah," I said. "They will."

We exited the elevator. Walked out onto cold, windy, and crowded Fifth Avenue.

"Would you mind taking me to my apartment?" she said. "I feel disgusting. I want to take a shower."

I hailed a cab. Escorted her to her front door. Told her to call me if she decided to file a complaint with the police. That I would accompany her and walk her through the process. When I got back to my apartment, I called Elite. Spoke to Casablancas. Told him what had happened to Jade.

"Alan's a pervert," Casablancas said. "Everybody knows that."

I was stunned. "I don't know it."

"He's not going to pull his routine in front of an ex-cop," Casablancas said. "Most of the models won't go anywhere near his studio."

"Then why the hell would you allow him to book a kid like Jade?"

"It's good for her," Casablancas said. "She wants to be a model, she has to grow up sometime."

Unbelievable.

I phoned Jade early the next day to check up on her. She thanked me for my kindness, said that she'd decided to quit the modeling business. That she was returning to the family farm in Kansas.

"Don't let a creep like Alan B. run you out of the business," I said as I padded to my front door and retrieved my daily newspapers. But she said it wasn't just Alan. She missed her family, friends, and life back home.

"Thanks for being a friend," Jade said and hung up. I'd never hear from her again.

I sat on my couch, began to read the headlines. The *Post*'s Cindy Adams was reporting that Donald and Ivana's divorce settlement was imminent. I was going to call Donald and congratulate him, but I didn't really know how he felt or if congratulations were in order.

A week later, I ran into him at a law firm's party at the Pierre Hotel. He was with a *Penthouse* pet named Sandi Korn. Donald was uncharacteristically quiet. I could tell that, although he was still dating beautiful women—last week he'd been photographed with *Star Search* contestant Rowanne Brewer—he was feeling down. And who could blame him? He was fighting with Ivana and Marla. He was still battling with his creditors and careening toward bankruptcy.

"What was the story with Collette?"

"Who?" Donald said.

We were standing at a food station, helping ourselves to assorted finger foods. Sandi Korn was off chatting with a group of young, moon-eyed male lawyers. "You know, we met her and Jade at John Casablancas's party."

"She was a dud." He placed a few steak skewers on his plate. "How'd you make out with—what did you say her name was? Jade?"

"I didn't."

"Two duds." After a moment, Donald said, "You think Marla misses me?"

"You were pretty hard on her."

"You know where she is?"

"LA."

"Know where in LA?"

I picked up a bacon-wrapped scallop. "Not really."

Donald went on to tell me that he'd had his security people looking for Marla for a week, but that they couldn't locate her. "Will you help me find her, Tom?"

"I've got a better idea," I said. "Her mother's your biggest fan. If I were you, I'd call Ann. Tell her how you feel. If you've got any chance of getting Marla back, Ann will know."

I phoned Ann the next morning, tipped her off, told her to expect a call from Donald. But Donald didn't call Ann. So, Ann called Donald. A few weeks later Marla was back in the city and living at Trump Parc on Central Park South. (She was now Larry Hagman's neighbor.) She called and asked me to join her, Ann, Kim, Chuck Jones, and Donald for dinner at the Oak Room Restaurant in the Plaza Hotel that evening.

Donald was no fun at dinner. Sure, he was happy to have Marla back in his life. But he brooded quite a bit, furious at Ivana, who he said was nickel-and-diming him to death, and the fact that his creditors were closely monitoring their divorce-settlement negotiations.

"They don't get it," Donald said, eyeballing, much to Marla's chagrin, my curvy, five-foot-one-inch-tall date who I'd met the day before while shopping in a women's erotic store called the Pleasure Chest. For obvious reasons, I nicknamed the sexy aspiring singer, "Peanut." I wouldn't normally have invited a total stranger to accompany me to a dinner with Donald and Marla, but Peanut hailed from Sweden and didn't have the faintest idea who the pair was.

"Ivana gets a big enough settlement from me," Donald said, drinking some Diet Coke, "and the banks will view me as insolvent." He poked at his appetizer. "That happens, no one gets a dime. Not the banks. Not Ivana." He speared a jumbo shrimp. "Guess what?" He leaned close, saw that Peanut was preoccupied speaking to Marla and Ann, and spoke conspiratorially. "The banks are going to loan me the money to pay off Ivana. They don't know it yet. But they don't have a choice." Donald smiled ear to ear, then bit into the shrimp.

I ate some of my lump crabmeat appetizer, heard a commotion, and glanced around the fabled, elegantly paneled Oak Room. Two burly ex-cops I knew were escorting the sultan of Brunei — one of the richest men in the world — and his family into the restaurant. They sat at a corner booth across the room, adjacent to a table occupied by author Gore Vidal and Liza Minnelli.

I sipped some wine, ate another piece of crab. Knew from reading the papers that what Donald said about the banks rang true. Apparently, he'd borrowed such enormous sums that they couldn't afford a Trump personal bankruptcy.

Our main courses were served and Ann, trying to steer the conversation away from Donald's divorce, asked me how my book and movie projects were going. I was saying that I had yet to get my story in front of someone who could actually green-light a movie project when Donald interrupted.

"Look," he said. "You ever need to use my name out in Hollywood, if it will get you through a door, you go ahead. Use the Trump name."

"Really?" I said. "Thanks, Donald."

Truth was, I had no intention of using his name with showbiz types because, unless he was willing to help finance my movie, it would do no good.

"Use my name any time." Donald cut into a well-done, ketchup-soaked sirloin steak. "The Trump name works wonders."

Chapter 29

Peanut landed a gig singing on some Miami-based, Caribbean cruise ship line. I borrowed one of Donald's gold Cadillac Allantés and drove her out to Newark Airport for a noon flight. We kissed passionately at the gate and promised to keep in touch. I knew that we wouldn't. Honestly, I was bummed to see her go. I felt that, even though she was eccentric as hell, we had a connection. But career comes first. I understand that. Probably just as well, because even though I was still working modeling and acting in TV commercials, money was tight. I could not afford to wine and dine anyone. The credit card companies were starting to hound me, sending late notices.

I used my sleeve to wipe Peanut's red lipstick off my white Irish face as I left the airport on my way to Atlantic City. I checked into Trump Castle. Donald had invited me to see a concert — I think it was Jerry Lee Lewis — that evening. After settling into my room, I phoned the Taj Mahal's blond-haired, blue-eyed assistant director of security. Invited Pam F., a stunning Viking of a woman who I'd dated before, to be my guest at the concert.

An hour later, I was sitting on the couch in Marla's Castle suite, watching a tennis match with Donald, when I mentioned my financial situation. He laughed out loud at my petty-cash crunch problem. Marla was stomping around the suite, slamming doors, glaring at Donald. She was pissed off about something. Kim and Ann had only just gone off to the hotel spa for massages and to have their hair and nails done.

"What you do is—" Donald used a remote to silence the tennis. "Run up your credit card bills as much as you can. Max them out. Then don't pay anyone. Let them take you to collections. Then offer ten cents on the dollar. Believe me, they'll take whatever you offer."

"I want to go to the fight!" Marla interrupted angrily from across the room. "Mama does too."

"It's only a closed-circuit boxing match," he told Marla.

The event they were referring to was the March 15, Mike Tyson-Razor Ruddock heavyweight championship. Donald turned the tennis sound back up, which further infuriated Marla. "Guys only," he shouted over the noise. "No one's bringing a date. No women are invited."

"You're a fucking liar!"

Oh, boy.

Donald planned to host the closed-circuit telecast of the Nevada boxing match in the grand ballroom of his Plaza Hotel and charge, I think it was, $100 per ticket. I'd been invited as Donald's guest, of course, and knew that Donald was fudging the truth. It was true that no one I knew was bringing a date. But female business associates and female members of the press were among the invited guests. As was John Casablancas, who never went anywhere without an entourage of leggy models. But Donald had another, more compelling reason for not wanting Marla at the fight.

He was suddenly and hopefully on the verge of finally settling his financial agreement with Ivana. His attorneys had advised him not to be seen in the city with his mistress until the settlement was finalized. But telling Marla that would only anger her and cause her to feel marginalized, again.

Marla stormed into the room, turned off the TV and glared at Donald, arms folded across her chest. I remember thinking to myself, *Please, Donald, don't say anything hurtful or stupid.* But Donald being Donald said, "Move your fat ass."

Marla dove on top of him, letting loose with a flurry of slaps and punches. I was about to grab the raging Southern belle and restrain her, but saw that Donald was laughing. Which only fueled Marla's anger.

"Watch the hair." Donald laughed and covered up his head, absorbing the blows on his arms. He pushed her away. Sprang to his feet. Dashed around behind the couch. "C'mon, wimp," he taunted. "Let's see you catch me."

Marla literally leaped over the couch and made a grab for Donald who, still laughing, raced across the suite and into the bedroom. Marla was hot on his heels. She screamed something unintelligible. I heard a loud bang. A crash. Another bang. Donald was still laughing. Then Marla was laughing. After a brief silence, there were different noises, and I knew they weren't fighting anymore. One of them pushed the bedroom door closed. I switched off the TV, got to my feet, and hightailed it out of the suite.

April 1991 was a busy month for me. Thanks to one of my cottontop mentors, Tom Counihan, I booked several high-paying modeling gigs. Began rewriting—seems I was always editing and rewriting my first novel—*Confessions of a Catholic Cop*. As per Donald's advice, I was running up my debt. Spending money like a fool. Buying clothes. Picking up dinner checks for my family and friends.

I finally got a bite on one of my short stories, or so I thought. Dick Wolf, a TV producer, sent me a first-class airline ticket, flew me out to LA, and put me up in the luxurious Beverly Hills Hotel. Although our next few days of meetings went well, I wound up thinking that Wolf intended to dazzle me with luxury perks — booze, food, and female companionship, then pick my brain about New York cops, their stories, attitudes, and not buy my story. Which he never did. I could swear that a few of the tales I told Wolf wound up as storylines on his TV series *Law & Order*.

I spent the following week with Larry and Maj Hagman at their Malibu beach house: seven days of star-studded beach parties and house parties and yacht parties and five-star restaurants. The week was a blur. Although I do remember bumping into the still-ravishing Alisa E. at a Jack Nicholson party. Her stalker, Michael Earp, had indeed stopped harassing her after she made the move to LA. She was still modeling, newly married, was three months pregnant, and still chained-smoked Marlboro Lights.

When I returned from LA, Marla and I had lunch together at my usual table, in the back room of P.J. Clarke's. Although there was a long waiting line, the haughty maître d' Leo — "There's a twenty-dollar wait, sir" — sat us immediately.

Marla went straight to our table as I veered off to say hello to a few other P. J. Clarke's regulars. The always-grumpy actor Anthony Quinn was, well, grumpy. At the next table, *Penthouse* publisher and famous cheapskate, Bob Guccione, shook my hand, then went back to arguing with his three underlings over his share of their $39 combined lunch check. I stepped across the room, bent to kiss my Upper East Side neighbor, Jackie Kennedy Onassis, on the cheek. Told her how wonderful she looked as I shook hands with her constant companion, Maurice.

"How's John-John?" Thanks to my cottontop friend, John McCooey—the ex-husband of Ann Skakel, the sister of Ethel Kennedy—I'd met JFK Jr. several times in Central Park and at McCooey's penthouse apartment.

I said hi to a few more regulars and joined Marla. Settled into my seat in the noisy back room and, ordering us food and drinks, I couldn't help but notice that in the restaurant's flattering light, Marla was aglow. She looked more beautiful and happier than I'd ever seen her. Apparently, hers and Donald's "breakup to make up" routine was working for the moment.

A middle-aged, Borscht Belt–funny waiter brought our drinks, along with a string of lousy jokes. A few minutes later, Patricia, a geriatric waitress, herself a former successful model, served our food along with a still cover girl–perfect smile.

"I've so much going on," Marla said breathlessly, tossing her large salad.

"Such as?" I took a bite of a famous P.J. Clarke's cheeseburger.

"I'll be shooting an episode of *Designing Women*. I'm reading for another soap opera next week. There's a Broadway play I'm considering."

"There's something else you're not telling me."

Marla beamed, morphed into the Southern belle. "Whatever do you mean, sir?"

I eyeballed her. Checked her ring finger. "Donald propose or something?"

"He's going to." Her smile brightened even more. "I just know he's going to."

A few weeks later, Marla, Donald, Ann, and I were flying back from a weekend of glitzy, high-roller parties on his yacht, *Trump Princess*, which was docked in AC. During the weekend I'd witnessed one of Donald's bodyguards, Scott Cummings, acting inappropriately toward his boss's main squeeze. I'd spotted Marla and Scott together in the yacht's master suite, locked in an embrace. She was obviously acting out a tit for tat, getting back at Donald for his past hurtful public and private comments about her, other women, and his views on marriage. Still, it bothered me that Marla would become so familiar with a member of Donald's own security staff; nonsensical conduct that might come back and bite her on the ass.

The helicopter was coming up on Manhattan. I was sitting alongside Ann, peering out of the window, straining to get a better view of the skyline when I heard Marla yelp. Looked and saw Donald present her with a Tiffany diamond engagement ring.

"Will you marry me?" Donald mouthed.

Marla was gaping at the ring.

"Will you?"

"Yes!" She plucked the ring from the box. Held it up to the light. "Mama. Look."

Ann shrieked.

I applauded. Said, "Bravo. Mazel tov. Félicitations." Found myself wishing very hard that my two friends would grow up. Stop the bullshit. Start appreciating each other. I hoped that they would learn to bring out the best in one another. Prayed that Marla and Donald would make it as a couple.

They say grief comes in cycles. A small inheritance check that I received from my mother's estate put me in a funk. But this time I fought the crippling melancholy.

I recalled how, whenever my mother came to stay with me, she loved to stroll around the Upper East Side. We'd visit the places she frequented back in the 1940s with my father when they were first dating. Funny how she knew the names and addresses of long-shuttered dance halls, restaurants, and even long-gone friends, but couldn't recall if or what she'd eaten for breakfast.

Around the middle of June, I received a gold-leafed invitation for the weekend of June 21–22 that read something like: *Donald Trump and Marla Maples invite you to celebrate the first anniversary of the Trump Taj Mahal and Donald's 45th birthday.*

That evening, a bunch of us were drinking champagne and eating a quick dinner at Sparks Steak House where, back in 1985, Mafia godfather Paul "Big Paul" Castellano had been assassinated by underling John Gotti. Marla, Kim, and Joni had just gone to the ladies' room.

Donald leaned close to Ann. "I'm gonna announce our engagement at my birthday party." Ann, who was eating off Marla's plate, nearly choked and then began to cry. When the ladies returned from the lavatory, there was more champagne and much celebration.

As you know from the Prologue, Donald did *not* announce his engagement to Marla as promised on his forty-fifth birthday party. He stood at the podium in the Taj's grand ballroom, in front of a roomful of decked-out high rollers, and talked about how great the Taj was doing financially. At one point, he looked over to my table where Marla, Ann, her husband David, Marla's dad Stan and his wife Baby Woman, and Marla's grandparents, Laura and Arnold Locklear, were sitting and introduced Ann to the audience. But there was no mention of his and Marla's engagement. Which led to that knock-down, drag-out fight later that evening in Ann's suite.

IT'S OVER! read the front-page headline of the *New York Post* on June 26. THE DONALD BOOTS MARLA FROM HIS WEST SIDE CONDO. *New York Newsday* got into the act with a competing headline: MOVE OVER, MARLA. They featured a photo of a stunning beauty, Carla Bruni, alongside a sub-headline: TRUMP'S NEW PAL.

A few days later, Donald called *People* magazine, pretending to be one John Miller, yet another—like John Barron—phony-baloney Trump Organization spokesman. "Miller" told *People* reporter Sue Carswell that Mr. Trump had indeed dumped Marla and repeated that there was never an engagement. That the Tiffany diamond ring was about giving the store Tiffany—a tenant in Trump Tower—some business and getting Marla something that would be nice.

"Miller" went on to say that Madonna and the actress Kim Basinger had been calling the office, asking for a date with Trump.

"Kim said it was about a real estate deal, but she really wants to go out with Mr. Trump. Important, beautiful women call Mr. Trump all the time," Miller said. "Competitively, it's tough. It was tough for Marla, and it will be tough for Carla."

What Donald didn't know at the time was that Sue Carswell recorded the entire conversation. Carswell then played the tape for gossip columnist and Trump ally Cindy Adams, who positively identified Miller's voice as Donald's. Then Carswell called Marla and played her the tape. Marla was predictably devastated.

That evening, under cover of darkness, she and Kim actually did move out of the Trump Parc apartment and fled to a new secret hideaway: Kathie Lee and Frank Gifford's estate up in Greenwich, Connecticut. A curious course of action, since Marla and I had only just met the multitalented Kathie Lee a few weeks prior, when she was singing at one of Donald's casinos. Personally, I found her genuine, warm, and friendly. But her husband Frank, a former football player, actor, television sports commentator, and a notorious philanderer, was self-important and aloof.

I wasn't surprised when Donald told me that Gifford had called him about five days later, ratted out Marla, and then demanded Donald get her the hell out of his house. Said that he didn't want to be involved in Donald's love life.

"Gifford's afraid," Donald sniggered, "that the press will catch on to his own girlfriends."

But Marla refused to answer Donald's calls.

Through Chuck Jones, she fed a retaliatory story to *Daily News* gossip columnist Richard Johnson. The July 2 headline read: NEW TILT ON THE JILT. Besides stating that she was indeed at the Gifford residence, the article reported that Marla was the one who dumped Donald. That Donald was still in love with the Georgia peach, insanely jealous, and begging her to reconcile.

"Get her out of here. Today," Gifford ranted to Donald after seeing the *Daily News* story. "Kathie and I are going out of town. I don't want her here when we get back. I don't need this shit."

But Marla refused to answer Donald's constant calls. And so, he drove up to Gifford's house. Planted himself in their sprawling living room and said he wouldn't leave until Marla agreed to talk to him. Which, at her guru Kim's urging, she eventually did.

"He proposed for the hundredth time," Marla told me that very evening by phone after she'd returned to her Trump Parc apartment. "I said yes."

Then she went on to explain, in her goofy, New Age spirituality speak, that Donald had changed for the better, which is why she'd decided to take him back.

"It's all about the issue of whether there is a greater reality or not," Marla said. "Donald and I now appreciate the vast evolutionary context in which our lives are being lived. We're now focused on the deepest love, the safety of truth, the wisdom of the universes." Honestly, I didn't understand what the hell Marla was talking about until she mentioned the engagement ring.

"It's 7.45-karat emerald-cut diamond," Marla gushed.

Now, that made sense.

Marla said, "Watch the Regis and Kathie Lee show tomorrow morning. Donald's serious this time."

I hung up with Marla. Was about to call the "changed" Donald and congratulate him, but then decided to wait and see what tomorrow would bring.

My phone rang at 8:55 the following morning.

"You watching Regis and Kathie Lee?" Chuck Jones said.

I picked up the remote and turned on the TV. "Watching it now."

I sat back. Drank some coffee. Sure enough, after Regis and Kathie Lee's usual opening shtick, Kathie made the exclusive announcement that Donald and Marla were officially engaged. Then Donald called into the show.

Regis said, "So, you're an engaged man this morning?"

Donald said, "I am indeed, and Marla's a very special girl."

Marla Gets Her Man reported various news sources on July 4, 1991. *The proposal came Tuesday night, in Connecticut. Maples had been left alone there while the Giffordses were in Washington, attending a state dinner at the White House. Trump appeared at the door with a serious diamond from Harry Winston. Almost eight karats. It has not been confirmed that he wept or fell on bended knee. But he didn't write* The Art of the Deal *for nothing. She caved.*

I had to hand it to Marla. She'd stood by her man, more or less, no matter his contentious divorce, dire financial circumstances, egocentric, puerile behavior, and volcanic mood swings. I turned off the TV and wondered if Donald was even capable of controlling his lascivious urges. Could he keep his roving eye from roving? I hoped so. Because if I knew Marla, she was keeping a few studs on a string.

Just in case.

Chapter 30

In early September the distant, staccato sounds of gunfire woke me from a dead sleep. I bolted to a sitting position, my heart pounding. Got my bearings. I was home. In bed. It was 2:03 a.m. I flopped back down. Knew that, judging by the reports, this time the running gun battle was taking place about four blocks north in East Harlem. I was taking deep breaths, slowing my heartbeat, wondering if Joni — a sound sleeper — had heard the shots when next to me, a groggy, accented voice murmured, "You hear that?"

Startled, I turned my head. Saw a lump in my bed. The lump moved. A fan of long blond hair cascaded from under the covers and covered a pillow.

Who the hell?

Wait. Yes, I remembered. I'd met Miss Brooke Waters, a grade-school teacher and tourist visiting from Zürich, Switzerland, last evening in a nightclub called Tunnel. I liked dating teachers. When you did something wrong, they made you do it over again.

"I heard." I snuggled up to Miss Waters.

"Vat *vus* that?" Miss Waters said.

"Fireworks."

Police sirens filled the air.

During the past few years, crack cocaine had slowly but surely seized the city by the throat and as a result, violent crime had become epidemic. Inner-city neighborhoods, especially black communities like Harlem, the South Bronx, and east Brooklyn, were being decimated. The New York City murder rate had hit a record high.

I'd lost count of the victims, usually the defenseless elderly, who'd been brutally assaulted and robbed in my Yorkville neighborhood. A senior citizen acquaintance of mine had been accosted after leaving a concert at the 92nd Street Y. Person or persons unknown had split his skull open, stolen his wallet, wristwatch, rings, and coat before leaving him for dead. The homicide was never solved.

I fell back to sleep.

Miss Waters, who turned out to be a superhot forty-year-old with grown kids and an ex-husband, woke me around 10:00 a.m. She jumped my bones, abused my body, then got dressed and walked out my front door with not so much as a toodle-oo. I felt used.

Only kidding.

I sat on the couch, opened the *Post*, and flipped to Page Six. Marla was backpedaling on her statement that she and Donald would not sign a prenuptial agreement, that their relationship would be "built on love and trust, and that's it." I was still laughing when my phone rang.

"Speak."

"Hello, Thomas," a familiar female voice said. "'Tis I." The breathtaking, raven-haired former Hooters girl — let's call her Desiree — was now an entertainment coordinator for Donald's three AC casinos. I'd met the dark-eyed beauty about a month ago when Marla, Donald, Kim, and I had gone backstage to meet members of the band Chicago. For me, it was lust at first sight.

"How're things, Des?" I said.

"I scored tickets for *Phantom of the Opera*'s Saturday matinee," she said. "I've made us reservations at the Algonquin afterward. Sunday, can we see the Statue of Liberty and the Empire State Building? I'd love to go to the Met at some point and I have to do some shopping."

"Anything you want to do is fine with me."

Desiree was coming to visit the city for the first time in a very long time. I was looking forward to being her... ahem... guide.

"Hey," Desiree said. "Want some dirt, just between us? I mean it. It gets back to Mr. Trump, I swear I'll kill you."

I raised my left hand. "Scout's honor."

Desiree went on to say that last week Donald, Marla, and Kim had gone backstage to meet Michael Bolton after one of his concerts. That Marla had made a fool of herself fawning over Bolton.

"I don't understand that girl," Desiree said. "She has everything. Why would she carry on like that in front of her fiancé? Unless he did something to deserve it."

I was sure he did. Three days ago, at a Ted Turner cocktail party, I'd witnessed Donald playing the ladies' man in Marla's presence. Witnessed Marla retaliate by flirting openly with the infamous horndog host. Which had escalated into another cringeworthy Donald-Marla brawl. Regardless, I really didn't want to hear anymore.

There was a knock at my front door.

"You still there?" Desiree said.

"Yes. Look, I've gotta run." I told Desiree that I was *really* looking forward to her visit, blew her a kiss, before hanging up the phone. I stepped across the room and looked through the front door peephole. "Miss Waters?"

I closed the peephole. Opened the door. "Back so soon?"

"I vorgot sometzing," Miss Waters said as she brushed past me and made a beeline to my bedroom. I watched as she flipped aside pillows and patted the rumpled sheets.

"Ah!" Miss Waters held up a dildo. "Vere you are, Samuel." She holstered Samuel. Pecked me on the cheek and yodeled "Toodle-oo," as she walked back out my front door.

Donald tore me a new one at dinner a few weeks later.

I have to say I was stunned. He'd never spoken to me in that manner before. But for months he'd been attacking everyone close to him — employees, family, friends — so I suppose I shouldn't have been so offended.

The modeling and TV commercial business had slowed down again, and I'd been looking for work. That morning, at 10:00 a.m. I was interviewed by a former Secret Service agent, Jim Heaphy, for a six-week bodyguard gig that paid a thousand dollars a day. The principal was the neer-do-well son of an A-list Hollywood icon. He was also an alcoholic drug addict and schizophrenic with violent tendencies. Basically, I'd be protecting the public from the principal, and not the principal from the public.

I turned that gig down.

Heaphy said, "That little prick, Ron Perelman, is looking for security guys again."

"Been there. Done that." I'd once taken a gig guarding the billionaire's East Sixty-third Street town house. Lasted about a month. Problem being that Perelman and his wife at the time, Claudia Cohen, were absolute horrors. (I went on to write a fictional account of that experience, *The Paranoid Elite*).

"Wanna give Perelman another shot?"

"I'd rather stick needles in my eyes," I said.

"Well, how about Sheldon Solow?" He was another billionaire real estate developer. "The salary's negotiable. But Solow's a yeller, likes to scream at everyone. He's your basic asswipe. If you don't mind being screamed at."

I shook my head. "Not for me."

"I've got a department store heir looking for a bodyguard-driver." He opened a folder, flipped some pages. "Nina R. Older woman. Rarely leaves her Fifth Avenue neighborhood. Spends her days going to lunches and dinners. Getting her hair and nails done. She contributes heavily to Jewish causes. Apparently, that caused the Islamic Jihad to put a price on her head."

"What else you have?" I said.

Heaphy tossed that folder aside, selected another. "A Wall Street guy. Decent money. Lots of overtime. There're no real security issues. The job's more about being a big brother to his five kids." He closed the folder. "Other than that, I've got some surveillance work out in Forest Hills, midnight to eight, if you're interested. It's a divorce case."

I got to my feet. "I'll pass."

That evening Marla, Donald, Anne, Kim, Chuck Jones, Joni, and I were once again at the Plaza Hotel's stately Edwardian Room, sipping cocktails, checking out the moneyed crowd, and looking over dinner menus. Several waiters hovered.

"It's only dinner," Marla was telling Kim. "But if he's really not your type, I'll tell him you're dating someone."

"I think he's handsome," Ann said from behind a sizable leather-bound menu. "Thomas, don't you think Bill O'Reilly is handsome?"

"An Adonis," I quipped. "A hunk if I ever saw one." I drank some of my martini. "Hell, if I were a girl, I'd go for him."

Donald laughed.

"You can meet him for a drink. See how it goes." Marla sipped her wine and flashed the 7.5-karat ring. "Mama, what do you think?"

"I'm hungry," Ann said.

The ladies ordered fish. Chuck and I ordered Caesar salads and shell steaks, creamed spinach and mushrooms as sides. Donald ordered thick-cut bacon to start, along with porterhouse steak, fries, and a bottle of ketchup.

"We could advertise a romantic weekend dinner, theater getaway package," Chuck said to Donald over salad. "Maybe get the hansom cabs involved."

Donald had recently appointed Chuck as the Plaza's publicity director—in a sense, a no-show job because Chuck's real function was as Marla's manager. Problem was that Chuck took the position seriously. He worked full-time at the hotel gig *and* full-time for Marla.

"Forget it," Donald said, gnawing at a slice of bacon thick as a human finger and twice as long. "How many times do I have to tell you? I've got people working on that stuff. You focus on Marla."

Chuck checked the time, laid down his fork, said he had to call home, excused himself, and headed to the pay phones.

"What's wrong with that guy?" Donald addressed the table when Chuck was out of earshot. "He stupid or something?"

"He's conscientious," I said.

Donald ignored my statement and proceeded to bad-mouth Chuck. I don't remember exactly what was said, but I recall being stunned by his mean-spirited words—a schoolyard bully making fun of a weaker kid. And he insinuated that since I introduced Chuck into our crowd, his supposed shortcomings were somehow my fault.

They were serving our main course when Chuck sat back down. Marla was talking excitedly about the script for her upcoming appearance on *Designing Women*. I cut into my steak — it was surprisingly tough — and mentioned that I'd recently met the show's producers-writers, Linda Bloodworth-Thomason and her husband, Harry Thomason. I'd actually met them with Larry Hagman out in LA, but decided that I'd make Donald feel good by saying that I'd used his name, as he told me to, in order to gain an introduction.

"You used my name?" His tone startled me.

"Yes," I lied.

"Don't you ever use my name again," Donald fumed. "Where do you get off using my name? I don't want you doing that again. Ever. Where the hell do you get off using my name?"

I felt my face flush. I could no longer hear Donald's words. I was focused on his sneering facial expression and nasty tone. I wanted to slap that look off his face. It was a good thing that he was on the other side of the table and out of my reach.

Ann piped up. "You told Thomas to use your name. At this very table. I heard you."

"No, I didn't," Donald said.

"Yes, you did," Marla said.

"You did," Kim said. "Ann's right. It was at this very table. You said to use your name anytime."

"Never happened," Donald said.

Outraged, I threw my napkin on the table, got to my feet, and strode out of the restaurant, knowing that my relationship with Donald had changed. And not for the better.

I called Chuck Jones the following morning.

"Don't say anything," I said when Chuck answered the phone. "I'm going to put you on conference call. I want you to hear what I have to say. But don't say a word."

"Okay," Chuck said.

I put Chuck on hold, toggled to another dial tone, dialed Donald's number. Then I toggled back to Chuck.

"Remember," I said to Chuck as Donald's office phone rang. "Not a word."

"Trump Organization," Norma said.

"It's me. He available?"

"I'll see." She put me on hold.

"Tommy Fitz," Donald said as if last night never happened. "Tommy Fitz."

"Look, you fucking asshole. Don't you ever speak to me that way again. You hear me?"

"Huh?"

"Don't give me 'huh?' I will beat the fuck out of you, you ever talk to me that way again. We clear on that? And don't think your bodyguards can protect you. I'll go through your boy Matt like a hot knife through butter. Oh, and where do you get off bad-mouthing Chuck Jones behind his back? What the hell is wrong with you? The guy breaks his ass for you and you make fun of him?"

Donald stammered.

"You're an asshole, Donald. Just watch your big mouth, or I swear I'll—oh, and by the way, you remember the steak I ordered last night?"

"Yeah," Donald said.

"It sucked!" I said and hung up.

Chapter 31

"Here comes your Uncle Frank," my mother whispered when I was about ten years old. My father, brother, three sisters, and I were sitting in a center pew, attending a Palm Sunday Mass at Woodlawn's St. Barnabas Church.

My mother said. "He's developed Irish Alzheimer's."

The bunch of us looked over our shoulders to the rear vestibule. Watched my father's brother as he dipped his right hand in holy water, blessed himself, and walked down the aisle. Uncle Frank looked normal to me.

"Irish Alzheimer's?" I said. "What's that?"

"All he remembers are the grudges."

I'm happy to say that I don't possess that chip. I anger slowly, explode, and forgive. Usually. When I walked into Nicola's with my dinner date Bessy on my arm, wove through the usual contingent of wealthy regulars and saw Donald sitting at a table in the back, I automatically smiled and waved.

Donald waved back, signaled for me to join him. I escorted my date to our reserved table, ordered us two martinis, up, olives. "Be right back," I told Bessy.

I should explain that Bessy was a neighbor. A sophisticated, charming eighty-year-old retired schoolteacher and Holocaust survivor. Three months ago, two Harlem crackheads had, after robbing the five-foot-four-inch, 100-pound "white bitch" of $6, decided to kick her teeth in. She'd spent four weeks in Lenox Hill Hospital.

Bessy was one of several octogenarians who a group of us eastsiders kept an eye on. When needed, we'd take them to doctor appointments. Make sure they had enough food, medications, companionship. Bessy was teaching me mah-jongg. And yes, before you give me too much credit, Bessy did indeed have two hot, sexy granddaughters that she'd been promising to introduce me to. Which had something to do with my taking her out for dinner in celebration of her receiving her new false teeth.

"Tommy Fitz," Donald said and introduced me to two stunning twentysomething ladies and their young male escorts. Donald said the ladies were beauty pageant titleholders and would be contestants in the upcoming Miss America pageant that he planned to host in AC. I knew all about Donald's fascination with beauty pageant winners, most recently the former Miss America, Carolyn Sapp. Unfortunately, so did Marla.

"Man," Donald said after I met the ladies. "You sure came on strong the other day." He addressed the two Miss something-or-others. "You should have heard him. He came on strong." Donald looked across the room at Bessy and grinned mischievously. "You and your… er… date want to join us?"

"No, thanks," I said. "We're in and out. Besides, it's past her bedtime."

The two ladies tittered.

"Let me ask you something," Donald said. "Marla say anything to you about a burglary at her apartment?"

I nodded. "She was really upset."

Last evening, I'd stopped by to collect Marla, Kim, and Ann on our way to Mickey Mantle's restaurant to meet Joni and other mutual friends. When I arrived at the apartment, Marla was in a full-blown panic. She told me that several pairs of shoes, nude photos that Donald had taken of her, and her personal diary were missing.

"We found a glove," Marla cried as she and Kim tore the apartment apart searching for the missing items. "One of those white surgical gloves was on the floor in my bedroom." That made me think of *To Catch a Thief,* an old Cary Grant movie. Grant played retired burglar John Robie, whose MO was to leave a white glove at crime scenes as a calling card. Was someone sending Marla a message?

"But your diamond ring is safe?" I asked her.

She held up her left hand and flashed the diamond.

"Your other valuables?"

Ann, who was relaxing on the couch, stuffing her face with Mallomars cookies, said that Marla's jewelry box hadn't been touched. Which didn't make sense. Marla's apartment building was manned twenty-four hours a day by doormen, a valet, and roving security. She had a Medeco lock on her front door. Not easy to pick. So, why would someone go through the trouble of breaking in, steal shoes, nude pictures, a diary, and leave behind a white glove, and not steal the famous diamond ring or, in its absence, the other valuables? Answer: They wouldn't. My guess was that there was no actual break-in. Whoever'd been in Marla's apartment — if in fact, someone had — must have had keys.

"Who has keys?" I said to Marla.

"Me, Kim, and Donald."

"What about the doormen?"

Marla looked at me as if the thought hadn't occurred to her. "They do have keys."

I picked up Marla's house phone. Asked the doorman on duty to check who'd signed out keys to Marla's apartment during the last week.

"Hold on," the doorman said.

After a few moments, I heard him flipping through pages.

"The super's been up there with the guys installing new window treatments," the doorman said. "Other than that, the valet brings up dry-cleaning and other deliveries all the time."

"No one else?"

"That's right."

Which I knew for a fact was BS.

I'd been in Marla's apartment myself with Chuck Jones a few days ago. Marla had been out in LA and had asked Chuck to pick up a stack of her new theatrical headshots, which she'd left on her kitchen counter, so he could submit them to casting directors. The doorman had given Chuck Marla's keys. I told the doorman thanks and hung up.

"Nothing unusual," I said to her.

"Right. You think I'm crazy," Marla sobbed. "So does Donald."

"No," I said, meaning it. "Someone's playing head games with you." But I didn't have the slightest idea who or why.

I saw Kim look behind a large living room Salvador Dalí print — I think it was *Woman with Head of Roses* — and wondered if she or Marla would stumble upon the bugs that I was sure Donald had had his security people plant. I didn't want to be around for that. "I'll head over to Mickey Mantle's," I said. "See you guys over there."

Donald sipped his soda, leaned close so the beauty pageant contestants and their escorts couldn't hear. "You think Marla made up the burglary looking for attention?"

I shook my head. "Somebody was in her apartment. I'm sure of it."

"I'm not so sure," Donald said. "She's been driving me batshit crazy."

"What else is new?"

"She's trying to talk me into some sort of counseling with Billy Graham. You know about that?" Graham was a famous American evangelist who owed his worldwide popularity to TV.

"I think she might have said something."

A waiter began serving Donald's table.

"Well," I said. "Gotta get back to my date."

"Call me," Donald said.

I made my way back to Bessy. Sat down just as a waiter set down our martinis. I picked mine up and raised my glass. "Here's to your new teeth, Bessy. And to your two lovely granddaughters who you promised I'm soon to meet."

"You know…" Bessy raised her glass. Took a sip. "If I were fifty years younger, you'd be mine."

I coughed the booze up through my nose.

Chapter 32

I WAS MOST SURPRISED WHEN Melanie Cain contacted me through our acting coach, Bob McAndrew, regarding me coauthoring a book/screenplay about Jack Tupper's murder at the hands of her ex, Buddy Jacobson. Since Bob knew I was acquainted with all the players, he felt I could add a unique perspective to the horrific, love-triangle story. I told him I was interested. He supplied me with Melanie's contact information.

But after speaking to Melanie, I discovered that there was no agent or publisher yet involved. That she had no money to pay me and that I'd be working on spec.

"So, I'd be doing all the work and, if we sold the project, I'd be paid half?"

"It's my story," she said. "You're the writer."

"I'll get back to you."

I did some research. Besides the two books that were already published about the murder — *Bad Dreams* by Anthony Haden-Guest and *Murder in the Penthouse* by Peter McCurtin — there were dozens of published articles and interviews with Buddy Jacobson and Melanie, all of which were public record. I decided that if I were going to work on spec, I'd someday write that story on my own. I phoned Melanie back. Turned down her proposal.

Bessy came through and introduced me to her two granddaughters. They were as advertised: beautiful and personable. But the older one was a brainiac and held a big job at NASA. She had absolutely no interest in me. The other was more my type: a black sheep wild child. But she was in and out of rehab, still heavily into drugs and, well, I wasn't. Although she did turn out to be a truly memorable one-night stand.

I got some unexpected good news when my agent called and said that a client had renewed a national network TV commercial that I'd shot back in 1985. The thirty-second Selsun blue shampoo spot had run for several years and had been the leadoff commercial during a Super Bowl; I forget which one. Regardless, for the next two years, I'd receive a paycheck every time the spot ran.

Even though my Selsun blue commercial had been renewed, the modeling and TV commercial business was still slow. I decided to inquire if the job bodyguarding and driving the department store heir that the former Secret Service agent, Jim Heaphy, had mentioned, was still open. Heaphy arranged for me to be interviewed.

"Nina acts ditzy sometimes," Nina's personal assistant, Katherine K., told me during the interview. "But she's got an MA in fine arts from NYU. She's really smart."

"Tell me about the death threats."

Katherine K. said that Nina was politically active and had made frequent and substantial donations to pro-Israel organizations. "There are those who see her activism as a form of Islamophobia. They want her dead."

Before accepting the position, I performed a risk assessment. Discovered a troubling cycle of routines. The same day and time hair appointments, nail appointments, shrink appointments, eating at the same restaurants. But my suggestions to change or at least modify those routines fell on deaf ears. It was obvious that Nina didn't take the death threats seriously.

After being hired, the first thing I did was ask her doormen if they'd noticed anyone suspicious watching the building. If any strangers had asked about Nina? Did she entertain frequently? What caterer she used. The only thing all the doormen agreed on was that Senator Daniel Patrick Moynihan, who I knew personally from Neary's restaurant, was—as one doorman said with a leering snicker—a frequent guest of Nina's.

After only six weeks I knew the job wouldn't work out. Not just because the fifty-year old social butterfly was putting my life in danger by not heeding my advice about how to thwart Islamic assassins, or because she worked me eighteen hours a day. Was infuriatingly late for every appointment and then expected me to speed, run stop signs and red lights. It was the fact she was the laziest person I'd ever known; she refused to walk. Anywhere. Period.

For example: One morning she had a 7:00 breakfast scheduled at the Pierre Hotel at Fifth Avenue and Sixty-first Street, which was located literally 131 feet from her front door. But she insisted that I drive her. At 7:35 a.m., late as usual, her doorman helped her into the rear of her limo. I shifted to *drive*. Tapped the gas. Rolled the 131 feet to the Pierre entrance. Two hours later, another doorman held the limo door as she stepped back inside. I put the car in reverse. Tapped the gas. Rolled back to her front door. I quit a few days later.

Later that week, I was sitting alone at the bar in Elaine's, face numb from a brutal dental appointment, nursing a club soda. Sinatra was singing "The Lady Is a Tramp" on the sound system. I'd said hello to a few regulars. The tables were busy with many of the usual celebrities. I spotted a group of unfamiliar attractive women at a prime table. Knew they had to be friends of Elaine's or related to one of the moneyed regulars. I was thinking about making a move, introducing myself, buying a round of drinks. But I realized that I had no interest in going through the same old routine: charming a woman back to my apartment, into my bed, then figuring out a way to get her out. I was tired. Tired of the dating game.

I drank some club soda. Took my drink and found a relatively quiet spot at the other end of the bar, by the pay phones and cash register. Elaine herself was working the register. I looked at her table and saw that the hound dog–faced Yankees owner,

George Steinbrenner, was sitting there along with Stump Merrill and pitcher Tom Seaver. Strangely, they weren't speaking to one another. I nodded to George. He nodded in return. I wondered what had "the boss" down in the dumps. Probably the fact his team had a less-than stellar season.

I sipped my soda, checked out other attractive women who were sitting at various tables. But I didn't flirt with any of them. Instead, I found myself brooding about the fact that the serial bed-hopping I'd engaged in, especially since my mother's death, no longer satisfied me. Dating had become a tedious, unfulfilling chore. There was an impersonal, dreary sameness about the sex.

As I finished my drink and ordered another, I decided that going forward, I'd stop screwing around and look for a lasting relationship. Stop dating beautiful, needy, loquacious airheads; depressives, Satanists, spiritualists, drunks, and those with more than five cats. Find someone intelligent, stable, responsible. Someone I cared about. Someone who cared about me. I drank the soda. Ordered another.

It must have been close to 3:00 a.m. when I walked out of Elaine's. Instinctively, I scanned the streets, searching the tall shadows, peering around the sharp angles, alert for bad guys. I walked north on an eerily deserted Second Avenue.

An out-of-service city bus rolled by. A lone cab cut across Ninetieth Street, heading to First Avenue. I heard a dog bark. There were sirens in the distance.

I walked past the dark, foreboding Ruppert Park. Several large rats scurried across my path. I turned left on East Ninety-first Street. Was about midway up the hill when I sensed movement. Looked and spotted the silhouette of a man in the tree-lined darkness to my right. I glanced to my rear. Two black males, hands in their pockets, were hustling up the block, heading in my direction—a robbery team. Adrenaline spurted into my system.

The guy to my right stepped out of the shadows. He was Hispanic. A kid. Big for his age. I'd guess eighteen years old. I could see his hands. They were empty. I glanced at the two-man backup coming up fast. Their hands were still in their pockets. I pulled my .38. But kept it low. Hid it behind my leg. I didn't wish to shoot anyone. Especially not three kids.

I'd been licensed to carry a concealed weapon my entire adult life and, not counting my days with the NYPD, was never forced to use it. Sure, there'd been a few close calls when I'd stumbled upon a mugging, an assault, or some crazy randomly attacking civilians with hammers, machetes, or baseball bats. I'd also been targeted a few times by Harlem and East Village street thugs. But I'd always found a way to escape. Duck into a bar, bodega, or drugstore. A few times I'd turned on my heels and simply run for my life. I'd do almost anything to avoid a gunfight.

The two-man backup was almost upon me.

"Julio," I said to the Hispanic kid. "That you?" I rushed forward. Slashed my S&W across his face. He went down. Hard. I spun. Pointed my weapon. The backup team froze. If they had guns and they were stupid, they'd pull them now. I waited. My finger tightened on the trigger. "Hands where I can see them."

The two raised their hands.

"Pick up your friend," I said, stepping back, giving them room. "And get the fuck out of here."

Chapter 33

"I've got someone I want you to meet," Joni said. We were sitting at the bar in the Four Seasons. Doing our best to ignore a heated, loud discussion between several men who, I assumed, were attorneys. They were sitting across the bar, debating the merits of the convictions of the defendants in the Central Park Jogger case.

"What does she look like?"

"You're a shallow dickhead. You know that, don't you?"

"Yeah," I said. "So?"

Joni sipped her drink. "What are you looking for in a lasting relationship?"

"Seriously?"

"Yes."

I thought a moment. "A great body, for starters."

Joni punched my arm. "I need you to grow up and be serious for five minutes."

"Okay." I took a minute. "Besides a great body, I want someone who's smart. Independent. Being employed would be a plus. She has to have a sense of humor."

"That's a given," Joni said, "if she's dating you."

"What I don't want is any more crazies. No drunks. Drug addicts. Manic-depressives. Satanic tattoos are a no-no."

"Hard to believe."

"And no cigarette smokers. I can't stand the constant bad breath."

Joni shook her head. "I worry about you."

"About me?" I made a face.

"Deep down, you're a wholly decent human being."

"Aw, shucks," I said, waiting for the zinging punch line.

"I'm serious. You keep your word, do what you say you'll do. You care about people. You're not mean." Joni sipped her drink. "You're positive, always smiling. There are people who hate you for being you."

"Hate me?" I said, flabbergasted.

"It's more jealousy."

"Why would anyone be jealous of me?"

"I just told you."

I took a moment to consider Joni's words. Frankly, I was taken aback. Sure, intellectually I knew that everyone had detractors, but I'd never given the issue any thought. Maybe I should start. Although the fact I'd never been jealous of anyone, was always too busy doing my own thing to worry about what others were doing, put me at a disadvantage. I wouldn't know what to look for. I was pretty sure that I had no enemies. At least, none that I knew of.

Joni sipped her vodka, rocks. "Any of your old relationships worth revisiting?"

"Funny you should mention that. I got a message on my answering machine last night. Someone I dated years ago." I wiggled my eyebrows. "We had a great time."

"What did the message say?"

"That she wanted to—" I used my fingers to make air quotes—"'see me.'"

"Maybe it's because you—" Joni made air quotes—"'knocked her up?'"

"Impossible," I said. "I haven't seen her in almost three years."

"So," Joni said, "she's bringing you a two-year-old."

I met Joni's friend in a local Greek diner. Turned out that Shelly was bright, attractive, gainfully employed, and geographically desirable; she lived in the East Seventies. But before we even ordered coffee, Shelly took out a wallet and showed me a picture of her "babies": two seventy-five-pound dogs. That's when I noticed that her clothing was covered with dog hair.

"Both are German shepherd–husky mixes." She produced a second photo. "That's Thunder on the left and Lightning on the right." She kissed the picture. "I love my babies." I looked closely at the photos, saw nicotine stains on Shelly's manicured fingers, caught the faint smell of tobacco.

Warning bells went off.

"You a smoker?"

"I'm quitting," she said.

Yeah. Right.

Not only was Shelly a smoker, but she was also obviously a devoted dog owner. Which meant she led her life around her dogs. Which meant if I became involved with her, I'd wind up living *my* life around her dogs. I was not interested in that arrangement.

"With dogs that size," I said, "you must live in a big apartment."

Shelly shook her head. "I live in a studio."

"A loft?"

She shook her head again. "Fifth-floor walk-up. A four-hundred-square-foot studio."

"With two seventy-five-pound dogs?" I couldn't help making a disgusted face. Her studio had to smell like a kennel.

"You have a problem with that?" Shelly said.

A waiter served our coffee.

"Not at all."

"Where's Marla?" Donald asked me a few days later. I think it was in early October. "She still with that Bolton guy?"

Here we go again.

After shooting *Designing Women* in LA, Marla had flown up to Washington State, where Bolton was giving a concert at the

Central Washington State Fair. The news of their romantic rendezvous had made the *Daily News*. Marla, through Chuck Jones, made sure it did. And made sure the papers spun the story to make it look like Marla had dumped Donald in order to be with her new beau, who the papers described as "younger and hunkier than Trump."

"Not sure where she is," I said. "But a bunch of us are going to see Bolton's concert at the Taj in a few days."

Silence. I could almost hear Donald processing that information. Deciding whether or not he felt betrayed by me going to the concert.

"She's just trying to hurt me," Donald said. "You know that. Right? That's what this is all about."

I drove to the Bolton concert at the Taj with my sister Patricia — a big Bolton fan — and another couple. Marla told me she'd left our names with Bolton's people so we could go backstage.

"I'm Thomas Fitzsimmons," I told Bolton's assistant after the concert. "We're friends of Marla Maples. We'd like to say hello to Michael. Tell him how much we enjoyed the show."

The assistant checked a backstage pass list, found my name, then said, "Wait here." She walked off, I assumed, to check with Bolton. "Sorry," the assistant told us an insulting twenty minutes later. "Michael's having dinner. If you'd like to wait—"

"No, thanks," I said, much to my sister's horror. "Tell him I'll see him another time."

"What did you just do?" my sister demanded to know as we walked out of the hall.

"Bolton's sending a message," I said.

"Message?" Patricia said. "What message?"

"I'm not sure," I said. "Maybe Marla's not as close to him as she wants everyone to believe."

The next day I woke to an unseasonably warm, sunny morning. Opened all my windows. Pulled on some sweats, slipped my .38, along with my ID and keys, into a custom-made, quick-draw holster/fanny pack. I did some stretching in my apartment and decided to jog over to Wards-Randalls Island. Not my usual choice for a run, since the islands are eerily deserted and its transient denizens potentially dangerous. But I was looking for a quiet place to think and Central Park, where I usually jogged, would be crowded on such a beautiful day.

Wards and Randalls Islands were conjoined back in the early 1960s. The islands once housed an orphanage, poorhouse, a potter's field (common burial ground for the poor), an "idiot" asylum, and a rest home for Civil War veterans. It was also once the headquarters of the New York House of Refuge, a reform school for juvenile delinquents. The islands were still home to several public facilities, including two psychiatric hospitals (one an asylum for the criminally insane), a wastewater treatment plant, and several homeless shelters.

I jogged over to the East River, breathed in the refreshing salt air, and turned north on a paved path alongside the FDR Drive. Traffic whizzed by to my left. There was boat and barge traffic to my right. At 103rd Street I climbed the stairs of the Wards Island pedestrian bridge. As I crossed the span and basked in the bright sunshine, I enjoyed spectacular views of the Harlem River to the north and the East River to the south.

I spotted a young woman sunbathing as soon as I came off the bridge. The sight of her startled me. She was lying on her back along the grassy shoreline, facing the city, eyes closed. I stopped jogging. Thought for a moment she was injured or dead. But then she lifted her left arm and glanced at her wristwatch, which glistened in the sunlight.

It was hard to determine what the woman looked like, but I could tell that she was white, had dark hair, was maybe in her mid-thirties. She was wearing street clothes; her high heels and purse were on the grass beside her. Her skirt was hiked up high and her top pulled down low to expose her pale skin to the sun. I wondered who she was. What the hell was she doing, alone, on the island?

She appeared to be too well-dressed to be homeless or a recently discharged psychiatric patient. So why, with schizophrenic homeless men roaming the island, would she place herself in harm's way? It didn't make sense.

I decided that she had to be a stranger to the city, a tourist. No local would be careless enough to visit those islands solo, let alone sunbathe. I was about to resume my run when I heard voices. Looked north along the shoreline. Four males in their late teens were sequestered in a thicket that surrounded a concrete storm drain. They were staring hungrily at the exposed woman. Nudging each other. Laughing. Egging each other on. It didn't take a genius to know what was about to happen: a purse snatching, robbery, or, God forbid, another Central Park Jogger–type attack.

I ran north along a bridle path. The four teens barely noticed as I strode by and then sat on the grass about fifty yards away. I lay back, propped up by my elbows, and let the sun hit my face. Squinted at the men. Watched and waited.

A tugboat plowed north on the East River. I checked the time. I was scheduled to meet two of my sisters at Mumbles for happy hour before going to the Palm down on Second Avenue for lobsters. Marla and her mother were supposed to make an appearance. Although I doubted they would. Marla was way too busy juggling an insanely jealous Donald, a reluctant Michael Bolton, and the various media outlets. Then there was the fact I'd seen another change in Marla during the last few months. The notoriety had gone to her head. The once-sweet Georgia peach who had made it a point to ingratiate herself to almost everyone was showing signs of pretention. Which meant to me that she was utterly secure in her relationship with Donald and rightfully so. Donald had only just flown her mother Ann to New York, first class, and put her up in the presidential suite at the Plaza Hotel. A few days later he'd shown up uninvited at a luncheon Marla was hosting (on Donald's dime) with Chuck Jones and another press agent at the Russian Tea Room. Last weekend Donald took Marla to play golf out in the Hamptons. Then pumpkin picking.

Donald had even reached out to Bolton during his stint at the Taj. Made sure the singer knew that he and Marla were still "very close." That their public breakup was temporary. There had been a photo of Donald, Marla, and Bolton in the papers taken at a celebrity softball game at Yankee Stadium. Trump vs. Bolton teams. Marla, a shit-eating grin on her face, posed for the cameras with Donald on her right and Bolton on her left.

Raised voices. The four teens were bickering with one another, looking and pointing in my direction. The woman was still sunbathing. I smiled at the men, hoping to project my intentions. I wasn't going anywhere.

It took another five minutes before the teens reluctantly straggled away. They slouched east, then south across the grass and disappeared over a rise. The woman had no idea the danger she'd been in.

I got to my feet. Approached the woman. "Miss?"

She opened her blue eyes, used her right hand to shield the sun. Used her left to pull her skirt down over shapely legs and reposition her blouse. She wore a wedding band–diamond ring combination. The gold watch appeared real.

"I work for the parks department."

"Yes?"

"You shouldn't lie here what with the snakes—"

"Snakes?!" The woman sprang to her feet. Did some sort of hysterical jig, like she was standing on hot coals. She pivoted a full 360, searched the grass. "Did you say snakes?"

"Relax," I said. "I don't see any now." I pretended to be looking. "But this is their nesting ground, by the water."

The woman had gone pale. Her hands trembled. She mumbled something in Spanish. Blessed herself. Snatched up her purse and shoes. "Thank you," she said and raced off, barefoot, to the pedestrian bridge, leaving a whiff of intoxicating perfume in her wake. The woman slipped on her shoes and started up the footbridge incline.

I watched until she walked down the ramp on the other side and was reasonably sure she was safe. Well, as safe as any lone, attractive female could be in East Harlem, El Barrio.

Chapter 34

THE WEATHER TURNED SERIOUSLY COLD. I'd closed all my apartment windows. Pumped up the electric baseboard heat before taking a shower. I shaved and slipped into a gray, pinstriped suit and black silk knit tie. One of Donald's Town Cars was scheduled to pick me up shortly.

I had time to kill, so I sat on the couch and perused the morning papers. Subway fares were being raised to an outrageous $1.50. Mafia kingpin John "the Teflon Don" Gotti was convicted in federal court of five murders, conspiracy to murder, loansharking, illegal gambling, obstruction of justice, bribery, and tax evasion and sentenced to life in prison. In Greenwich, Connecticut there was speculation that police were reopening the 1975 unsolved murder of fifteen-year-old Martha Moxley.

Joni high-heeled into the living room, coffee cup in hand, and sat on her usual chair. "Think Donald will be pissed at Marla?" Joni said, referring to Marla's *Designing Women* episode that she and I had watched the evening before. "She made a fool of him. Sort of."

"He's thin-skinned," I said. "He won't be happy."

"See the story in the *Post* about the engagement ring?"

I had. Gossip columnist Cindy Adams had reported that jeweler Harry Winston was demanding payment for Marla's 7.5-karat engagement ring. And there was speculation among some of us insiders that, since there had been yet another break-in at Marla's Trump Parc apartment, and more shoes were missing, that Donald was trying to steal the ring back. I didn't believe that for a second.

"I'll be at the Four Seasons after work," Joni said as she finished her coffee, placed the cup in the dishwasher, and walked out the front door.

I turned back to the article about the Martha Moxley murder. Bear in mind that because two of the suspects, Thomas and Michael Skakel, were the nephews of Ethel Skakel Kennedy, the widow of Senator Robert F. Kennedy, the homicide had received worldwide attention. (You'll recall my friend John McCooey had married and divorced Ethel's sister Ann.).

On the evening of October 30, 1975, high school student Martha Moxley had been in the company of, among others, Belle Haven neighbors Thomas and Michael Skakel. Martha began making out with Thomas and they were last seen "falling together behind a fence" near the pool on the Skakel property.

The next day, Moxley's body was found underneath a tree in her family's backyard. Her pants and underwear were pulled down. However, she had not been sexually molested. Several pieces of a broken golf club were found near the body. An autopsy indicated she had been bludgeoned and stabbed with the club. The six iron was traced back to the Skakel home. Yet no arrests were ever made.

I sipped my coffee and thought about the fact that, thanks to John McCooey, I was acquainted with some of the players in that sensational drama. I'd once met young Michael and Thomas, their father Rushton Skakel, and his sister Ethel Kennedy at the exclusive, classic, shingle-style clubhouse of the Belle Haven Beach Club in Greenwich.

McCooey and I had spoken at length about the Moxley murder several times over the years. I told him that as an ex-cop who didn't believe in coincidence, the identity of the killer or killers was obvious: One or both of the Skakel boys. However, McCooey was adamant that the Skakels, who, like JFK Jr. were frequent guests at his penthouse, were innocent.

I closed the paper, wondering if the Moxley case would ever be reopened. If her killer would ever be unmasked and prosecuted. I wondered if her family would ever find closure.

My doorman buzzed. The Trump Town Car was waiting to drive me to the eastside heliport. I was on my way to AC to attend a Doobie Brothers concert. Meeting up with Marla, Donald, Kim, Ann, Marla's stepdad David, and Chuck Jones. The group was flying in from Dalton, Georgia, where Marla had crowned the newest Whitfield High School football homecoming queen and answered questions from the press like, "Why do you keep taking Donald back?"

At the preconcert dinner that evening, there was no mention of the *Designing Women* episode. However, there was much-excited speculation about Marla's having auditioned for the Broadway play *The Will Rogers Follies* and her upcoming appearance as a segment reporter on Bill O'Reilly's *Inside Edition*. Also, the daytime drama *Loving* had offered her a starring role; Chuck Jones had come through as usual. There was also more talk about that Kim-O'Reilly fix-up: Where to go on a blind date? What to wear?

Although part of me thought that Donald had gotten us all together so he could announce his reengagement to Marla. Maybe even set a wedding date.

That didn't happen.

Maybe that was because Marla kept gushing about how charming and good-looking O'Reilly was. Or maybe it was because she was evasive whenever Michael Bolton's name was mentioned; Kim, who had a crush on Bolton, was visibly upset about that. Another thing I remember: Marla had acted uncharacteristically imperious toward Kim and the casino's restaurant waitstaff.

"You see it?" Donald said to Chuck and me as we walked out of the restaurant. "Can you believe how Marla spoke to our waiter?"

Marla, Kim, Ann, and David had walked on ahead.

"Yes," I said. "What's her problem?"

Donald lowered his voice. "Marla's becoming Ivana."

I caught sight of Pam F., the Taj's stunning assistant director of security, across the lobby. Pam flashed a quick little smile. I nodded back. My plan was to beg off going to the concert, basically ditch Donald, Marla, and family ASAP, and hook up with Pam. Which I managed to do about half an hour later. I loved it when a plan came together.

I was speaking to Donald on the phone at the end of October, discussing our attending an upcoming Paula Abdul concert at the Meadowlands, when he was interrupted by an emergency message. I could hear Norma telling him that his mother was mugged while shopping near her Jamaica Estates home. (Fred and Mary Trump had been neighbors of mine when I lived in Jamaica Estates for a short time back in the late 1970s.) Donald said he had to go, hung up with me, and rushed to his mother's side.

The sixteen-year-old assailant robbed Mary Trump of $14, then knocked her onto a sidewalk. She suffered two broken ribs, facial bruises, several fractures, a brain hemorrhage, as well as permanent damage to her sight and hearing. A Good Samaritan, delivery truck driver Lawrence Herbert, apprehended the assailant and held him for police.

I learned something about Donald after that incident. I'd assumed that with the nefarious characters he was forced to deal with in the New York construction trade, he'd make one phone call and his mother's assailant would simply disappear. Or that he'd have his bodyguard, Matt — who swore he'd kill for him — take care of things. Or maybe even ask me to use my contacts to make sure the mugger had a less-than pleasant stay in jail. But although Donald was outraged that the robber was out on bail while his mother was in the hospital suffering, he took no vindictive action that I knew of. What he did do was reward the

Good Samaritan with a check that kept him from losing his home to foreclosure. Incidentally, the assailant was eventually sentenced to three to nine years in prison.

"You coming with us to the Paula Abdul concert?" Donald asked me.

"Who's *us*?"

"Kim. Bill O'Reilly. Me and Marla."

So, Kim's blind date with O'Reilly had morphed into a double or triple date, which wasn't surprising. Regardless, spending time with the spacey Kim and uptight O'Reilly didn't sound like much fun to me.

"No can do," I said. "But thanks for the invitation. Let me know how it goes."

MUGGERS TRUMPED—DONALD STOPS ATTACK read the article in the *Daily News*. I was sitting in a local diner, eating breakfast with Joni. I'd ordered bacon and eggs. Joni had ordered a lox and bagel platter duplex, a monster meal. I set aside the paper as the waiter served our food. I looked at Joni's overflowing plate and wondered how she could eat like that and stay so thin. Joni needed three hands to pick up the overstuffed sandwich, but managed with two. She chomped down, took a man-sized bite. I ate some bacon, went back to reading the paper.

Though it wasn't clear how the *News* was tipped off—probably another phony-baloney Trump spokesperson—the paper reported that Donald, Marla, and another unnamed couple (Kim and O'Reilly) were heading toward the Lincoln Tunnel on their way to the Meadowlands in New Jersey for the Paula Abdul concert. Their limo stopped for a red light on Ninth Avenue and West Forty-fifth Street.

Someone in the limo commented, "Gee, look at that, it's a mugging."

Donald said, "I told my driver to stop the car because it was brutal-looking." He claimed he exited his vehicle and confronted the thug. "The guy with the bat looked at me, and I said, 'Look, you've gotta stop this. Put down the bat.' I guess he recognized me because he said, 'Mr. Trump, I didn't do anything wrong.' I said, 'How could you not do anything wrong when you're whacking a guy with a bat?' Then he ran away."

I forked some eggs and considered the fact that the Donald I knew wasn't that crazy or that brave. Leaving the protection of his limo and pistol-packing driver to confront an armed, violent thug didn't make sense. But then I thought about the fact that Donald's mother had been mugged the month before. Maybe he was looking for payback? But then why hadn't his driver and O'Reilly, who I assumed was a two-fisted Irishman, get out of the limo and back him up? Then again, why would Donald fabricate a story with the journalist O'Reilly in the car? If it was bullshit, why had O'Reilly kept silent? I ate some buttered rye toast and decided to find out what really happened. I knew if I asked Donald, he'd stick with the published heroic version. I decided to ask Marla, call her on the pretext of asking how the blind date went.

"How'd Kim and O'Reilly get along?" I said over the phone later that day.

"Well," Marla sighed. "They're going out again."

I detected something derisive in her voice.

"Which reminds me," Marla said. "I need to find a full-time personal assistant."

"Kim going somewhere?"

"You know someone?"

So, Kim was about to become history.

"Donald's people will find one if I want," Marla said.

"If I were you," I said, "I'd find my own assistant. If Donald's people do the hiring, you can bet that their loyalty will be to Donald. You want someone loyal to you."

"You're right."

"You know who'd be perfect? Janie." North Carolina native Janie Elder Porco, wife of my Navy buddy Dominick, was one of my most favorite people in the world.

"Janie?" Marla said, incredulous.

"Sure," I said. "She's smart. Reliable."

"Janie's too much of a redneck," Marla said.

Which pissed me off. "You love Janie."

"I know, but—"

"She's great with people. Fun. Easy to get along with. You already know she's honest. Hardworking. And you know she'll be loyal to you."

"Maybe you're right," Marla said.

"Let's not get ahead of ourselves," I said. "I'll ask if she even wants the job."

"Thanks, Fitzy."

"By the way, the story in today's paper about Donald stopping a mugging. That really happen?"

Marla sighed. "The mugging happened."

"Yeah?"

"Donald never got out of the limo."

Chapter 35

It was unseasonably warm on Thursday, New Year's Eve 1992. As I stepped into my tuxedo slacks and slipped on my tux-loafers, I recalled that every year, before her death, my brother, sisters, and I all called my mother just before midnight. She loved receiving those calls. We loved making them.

I pulled on a pleated wingtip collared shirt, fastened the black onyx shirt studs and cuff links, tied my bow tie and shrugged into my jacket. Checked myself in a full-length mirror. I slipped a white silk handkerchief into the tux jacket pocket, squared it off, and thought about the fact that for the first time in my adult life I didn't have a date for New Year's Eve.

For a while, I had considered reconnecting with that old girlfriend who wanted to — air quotes—"see me." But when we met for a drink at Elaine's, she gave me a huge hug, a wet kiss, and handed me an envelope with $500 cash. It was rent money I'd lent her, and forgotten about, years ago. Then she introduced me to her successful businessman husband — his chauffeur-driven Bentley was waiting outside —and adorable two-year-old son.

Chuck and Lynn Jones had invited me to a party at their home in Greenwich, Connecticut, just blocks away from the exclusive Belle Haven enclave where Martha Moxley had been murdered. I thanked them for the invite, but I wasn't about to leave the city on New Year's Eve.

Donald invited me to AC for the casino's New Year's Eve festivities. But he'd been in another deep funk, fueled in part by the fact that Ivana had written a tell-all book which, even though it was a novel, he claimed violated their divorce agreement.

"If the book's as bad as I think it is, I'm gonna sue Ivana's ass off. Then I'm going to sue for full custody of the children."

I sent Donald my regrets.

I draped a white silk scarf around my neck, grabbed my black Chesterfield overcoat, and headed out the door. I'd rented a limo for the evening along with two friends: actor/producer David Broadnax and William L., the former FBI associate turned PI who I sometimes worked for. They both brought dates.

David, William L., and I pooled our lists of parties we'd been invited to. David's date, a tourist from Canada, wanted to visit Times Square. Bad idea. Not just because of the rowdy, overflowing crowds waiting for the midnight countdown and ball drop. It was the fact that Times Square was still outright dangerous.

We made an appearance at Café Carlyle, sat at the bar, and watched Bobby Short's opening set. Then we moved onto Le Club. Left after an hour. Wound up settling in at the notorious party-animal Huntington Hartford's (heir to the A&P supermarket fortune) penthouse, on the thirteenth and fourteenth floors of One Beekman Place. I became bored after we all watched the ball drop on TV and the kissing and hugging and the happy New Year's cheerfulness died down. I pulled an Irish good-bye, slipped out without fanfare, and had the limo drop me in front of Elaine's. I didn't wish to be alone.

Although Elaine's was closed for a private New Year's party, the bouncer, another ex-cop, saw me and let me in. The joint was jumping. Sinatra was singing "New York, New York" on the restaurant's sound system.

I took off my overcoat, but held onto it. The bartender, Tom Carney, handed me a martini. I looked around and saw a few neighbors and a dozen celebrity faces. There were several attractive women. But it was impossible to tell if they were with escorts. I sipped my drink. Continued to scan the room. The sad fact was that although I was in the midst of a rousing party, I was still alone.

I wandered through the throng for a while, wished everyone I knew and those I didn't a happy and healthy New Year. I tried in vain to catch the eye of a striking brunette and then a stunning redhead and wondered what the hell I was doing with my life.

I'd be forty-four years old in February. I hadn't held, or wanted, a steady job since leaving the NYPD more than a decade ago. I'd been married to two breathtakingly beautiful women and had shared a sense of humor with both. For a while.

I was still struggling financially and had no life plan. Didn't know how I was going to make a living. Sure, I knew successful, influential people, but I'd never figured out how to parlay those relationships into gainful employment. Maybe that was one of the reasons the swells enjoyed my company.

I continued to make the rounds. Was mildly surprised to see the famous and famously cheap author sitting at a table with his stalker, the schnook who'd made death threats. If you'll remember, I'd run him off on the author's behalf. They looked awfully cozy. I considered making my way over to their table, wishing them a happy New Year, when a distant memory niggled my subconscious. I suddenly recalled that the famously cheap author never paid me. I remembered sending him an invoice. But not receiving payment. I made a mental note to call the SOB in the morning.

I used the lavatory. Then headed back to the bar, flirting every chance I got but to no avail. Bellying up to the bar, I signaled the bartender for another martini. Decided that whatever I chose to do with the rest of my life, whoever I wound up in a relationship with, the lady had to be fun. I mean, isn't that what life's all about? Having fun, albeit without knowingly hurting anyone? That was my philosophy. Always had been. Probably always would be.

I heard laughter. Noticed that there was a group of attractive females clustered beside me. "Excuse me," I said. "Would any of you ladies like to have some fun?"

"Me!" someone shouted.

I knew that voice.

"Yeee-haaawww!" a hungry woman in a skimpy, sequined green cocktail dress hollered. My lord, it was the whack-a-doodle I'd had that riotous one-night stand with some years ago. Brandy, Randy, or Candy swooped into the corner. Bear-hugged me. Flung her arms around my neck. Whispered a string of erotic suggestions into my ear. Then stuck her tongue down my throat. I struggled to break the embrace.

"I have to—er—go to the—er—men's room."

"Hurry back," Brandy, Randy, or Candy said and stroked my crotch.

I wove through the crowd, toward the men's room, looped around by the kitchen, pulled yet another Irish good-bye, and slipped out the side door. Whew.

Second Avenue was like Mardi Gras. I shrugged into my coat. Sidestepped a group of well-dressed couples who were arguing about where to go next. I hurried north, turned up Ninety-first Street. A brisk wind struck me. I buttoned my coat and flipped up the collar. Was almost to Third Avenue when I spotted a ghostly figure loitering at the top of the hill. It took a moment for me to recognize Bessy. She was in her nightclothes and bedroom slippers. I dashed up the hill.

"Bessy." I took off my overcoat and draped it over her shoulders. "What are you doing out here?"

"Thomas?" She squinted at me. "Looking for Abraham."

Her long-dead husband.

"He's here somewhere." Bessy scanned the area. "I heard him. He called me."

"I'll take you to Abraham." I put my arm around her. It took a good fifteen minutes to shuffle the block and a half to her apartment. Bessy had left her front door wide open. I sat her on the couch. Then checked the apartment for intruders. Finding no one, I closed and locked the door. As usual, Bessy's railroad apartment was immaculate. The furnishings were old, but meticulously maintained.

"Where do you keep your phone book?"

Bessy was staring out a window.

"Bessy?"

She didn't answer. I looked around, located her phone book lying alongside an old rotary phone. I started calling relatives. On the third try, the NASA brainiac answered and said she'd be there within the hour. I checked the time: 3:05 a.m.

I wandered into Bessy's kitchen. Opened the refrigerator. On the top shelf in the rear was an open bottle of Manischewitz wine. I found two wineglasses, poured.

"Where's Abraham?" Bessy said.

"He's on his way."

"Who are you?"

"Thomas. I'm your date for New Year's Eve."

Bessy looked confused for a moment. "Don't tell Abraham."

"That meshuggener?"

Bessy laughed. "So, you've met my Abraham."

I handed her the wine. We toasted and clinked glasses.

"Happy New Year, Bessy," I said.

"Happy New Year, Thomas," Bessy said and gulped down the entire glass of wine.

Chapter 36

I SWORE OFF DATING FOR the next few months. Spent my time hanging out, cocktailing, and dining with family and friends. I trained at a health club almost every day. Altered between Hell's Kitchen's rough-and-tumble Mid City Gym—where I still sometimes ran into actor Michael Douglas—the New York Athletic Club, and the University Club. I jogged. Skipped rope. Hit the heavy bag. Was happy to work a few low-pressure bodyguard gigs for clients with more money and ego than any genuine security concerns. There were a few modeling gigs. A dozen TV auditions that I didn't book. Although I was on hold for a national network Preparation H spot, I hoped I didn't book it.

Nights I worked on my writing.

In late June, Marla's new assistant, Dominick's wife, Janie Elder Porco, phoned. "Marla got the role with *The Will Rogers Follies.*"

"What about the soap opera, *Loving?*"

Thanks to the tireless efforts of Chuck Jones and the entertainment attorney Michael Collyer, the daytime drama *Loving* had not only offered Marla a role, but to write the entire soap around her yet-to-be-created character. Collyer had negotiated her a fat salary, far more than she'd earn on Broadway, and some creative control. Working on *Loving*, in the opinion of Chuck and Collyer, was the far better opportunity if Marla was serious about a film career.

"She turned *Loving* down," Janie said.

Had to have been Donald's influence.

He'd told me over dinner at the Old Homestead Steakhouse that landing a role in a Broadway play would force the press to take Marla seriously; a tacky soap opera wouldn't. Donald said that acting on Broadway might even rehabilitate her jezebel image. Personally, I thought that only Donald marrying her would make a difference, but kept that to myself. Regardless, I had to give Marla credit. With her mother Ann as her stage mother/coach, she'd come to the city, a starry-eyed Southern belle with a plan: Snag herself a rich man and use his money and connections to further her acting career. Honestly, I had no problem with that. I mean, I could name several successful actors, businesspeople, and politicians who'd done far worse for the same purpose.

"Here's Marla," Janie said.

"Hiya, Fitzy."

"Congratulations," I said. "I couldn't be prouder of you." We spoke for a while about the play's cast, music, and grueling rehearsal schedule. Then Marla said that she didn't think in a million years that she'd win the singularly apt role. She was to play the legendary Broadway producer Flo Ziegfeld's favorite: the sexy other woman. I never doubted that she'd land the gig. And not just because of her acting chops. All the press she'd received since hooking up with Donald made her an international celebrity, a novelty. Which was good for the fledgling show's box office.

"Break a leg," I told Marla as I hung up.

I glanced out at East Harlem as police cars, lights flashing, raced up Third Avenue and prayed the officers would be safe. I poured myself a coffee and wished with all my being that Marla would do well. Become a Broadway sensation. Knock 'em dead. Then I phoned Donald. Norma put my call straight through.

"So, Marla's headed to Broadway."

"If she doesn't drive me nuts first."

"Now what?"

"Shoes," Donald said. "She keeps saying someone's stealing her shoes."

"Again?"

"Three hundred pairs so far."

That sounded like an exaggeration. I mean, who besides Imelda Marcos had three hundred pairs of shoes? I seem to remember that when Marla lived with me, she owned a few pairs of high heels and a pair of Tony Lama cowboy boots, but wore the same white tennis shoes most of the time?

"Have Matt put a hidden camera in the apartment," I said. "See who comes and goes."

"Already done," Donald said.

A few days later: "Fitz? It's Janie. You sitting down?"

I'd just walked into my apartment after working as a hand model for an upscale woman's fragrance. I'd spent most of the day standing behind a top model. My bare right arm draped provocatively over her partially veiled right shoulder. My hand fondling her left boob. For six full hours. Seriously.

"What's up, Janie?"

"They just arrested Chuck Jones for stealing Marla's shoes."

"What?" I nearly burst out laughing. Anyone who knew Chuck knew that he had a quirky sense of humor. Snatching Marla's shoes as a joke wouldn't surprise me in the least.

Chuck was arraigned later that day in Manhattan criminal court, charged with burglary in the second degree, a class C violent felony punishable by a mandatory minimum term of incarceration of three-and one-half years up to a maximum fifteen years in state prison, as well as fines and surcharges. He made bail. Went home to Greenwich to be with his family. I called Chuck to ask what the hell was going on. Left a message on his answering machine. He didn't call me back.

Donald, Dominick and his wife Janie Elder, and two hundred of Donald's other friends attended the August 3 opening night of the *The Will Rogers Follies*. Giant movie spotlights swept the night sky. The sidewalks outside the theater were jammed with ticket holders, gawkers, and paparazzi. I thought I recognized at least one male-female pickpocket team slithering through the crowd, but they were gone before I could make a positive ID. The play was highly entertaining.

Marla and the entire cast were excellent.

After the show, Donald held a Western theme party for five hundred in the grand ballroom of the Plaza Hotel. All the celebrities who'd attended the show, and more, were there. I saw John Casablancas, who had four stunning models in tow. Spotted Grayman speaking to LaToya Jackson. Wondered what, if any, was his connection to LaToya, another former Chuck Jones client. I talked to Tommy Tune, the show's multi–Tony Award–winning choreographer. Tune had been a guest of mine when I cohosted the WNBC show *Now!*

"Can you believe how great Marla was?" Donald, beaming with pride, said to me, his arm draped possessively around her shoulder. "She was great. Right? Great."

"Great," Tommy Tune and I said in unison.

I'd never seen Donald and Marla happier.

I read Alessandra Stanley's snarky review in the *New York Times* the next morning. Apparently, some female journalists looked upon Marla as a five-eight, 125-pound barracuda—a blond-haired, blue-eyed aberration, a larger-than-life 14-karat-gold predatory husband snatcher.

Another female journalist interviewed Marla that week at her Trump Parc apartment and wrote: *At first glance, the amount of makeup she wears reads cheap. The foundation is as thick as frosting, the off shade of pink lipstick conjuring eighth-grade shopping sprees at Woolworth's.*

A few weeks later, on a Wednesday between shows, I ate an early dinner with Donald and Marla at Joe Allen Restaurant in the theater district.

"I've been telling Marla to fire Chuck for years." Donald looked at my martini. "I don't understand how you can drink that and stay awake."

"I'm Irish." I carefully lifted the full glass to my mouth and drank. "It's a gift."

"Chuck has my diary," Marla said. "And Polaroids. He won't give them back."

"You sure he has them?" I said.

"Positive." She made a face. "I don't need this. Doing the play is hard enough without having Chuck as a distraction."

Our food was served. Conversation drifted to a hurricane named Andrew. The category 5 storm had made landfall at Miami-Dade County. With sustained wind speeds as high as 165 mph, Andrew destroyed more than 63,500 houses, damaged more than 124,000 others, and caused $27.4 billion in damage. Sixty-five people were left dead.

"Any damage to Mar-a-Largo?" I said.

"Minimal," Donald said. "Some downed trees."

We finished eating when Donald's driver, Barry, suddenly appeared at the table.

"It's time for your next meeting, Mr. Trump," Barry said, pointing at his wristwatch. "We'll have to hurry."

I'd seen this "time to go" ruse before.

"Thanks, Barry."

"Who's your meeting with?" Marla said suspiciously. "Don't lie to me, Donald."

"Bankers," Donald said with a goofy smile.

Marla's face flushed with anger. I held my breath, hoping that she didn't start throwing silverware, plates of food, or roundhouse punches.

"You're a liar," Marla said.

For once, Donald kept his mouth shut. He paid the tab. Got to his feet and went to peck Marla on the cheek. She turned a cold shoulder.

"See ya, Tom," he said and made a quick exit.

"That fucker," Marla said, tears in her eyes. She threw down her napkin, shot to her feet. Picked up her jacket and purse. I walked her back to the Palace Theatre.

"Look, Fitzy," Marla said in that newly acquired, thoroughly annoying pretentious way of hers. Like I worked for her. "I need you to get Chuck to give back my diary and the Polaroids." We arrived at the theater's stage door. "Let's see how you handle that."

"I'll talk to him."

Which I did the next morning.

"I don't have Marla's diary," Chuck told me over the phone from his house in Greenwich.

"She says you do."

"She's a flake. You of all people know that. She probably left her diary in some hotel room like she's done before."

I knew what he was talking about. When Marla lived with me, I'd seen her diary lying around in my living room, dining room, bathroom, and bedroom.

"What about the Polaroids?"

"I don't have any Polaroids."

"He's a liar," Marla said angrily over the phone from her Palace Theatre dressing room. It was a Monday. All the Broadway theaters were dark. But Marla hadn't paid close enough attention to her contract's fine print and, as a result, she was being forced to attend day and night press functions promoting the play on her days off while Donald was off doing "business."

"Look," I said. "I don't want to be caught in the middle of this thing. But maybe if you offer to drop the criminal charges, Chuck'll have some incentive to return your stuff."

"I can't do that," Marla said.

"Why not?"

"I have to protect Donald."

"From who? What does Chuck's larceny have to do with protecting Donald?"

Marla hung up.

Now I was curious about what was in that diary.

The Trump Organization's reception area was eerily deserted when I walked in late that afternoon. There was no blue-suited security guard to greet me. Except for the hum of the ventilation system, the place was quiet. Absent were the usual groups of anxious businessmen hoping to secure Donald's cash for their "can't miss" schemes. No clergy or representatives of so-called nonprofits were there to beg for charitable donations. Not to mention the slimy politicians looking for the usual handouts. And no one seemed to be staffing the reception desk.

"Hello?" I called out. When no one answered, I walked around the desk and opened the door that led to the inner sanctum. Most of the workstations in the large room were unoccupied. I was relieved to see that Norma was at her desk.

"Thomas," she said, smiling, opened her desk drawer, lifted out an envelope, and handed it over. "Four Knicks tickets."

"Thanks," I said. "He in?"

"Norma!" Donald shouted. "Who's out there?"

"Tommy Fitz," I said.

"C'mon in."

I stepped into Donald's office. Sat. Thanked him for the tickets.

"Tell me," Donald said. "Who do you like in the election?"

Don't know if I mentioned it earlier, but I'm not political. I do try to pay attention, and the Clinton-Bush race was, as expected, dominating the local and national news. But I quickly grow tired and numb by all the absolute, never-ending BS from both parties.

Norma poked her head in. "Chuck Jones is on the line."

"I'm not in." Donald looked at me. "He keeps calling, wanting me to tell Marla to drop the criminal charges."

"She won't, right?"

Donald nodded. "She says Chuck betrayed her."

I didn't know who betrayed who. But Chuck had devoted the last five or six years of his life to Marla Maples. He was her confidant, big brother, protector, lackey, shrink, agent, and manager. Hell, if it weren't for Chuck, Marla and Donald probably wouldn't even be together.

"You know," Donald said, "the DA's office offered to let Chuck plead guilty to a lesser charge. No jail time."

I knew that. Still proclaiming his innocence, Chuck wouldn't take any deal. He was steadfast in insisting that Marla drop all charges. Period.

"I'm staying out of it," Donald said. "That's what I told Chuck and Marla. I've got my own problems. Let them work it out."

Chapter 37

THE CREDIT CARD COMPANIES BEGAN harassing me in earnest in early February. No matter their threats or verbal abuse, I remained cooperative and courteous. Eventually, I offered to settle with each company for substantially less than I owed. They all agreed. Just like Donald said they would. Within weeks I was no longer burdened with credit card debt.

From out of the blue, a future Academy Award, Golden Globe–winning movie producer, Doug Wick, phoned me. He'd read "Rockers"—a based-in-fact short story I'd written about vigilante New York City cops. Doug told me how much he liked the story, my writing style, dialogue, characters, and said he wanted to option the story to be produced as a feature film. I was ecstatic, of course, and asked Michael Collyer to handle the negotiations. I was to receive a $10,000 advance plus another $170,000 and 5 percent of the net, if the picture was actually made.

"This calls for a celebration," Larry Hagman, who happened to be in town that week, said. And so, we celebrated. Well, *I* celebrated. Hagman was ordering club soda. He'd just been informed by his doctors that he needed a liver transplant. Said he was on a —wink, wink—transplant waiting list. It's common knowledge that celebrities automatically go to the head of any organ replacement waiting list.

We were seated at the bar in Dorian's Red Hand, where, if you'll remember, Robert Chambers, the "Preppy Killer," met his victim Jennifer Levin the night he murdered her. First Grade

Detective Mike Sheehan, who'd arrested Chambers, was sitting beside Hagman, discussing another case he was working on: a serial rapist was stalking the Washington Houses, a project in East Harlem, just twelve blocks north.

"He's targeting children and teenage girls," Sheehan, the father of a six-month-old girl, said. "He'd better hope we arrest him before his victims' families find him. Not that I have a problem with that."

All at once a group of giggling middle-aged women surrounded Hagman, thrusting bar napkins at him, asking for autographs. One of them produced an Instamatic camera and asked if he'd take a group picture with them. As usual, Hagman happily complied. I took the photo.

About 2:00 a.m. Hagman — who'd broken down and drank a bottle of Moët & Chandon — and I exited Dorian's. Rainy Second Avenue was all but deserted.

"Look, something I've been meaning to ask you," I said as I popped open an umbrella, locked arms with my tottering friend and helped him to the curb in search of a cab. "I'm curious."

"Ask away, my boy."

"Were you serious about hiring a hit man to kill your blackmailer pal, Albert F., upon your death?" A taxi pulled to the curb. Hagman graced me with the evil J.R. Ewing grin, and patted my arm as he disengaged himself, opened the cab's rear door, stepped inside, and pulled the door closed. I watched as the cab moved south, cut across four lanes, and turned right.

I decided to head up to Elaine's for a totally unnecessary nightcap. Just then a Checker cab pulled to the curb and three loud, querulous, twentysomething guys wearing rugby jackets exited and, jostling each other, entered Dorian's.

I stepped into the cab.

"Take me to Elaine's, please."

"Where?" the driver said.

"You kidding?" I looked at the driver's rearview mirror. A set of large blue eyes were focused on mine. The driver was female.

And a good-looking one at that—something was amiss. In a city where cabdriver robberies and murders were not uncommon, I'd never even *heard* of a female cabdriver. I squinted at the driver's hack license. Whoever she was, she was using the name Cathy C. I glanced out the rear window. An undercover, unmarked police car—as obvious as a lights-flashing blue-and-white—was idling on the corner.

"Eighty-eighth and Second," I said. "Maybe you and your backup team would like to join me for a drink, Officer?"

Cathy C. did a double take. "Excuse me, sir?"

"Relax," I said. "I'm retired from the job. And I'm buying."

The following afternoon, I was home, nursing a hangover with the blue-eyed lady cabdriver/undercover policewoman, Cathy C. She had only just un-handcuffed me from my bedpost. We were sitting on my bed, drinking coffee. Eating buttered toast. A game show was on the TV. I was admiring the way she filled out the thick, terry-cloth Trump Plaza hotel robe I'd lent her when a special bulletin flashed on the TV screen. A talking head stated that an explosion had occurred at the north tower of the World Trade Center, in its underground garage.

"Holy shit," Cathy C. said. I turned up the sound. There were reports of unconfirmed fatalities. Authorities suspected a gas or transformer explosion.

It would turn out that a truck bomb had killed six people and injured over a thousand. The 1,336-pound urea nitrate–hydrogen gas–enhanced device was intended to "timber" the north tower into the south tower, resulting in the deaths of thousands. No one knew it at the time, but the world had changed. Islamic terrorism had come to our shores.

"I'd better get the precinct," Cathy C. said as she sprung off my bed, allowing the Trump robe to slip off her shoulders and pool on the floor. I followed her into my shower.

A week later, I was sitting at a table in the crowded back room of P.J. Clarke's.

"Hiya, Fitzy," Marla said as she hung her coat on a wall hook and sat across from me. As was usual these days, she was dressed to the nines. I must admit that I missed the old Marla: the jeans, cowgirl boots, and beauty pageant hair.

Marla ordered iced tea. I was working on a beer.

I closed a copy of the *New York Post*. Returned a wave across the room to actress Suzanne Somers and her TV host husband, Alan Hamel. I picked up my beer, took a sip.

"I'm pregnant," Marla said.

I spit up some beer.

A waiter delivered Marla's iced tea.

"I'm expecting in October."

I raised my glass in a toast. "Congratulations."

We touched glasses. Drank.

"What did Donald say?"

Marla forced a giggle. "He doesn't know yet."

"Oy vey," I said.

Marla smiled tightly. "I'm telling him tonight."

I phoned Donald a few days later.

"You think she did it on purpose?" he said before I had a chance to congratulate him. "Force me to marry her? What do you think?"

"Didn't you want kids with Marla?"

"No," Donald said.

"But I heard you tell her you wanted her to have your babies."

"Never happened."

"We were up in your apartment."

"I bet her mother is behind this," Donald said. "Ann's a disaster. A fucking disaster." He lowered his voice. "I've gotta figure out what to do about this." He hung up.

I wondered what he meant by that. Didn't have to wonder long.

"Donald wants Marla to have an abortion," Ann cried over the phone. "First he tells her he wants her to have his babies—"

"I was there," I said. "I remember."

Donald and I had never discussed being pro-life or pro-choice. Regardless, if Marla had the baby, Donald would not shirk his responsibilities. I knew that. Ann and Marla knew that.

"Hold on," Ann said, "Marla wants to talk to you."

"I'm not having a fucking abortion," Marla screamed in my ear. "I'm not."

Sometime after 2:00 on a Sunday morning about a month later, I was lying in bed, struggling to get through a well-reviewed, highly recommended (by a couple of female friends) newly released book titled *Bridges of Madison County* when I heard gunfire: three quick pops. Pause. Then two more rounds, but from a different gun. I could tell that the firefight was no more than a block or two away.

"Thomas!" Joni called from her room. "You hearing that?"

"Yes. Stay away from the window."

"No shit, Dick Tracy."

I took that opportunity to close the book — a total snooze — and toss it aside. I adjusted my pillow. Turned out the light. Closed my eyes. But it was hard to fall asleep to the sound of approaching police sirens.

I didn't think it was possible, but my neighborhood had seen yet another surge in violent crime: gunpoint muggings, armed robberies of bodegas and liquor stores. There was also a new rapist terrorizing the hood. And then there was the string of residential burglaries. Most occurred in five-floor walk-ups.

I had a different kind of problem. Much as I tried to avoid it, I wound up smack in the middle of the Donald, Marla, Chuck Jones debacle. Months-long negotiations between Chuck's attorney and the DA's office broke down. Chuck still refused to accept any deal. And so, the DA put on the pressure. Chuck was looking at serious jail time.

"They can't do this to me," Chuck told me on more than one occasion. "I was allowed access to her apartment. You were a witness."

Since I'd accompanied Chuck to Marla's apartment on numerous occasions, saw the doorman hand over her keys, I knew he was telling the truth. Sure, the DA could charge him with misdemeanor petty larceny, stealing Marla's used shoes, but the C felony charge of burglary was bogus. And to make the charge stick, Donald, Marla, the Trump Park doorman, and building superintendent would all have to commit perjury in open court. Testify, under oath, that Chuck was never authorized to enter Marla's apartment. I was positive that would never happen. Figured that the heavy charge was a ruse meant to force Chuck to give back Marla's diary and Polaroids. If he complied, I was sure that the case would be dismissed. But Chuck continued to insist that he didn't have Marla's property. Marla insisted that she knew for a fact he did.

Personally, I didn't know who to believe. Since a trial would destroy Chuck's business and personal life, I found it hard to believe that he was holding onto Marla's possessions. Why would he? But if he didn't steal her diary and photos, who did? I suspected that, since Marla might have written unflattering things about Donald in the diary, that he was the most obvious suspect; he had motive and opportunity. But would Donald allow Chuck to take a fall, go to prison for something he didn't do?

No. He wouldn't.

I was at a loss. Frustrated with both sides. I advised Chuck that if he had Marla's possessions or knew who did, to "Get Marla her shit back!"

Told Marla that embarrassing Chuck in the press and destroying his reputation had done enough damage. "Chuck's been your biggest supporter, best friend, and fan. That should count for something." But Marla didn't want to hear it.

On October 13, Marla gave birth to a girl, Tiffany Ariana Trump, at St. Mary's Medical Center in West Palm Beach,

Florida. I phoned Donald and Marla at Mar-a-Largo a few days later. Ann answered the phone.

"Isn't it exciting?" Ann said.

"Very," I said. "When are they coming back to the city?"

"Soon," she said. "We have to plan the wedding."

Wedding? Did she say *wedding*? I didn't know anything about that. Last time I spoke to Donald, he told me there was no way in hell he was getting married, jumping from the frying pan into the fire.

"Everyone's telling me to get married," Donald complained. We were sitting in the back of his limo. I'd bumped into him as I exited the Oak Room Bar. He'd offered to give me a lift uptown to Elaine's.

"People are telling me I have to marry her," Donald griped. "I have to do the right thing. My father and mother are the worst. And my lawyer's saying some Japanese corporations won't do business with me if I don't marry Marla. Like I give a shit what the Japs think."

Ann was saying, "Marla has to design the invitations. Pick out a dress. Photographer. A band. As far as venue, we're thinking the grand ballroom at the Plaza is a good choice. What do you think about the venue, Thomas?"

"Venue's great." I was tempted to be a wiseass and ask Ann if Donald knew anything about the wedding, but said instead, "They set a date yet?"

"No," Ann said.

That's what I thought.

"But they will," she said. "And soon."

I was mugged about two weeks later on an appropriately otherworldly night, in the West Village's Halloween parade. It was a miserable evening. A windswept nor'easter was pounding the city. Elaborately costumed ghosts, goblins, and witches carrying eye-poking umbrellas swarmed the streets and sidewalks.

I'd become separated from Joni and a group of friends. Was making my way north along the jam-packed parade route, fighting the gusty winds with my useless umbrella, when someone shoved me from behind. Next thing I knew I was face down on the wet pavement. Then a knee pressed on the center of my back forced the air from my lungs and kept me pinned to the sidewalk. Frantic hands searched my pockets.

Then they were gone.

I had some difficulty getting up and catching my breath. A muscular guy in a Marilyn Monroe costume helped me to my feet.

"You all right, honey?" Marilyn said, brushing the wet dirt off my tuxedo jacket with a perfumed, lacy handkerchief.

"I think so." I checked my pockets. The gold money clip I kept in my right-hand pocket was gone; they'd gotten about $100 cash. The clip was worth another $200. But my wallet, which I kept in my front, left-hand pocket in crowd situations, was still there. And my weapon was still in my ankle holster. My pants were torn at the knees. My jacket was torn at the shoulders. The heels of my hands were bleeding and my forearms hurt from breaking my fall. I looked angrily around for my attackers.

"Did you see who did it?" I asked Marilyn.

"The Village People."

"Huh?" I picked up my broken umbrella.

"The singing group? They were in Village People costumes. You know, a cowboy, biker, Indian, construction worker." Marilyn pointed to the parade. "They went that way."

My eyes couldn't penetrate the wall of wet umbrellas, not that I could ID anyone.

I thanked Marilyn for the help. Continued north on Sixth Avenue, troubled by the fact that ambush predators had taken me by surprise. I must be getting old.

I caught up with my friends a few blocks later.

"What happened to you?" Joni said.

I thought about telling her the truth, but I was too embarrassed.

"I tripped."

I never told anyone that I'd been robbed that night.

"So," I said to Donald over the phone in early December. "I spoke to Chuck Jones's lawyer. They want me to testify in court. They're planning on subpoenaing me. I don't wanna be involved in this bullshit. Can't you talk to Marla?"

"Did you hear about the shooting?" Donald said.

"Didn't you hear what I said?"

"On the Long Island Railroad."

"I heard."

Donald was speaking about a crazed gunman named Colin Ferguson who'd pulled a Ruger-89 semiautomatic handgun, killed six random Long Island Railroad commuters, and wounded nineteen others.

"I used to ride that train," Donald said. "So have my brothers, sisters, parents. My kids. That could have been any one of us."

"Yeah," I said. "It's terrible. Now, about Marla…."

"I can't believe this," Donald said. "This changes everything. Life is too short."

"Will you talk to Marla?"

"That's what I'm saying," Donald said. "I'm going to talk to her now. We're getting married. Life is too dammed short."

Chapter 38

THE DECEMBER 20 NUPTIALS AT the Plaza Hotel's grand ballroom were, as expected, extravagant, first class, very-very Trump. Which was surprising, since Marla told me several times that she had planned a small, intimate ceremony with family and a few close friends. But, Marla told me, you know Donald.

I stepped from a cab on Fifth Avenue and, as I walked across Grand Army Plaza, saw that a dozen rubberneckers had climbed the Pulitzer Fountain across from the hotel's entrance. Crowds kept in check by barricades and a dozen uniformed police officers jammed the sidewalk. Some fifteen news vans were parked and double-parked along both sides of the street. At least 100 paparazzi were queued up on the hotel's steps, cameras at the ready.

As I threaded my way through the crowd, I couldn't help but revel in the irony. The brash, bombastic businessman and the Georgia jezebel, the couple that the media and everyone else predicted would never marry, were doing just that.

I skirted the red carpet, where boldfaced names hammed it up for the cameras. Made my way through the lobby to the grand ballroom and the mezzanine VIP section. I shook hands with the guys working security as I strode up the mezzanine stairs. Said hello to Stan Maples and Baby Woman, to Marla's grandparents, and the rest of the Maples clan. They were all standoffish and I knew why. Even though I'd told them repeatedly that I did not want to be involved in the Chuck Jones criminal case, they believed that because I was about to be subpoenaed, I was somehow taking Chuck Jones's side.

I scanned the VIP section. Spotted Dominick Porco speaking to O.J. Simpson. Dominick's wife Janie Elder was to be Marla's maid of honor; I wondered what her former best-friend-forever and guru Kim Knapp thought about that.

I joined Dominick and O.J. and we bellied up to one of many bars. I glanced around and realized that there must be a thousand guests. I spotted soon-to-be ex-Mayor David Dinkins and a host of other politicians. And there was the Manhattan district attorney himself, Robert M. Morgenthau, the man who was prosecuting Chuck Jones. Conflict of interest, anyone? You tell me.

I was on my third glass of champagne when I noticed that there was more security working the event than I would have anticipated. And they looked on high alert like they were expecting trouble. I mentioned that to Dominick.

"It's Marla's doing," Dominick said. "She's afraid of Chuck Jones."

"What's she think Chuck's gonna do?"

"Crash the party. Shoot up the place."

I suppose I could see Marla's point of view. As a Vietnam veteran and combat Marine, Chuck knew how to handle weapons. Add to that the fact that Marla, along with Donald's pal, DA Morgenthau, were doing their level best to put him in prison.

"Watch this," I said to Dominick and O.J. Then I eased from the VIP section and walked across the ballroom floor. Positioned myself behind Matt, Brian, and two other bodyguards.

"Look!" I stage-whispered. "There's Chuck Jones!" Talk about a cartoon-style freak-out. All four men snapped to, practically leaped into the air, made ready to pull weapons, and frantically scanned the area.

"Where?" Matt demanded to know. "Where is he?"

I burst out laughing. "Only kidding, guys."

It took a minute before the bodyguards realized I really was joking.

"Not funny," Matt said.

Someone said the ceremony was about to begin. Chairs were lined up across the room facing another mezzanine. I claimed a seat with Dominick and O.J. Then, Dr. Arthur Caliandro, pastor of the Marble Collegiate Church, took a position at the makeshift altar, which was decked with white orchids and white birches.

Donald, trim and handsome in a Baroni tux, appeared on one side of the altar. He looked nervous as hell. His father and best man was obviously trying to calm him down. Then Marla came into view, wearing a low-cut, white-satin sheath dress, floor-length train veil, and diamond tiara. She looked gorgeous. Donald regarded his bride-to-be. Gaped. Smiled and seemed to relax.

Dominick whispered, "Janie told me that dress cost ten grand. The diamond tiara's worth two million. They borrowed it from Harry Winston."

"Yeah? What about her shoes?" I said, louder than necessary, trying again for funny. No one laughed.

As Dr. Caliandro began the double-ring ceremony, I glanced around at the grinning, fidgety guests. I'd attended countless weddings of most every religion or denomination. Regardless, there was usually a contingent of dramatic, weepy women vying for attention. Not at this ceremony. There wasn't a wet eye in the room.

A few moments later, when Caliandro came to the part "If anyone can show just cause why this couple cannot lawfully be joined together in matrimony, let them speak now or forever hold your peace," I could sense the entire congregation holding their collective breath. A few people coughed. Someone giggled. A guy behind us made a fart noise. But no one objected. And Chuck Jones didn't come charging out of the crowd, guns blazing. When the ceremony was over and Caliandro pronounced the couple man and wife, everyone shot to their feet and applauded.

Afterward, I made my way to the bride and groom. Shook Donald's hand, kissed Marla's cheek, and congratulated them.

Then we all we sat down to a veritable feast of caviar, smoked fish, lamb, beef, tuna, and turkey. And I fell in lust with a leggy, exotic brunette who was falling out of a clingy purple cocktail dress.

Later, as the lady in purple and I cabbed up to Elaine's, I thought about the fact that around 70 percent of all marriages fail. I hoped with all my being that Donald and Marla would be the exception. That they'd live happily ever after.

As the cab sped north on Park Avenue, I raised the full glass of champagne that I'd snuck out of the Plaza. "Mazel tov, Donald and Marla," I said and drank it down. The lady in purple followed suit. Downed her own glass, then puked out the cab window.

I'd just left the 92nd Street Y about two weeks later, still sweating from a cardio workout. Was walking into my building lobby when a guy in a rumpled suit approached me, a big, friendly smile on his face.

"Thomas?" the guy said and stuck out his hand. "Thomas Fitzsimmons. Right?"

I eyeballed the guy. He did look somewhat familiar. "Yes," I said, and as I reached out to shake his hand, he slapped a subpoena into mine.

"You've been served," he said. "Have a nice day."

That's when I remembered he was the same process server who'd served Marla with a subpoena at the Four Seasons in the *Trump vs. Trump* divorce.

I called Marla from my apartment about five minutes later. Janie answered the phone. "I need to speak to Marla."

Janie hemmed and hawed and then handed me off to Ann.

"A process server just served me with a subpoena," I told Ann. "This shit has to stop. I mean, come on."

"I think it's awful what they're doing to Chuck," Ann said. "Just terrible. But Marla hates Chuck."

"Hates him?" I said, incredulous. "Why?"

"I don't know." Ann was holding something back.

"Tell Marla I called." I hung up, remembering the old saying: "There's a thin line between love and hate." I found myself wondering for the first time: What if Chuck had been more than Marla's confidant, big brother, protector, lackey, shrink, agent, and manager? What if they'd been intimate? I called Donald at his office. Finally reached him on his car phone. Told him about the subpoena.

"Ignore it," Donald said.

"I could be held in contempt of court. I have to testify."

"Why're you sticking up for Chuck anyway?"

"I'm not."

"Yes, you are."

I thought about that.

Chuck *had* been a good friend to me over the years. Who wanted to see a friend sent to state prison? Sure, he was guilty of petty larceny; how much are used shoes worth? But it's not like he shot or stabbed anyone, embezzled the church funds, or stole anything of real value.

"Granted, Chuck has problems," I said to Donald. "But he needs a shrink. Not prison. I mean, yes, he's my friend. But he's been a friend to you too."

"So?" Donald said. "What difference does that make?"

I shouldn't have been surprised to hear Donald say that. I mean, I've always known that he wasn't like anyone else. He had his own abstruse standards. Played by his own set of ever-changing rules. His loyalties, personal and business, were reserved for whomever he considered to be a "winner" at any given moment. And he was quick to turn his back on anyone he perceived to be a "loser." And so, his allegiances were fluid, undefined, a matter of shifting conveyances. Which didn't necessarily make him a bad person. Just different. More transparent than some others of his ilk, that's for sure.

"Look, Tom," Donald said. "I don't have time for this shit. I'm fighting for my financial life here. I could lose billions."

"But Chuck—"

"Forget Chuck," Donald said. "What about me?"

"You won't talk to Marla one last time?"

"No. We done?" Donald said. "I've got another call."

"We're done, Donald," I said and hung up the phone.

Much as I hated to be in the middle of all the drama yet again, I was compelled to appear at Chuck's trial. Testified under oath that I'd accompanied Chuck to Marla's Trump Parc residence on several occasions. That I'd witnessed Chuck ask the doorman for Marla's keys, the doorman hand them over. Saw Chuck return the keys to the doorman on the way out. Basically, that was all I had to offer.

Regardless, Chuck was convicted of the "trumped-up" burglary charge and possession of stolen property (worth over $250), and sentenced to four-and-a-half-years in state prison. Which sickened me because I knew for a fact Chuck's prosecution was not about unlawful entry, or stolen shoes, but about Marla's missing diary and nude pictures.

After only four months in jail, Chuck had his conviction overturned on a technicality. But the DA retried him. Acting as his own attorney this time, Chuck was convicted and sent back to prison.

Chapter 39

"You're a fucking snake!" a drunken attorney, Salvatore "Fat Sal" Albino shouted at me from across the bar at Mumbles. It was around seven in the evening. The restaurant was crowded with early-bird diners. I was sitting on a stool alongside Larry Hagman and his wife, Maj. I wasn't in the best of moods, was still processing last week's shocking, accidental death of my acquaintance and onetime potential investor, Dodi Fayed, who'd died in a catastrophic car accident with Princes Diana.

Maj was saying that she wanted to go to the movies and see *Saving Private Ryan*, which had only just premiered. Larry wanted to see another new release *Men In Black*. A few Mumbles regulars were discussing the murder of fashion designer Gianni Versace by Spree killer Andrew Cunanan outside Versace's Miami Beach, Florida, residence. Others were debating why, during the Evander Holyfield vs. Mike Tyson II boxing match in Las Vegas, Mike Tyson had bitten off part of Evander Holyfield's ear. Venessa Williams's new song "Save the Best for Last" played on the bar's sound system.

Fat Sal, who was being held upright and egged-on by an angry and equally drunk policewoman I'd nicknamed "Trench coat Beth," glared at me.

"Him," Fat Sal blubbered and pointed across the bar. "He's a fucking snake!"

Fat Sal was a criminal defense attorney who had defended a cop killer and was a former partner with Bruce Cutler, the "in-house counsel"—according to federal Judge Leo Glasser—for Mafia kingpin John Gotti and the Gambino crime family. Fat Sal was also madly in love with my BFF Joni. Would never believe that Joni and I were best friends and had never been intimate. In his mind, I'd stolen Joni away from him. Joni told me that Fat Sal was a friend, but that they'd never had a dating relationship.

Trench coat Beth—she always wore a grimy Burberry trench coat and chain-smoked cigarettes—scowled at me with hatred in her eyes. Beth, who would one day become one of the highest-ranking female police officials in the NYPD, had had an affair with a married detective friend of mine. Since Beth knew that I knew of the affair, and that I also knew the detective's wife, she deduced that I was the one who outed her and tipped off the wife. Bullshit, of course, but I wouldn't be surprised if Fat Sal put that piece of fiction into her head.

Fat Sal yowled something unintelligible. Broke away from Trench coat Beth. Shot to his feet. Pushed and shoved his way through the crowd, making his way around the bar to confront me. Fortunately for Sal, a Mumbles manager and waiter stopped him.

Hagman whispered to me, "I don't want any trouble."

"There won't be any." I shook my head. "Fat Sal's just drunk."

"Let's go," Hagman said.

I paid our check. We filed out the door, walked one block south to Victory Café, and found spots at the crowded neighborhood pub. Within moments, Hagman had half the bar in stitches mimicking Fat Sal: blubbering, spitting beer up, and calling me a snake.

That was when William L. walked in, accompanied by four attractive young ladies. My radar went up. I waved to William L., who acknowledged me and threaded through the crowd. He introduced us to the ladies, who he said were newly hired American Airlines stewardesses. They were young enough that, until someone mentioned *I Dream of Jennie*, they had no idea who Larry Hagman was.

Blond-haired, blue-eyed with alabaster skin, Sheila G.—who Hagman would nickname "the Ice Princess"—caught my eye. She dazzled me with her smile and I couldn't help but notice that she had the greatest pair of legs I'd ever seen. We chatted and sport flirted for a bit, and I discovered that she was a Stamford, Connecticut native, studied marketing/advertising at Johnson & Wales University, came from a large Irish Catholic family, and was eighteen years my junior. She said she'd worked her way through college as a cocktail waitress. Upon graduation, become a flight attendant because she was bored with her job prospects, loved to travel, and wanted to distance herself from her family.

"I'm the youngest of eleven children," Sheila informed me. "I was a mistake, unplanned." She looked off and the smile slipped from her face. "Unwanted."

My heart went out to her.

Hagman entertained us by being Hagman. We laughed and drank and listened to music. As the night wore on, I felt that Sheila and I had a connection. Told her I'd like to see her again. We began our liaison slowly. Brunches. Movies. Walks in Central Park and along the East River. I showed her around the East and West Village. She showed me around Connecticut. We'd order takeout and watch movies at my apartment, where she met Joni who, having known many of my lady friends, seemed unimpressed. Regardless, it didn't take long before I knew that I wanted to get closer to this sad young girl. Make her happy. Fix her world. We began to date seriously.

Sheila shared an East Eighties apartment with a kookie, emotional waitress/actress who, among other oddities, was in the habit of wearing white geisha makeup daily. When she and her roomie had a falling out, she began to stay overnight at my apartment and before I knew it, she'd moved in. I joked that Joni, Sheila, and I were like the TV show *Three's Company*. Would it were true.

Although my inner circle—i.e., my three sisters, Tom Counihan, John McCooey, Dominick Porco, Larry Hagman, et al.—approved of Sheila G., Joni was circumspect.

"It's not that I don't like Sheila personally," Joni told me on one occasion. She picked up a remote and lowered the sound on one of my favorite TV sitcoms, *Murphy Brown*; I had a crush on Candice Bergen since meeting her at Studio 54. "I don't like her for you," Joni continued. "I mean, what does she bring to the table?"

"She's nice to me," I told Joni.

"So?"

"It's a good start."

"You're an idiot," Joni said.

I turned the TV sound back up.

Soon there was tension between the two women. There was some door slamming. Muttered invectives. They stopped speaking to one another. It became apparent that I was being forced to make a choice; Joni or Sheila had to go. I called my sisters for advice. Their collective response was: "Two beautiful women in the house? You must be insane."

Then Sheila confronted me and demanded I explain a couple of long black hairs she'd found in our bedroom shower, obviously Joni's. I had no idea how they'd gotten there. Had Joni used my shower? She never had before. Was Sheila the type who'd plant those hairs in order to cause a riff and drive Joni out of the apartment? I think I got my answer when I overheard Sheila speak on the phone to one of her girlfriends and realized that, like Fat Sal, she didn't believe that I'd never been intimate with Joni. Didn't believe that any man could be just friends with someone as attractive and vivacious.

"Joni has to go," Sheila told me. "Either she goes or I go."

"I can't kick her out."

"Why? You sleeping with her too?"

Things suddenly worked out when a cop from the 17th precinct who I had sublet mine and Constance's former East

Forty-seventh Street apartment moved out. Joni happily moved in. Just like that, the two women began to get along.

I heard from Ivana Trump soon after Joni moved out — that is, I heard from her attorney. Seems Ivana's former assistant of ten years, Lisa Calandra, was suing Ivana, claiming that she was owed $1.5 million from a Home Shopping Network deal that earned Ivana $30 million. She was also threatening to write a scathing tell-all book. But Calandra had disappeared, gone underground. Ivana's attorney hired me to find her.

Not that I had a relationship with Donald's ex-wife. She would have associated me with Marla, who she saw as an adulteress who'd broken up her marriage. But Ivana needed a decreet investigator, someone who wouldn't sell the story to the tabloids. The attorney knew that I was part of the Trump trusted inner circle.

I contacted friends at the phone and electric companies and found Calandra was living in the same East Forty-seventh Street address where my studio was located and where Joni now lived. I actually spotted Ivana's former assistant in the mail room. Calandra had no idea who I was.

By the way, collecting my fee from Ivana was like pulling teeth. When I complained to the attorney, he said, "You know these people as well as anyone, Thomas. Ivana and Donald don't pay their bills."

I woke at 3:00 a.m. in a cold sweat, a scream caught in my throat. I'd had one of those mind-racing sleepless nights. Dreamed that I was in a plane crash. It was the most frightening, realistic dream I'd ever had in my life.

"You okay?" Sheila said groggily.

I told her I was. Lay back down and took some deep breaths.

My phone rang around 9:00.

"Thomas? It's Diana King," the sister of Roger King, said. "I need your help. Someone tried to kidnap me and my sister."

"When?"
"Last night."
"You call the police?"
"No."
"Where are you?"
"My parents' old place in Fort Lauderdale off of Bayview Drive."

Thanks to Michael Collyer, who I discovered had originally recommended me to Roger King's LA attorney, Harrigan, I'd already handled several minor investigations for Diana and her sister Karen. Background checks mostly for King World new hires. When Diana decided to add safe rooms and state-of-the-art alarm systems in her Manhattan town house and New Jersey estate, I researched construction companies, solicited bids, and suggested the best candidate.

"Keep your doors locked," I told Diana. "I'll have my people there within the hour." I hung up, called my twin brother and Kyle S.—from the old Kew Gardens, Maxwell's Plum days—both of whom had retired from the NYPD and moved to Florida. Told them to get to Diana's house ASAP and secure the premises. I told Sheila what was going on. Then called the airline. Booked the first flight to Fort Lauderdale. It left in two hours. I packed a bag and laptop computer and called a car service.

"LaGuardia," I told the car service driver. "Take the Triboro Bridge." I sat back, gazed out at the heavy traffic. Hoped I'd make my flight.

"They're expecting a foot of snow," the driver informed me. "Supposed to start soon."

I exited the vehicle in front of the American Airlines terminal and dashed inside. Arrived at the gate just as they were boarding. I showed my first-class ticket to the gate agent, walked down the jet bridge, entered the 727, started down the aisle to my seat and all at once remembered the plane crash nightmare from last night. I froze. Looked at my seat. And for the first and only time in my life, I was overcome with paralyzing anxiety. There was no way I could stay on that plane. I spun in panic, knocking into other boarding passengers, excused myself, pushed through them, mumbled something about coming right back, and raced off the plane.

I sat down in the boarding area and caught my breath. What the hell just happened? What was wrong with me? I'd never had a panic attack before. I did some deep breathing exercises, told myself to calm down. I thought about getting back on the plane. I had a job to do. Diana and Karen were depending on me. But the gate agent closed and secured the jet bridge door. The jet pushed back. Heavy snow had begun to fall. The airlines began to delay and cancel flights. Now, how the hell was I going to get to Diana King's Florida residence?

I raced to an Avis counter, rented a car, and headed south.

My twin was standing guard out front when I arrived at Diana King's Bayview Drive home. I stepped out of the rental car. Judging by the clothing bulges, my bro was carrying two weapons, probably a Glock .9mm and a S&W .38 under his Hawaiian shirt.

We shook hands.

"How're things?" I asked him.

"She's frightened, all right. But the whole kidnapping thing sounds off."

"How so?"

"You'll see." He pointed at the rear of the house. "She out back. Her sister Karen left an hour ago. Flew back to LA."

I walked around back. Acknowledged Kyle S., who was across the narrow lawn, guarding the intercostal waterway access. A Walther PPK .9mm hung from a shoulder holster under his right arm.

I took in the spectacular waterfront views. Found Diana in shorts and tank top, sitting inside a large screened-in patio, on a lounge chair alongside a hot tub.

She closed a book, placed it on a side table, greeted me warmly. A servant served iced tea and finger sandwiches while we discussed what had transpired the night before. Bottom line: A man she and her sister had never seen before had rung her doorbell around 10:00. Said he was delivering pizza.

"We didn't open the door, of course," Diana said. "Karen told him we didn't order pizza. But the guy kept insisting we did. Then he pounded on the door, kept trying to get in."

"Did you get a good look at him?"

She said they didn't. That the guy kept a ball cap low, his shirt collar up; he made sure to obscure his face.

"Could you tell his height? Weight? Skin color?"

"White. Five foot ten. Maybe early forties."

"Did you see what he was driving?"

"We didn't think to look. But he had a pizza box in his hand."

I knew what my brother meant by saying he thought the kidnapping attempt sounded off. Not that Diana wasn't being sincere. When you're as rich as she was, kidnapping was always a very real possibility. But this sounded like some kook, maybe even a drunken neighbor, who knew two women were alone in the house and decided to make his move.

"What would you like me to do?" I said.

"Find who the guy was. Make him stop."

That evening, under the cover of darkness, I escorted Diana to her brother Roger's secure compound up in Boca Raton. Then I hired a local, all ex-cop security team, including a female Diana look-alike and staged the Bayview house. Made it look like Diana was home. Alone. I had Sheila G. fly down to act as my assistant.

First thing we did was canvass all pizzerias and fast-food restaurants in a two-square-mile radius. Spread cash-for-information when necessary. No one had received a delivery order from the King women. At the end of two weeks, I was pretty sure I knew who the bogus pizza delivery guy was. Diana employed a part-time maintenance man I'll call Gimpy, who walked with a slight limp and fit the general description. A weirdo who, while we were there, kept showing up unannounced at the Bayview Drive house, booze on his breath. When I asked Gimpy to stay away, he became agitated. I pressed him about his whereabouts the night of the phony pizza delivery. Gimpy said he was home alone watching TV. That, no, he hadn't made or received any phone calls. No neighbor or acquaintance could vouch for him. In other words, Gimpy had no alibi. I had Kyle S. take a clandestine photograph of him. Had prints made. Showed it to local pizzerias. Two recognized Gimpy as a regular customer. But they didn't remember if he'd been in the night in question.

We wrapped things up. I submitted a written report to Diana, which included my suspicions about Gimpy. She didn't fire the guy, just stopped communicating with him. Told me that she'd never feel safe in the Bayview Drive house ever again.

"Would you like me to arrange for full-time personal security?" I said. "An ex-cop who would take care of your security concerns." Diana thought that that was a great idea. And it was. But it turned out to be a dumbassed business move on my part. Because once I found her the right man for the job—a retired lieutenant—I'd never work for Diana King again.

A month later I took Sheila G. to Trump Tower to meet the Trumps. Donald was still at his office when we arrived. Marla was borderline rude and as cold as I've ever seen her. I didn't know if it was her old jealousy—she never did like seeing me with other women—or if she was butting heads with Donald as usual. A phone rang somewhere in the apartment. Marla left us standing in the foyer while she answered. Sheila and I waited for about ten minutes, took the hint, left without saying goodbye.

Soon after, Sheila G. and I decided to marry. Which, in retrospect, didn't make much sense, since we weren't madly in love with each other. I think we were just two lonely people, who got along well and didn't want to be lonely anymore. Although she insisted that I speak to her father first; a quaint, old-fashioned idea. But I played along. Thinking that her parents, who were not as stiff as my first set of in-laws and not as fun as the second, liked me well enough.

"Let's put it this way," her father said when I asked him for his daughter's hand in marriage. We were sitting in his Connecticut living room, enjoying some beer. "I won't interfere."

Not exactly a glowing endorsement.

"Let's elope," Sheila suggested in response to her father's lack of enthusiasm.

I thought that was a great idea.

And so, Joni and actor/producer David Broadnax witnessed at the 141 Worth Street marriage bureau ceremony. We celebrated at Fraunces Tavern at 54 Pearl Street. Opened in 1762, it was New York's oldest and most historic bar.

Afterwards, Sheila insisted that we plan a formal wedding reception. Which I thought was weird. Her thinking, as I recall, was that she wanted her share of wedding gifts. She purchased a full-blown white and frilly wedding dress. We hired a photographer. Took pictures. As a party venue, we chose Dakota, an Upper East Side restaurant owned by a pal of mine, CBS sports producer Tommy O'Neil. We invited about 100 family and friends to the party, including Donald and Marla—they sent regrets. Not that I took offense. I knew from sources that there was trouble in their marriage. Go figure.

The reception was a success. Sheila got her wedding gifts. But she became disenchanted around eight months into our marriage. She wanted to give up the Manhattan apartment, move up to Connecticut, buy a house, and have kids ASAP. But I had no steady income and was still experiencing financial ups and downs; there was no way we could afford a house.

"If you didn't spend so much time writing, you could get a steady job and we could have kids. How long before you give up on writing?"

"Writers don't stop writing," I told her. "It's something I have to do."

That wasn't the answer she wanted.

And so, although we'd only been married for about a year, Sheila decided that if I didn't do things her way, she wanted a divorce. One day she showed up with her mother in tow, packed her belongings, and moved out.

I honestly don't remember much about our short-term marriage. What I do remember was that she was in love with me one day, and not in love with me the next. Like our marriage, my divorce from Sheila G. was short and sweet.

Chapter 40

I WAS SITTING AT HOME, feeling down in the dumps after my third divorce. Wondering why I couldn't make a lasting connection, if I'd ever meet the right one, when Paul Derounian called.

"Coach," Paul said over the phone. "I'm throwing a belated birthday party for Stan Dragoti. I want you to attend. There'll be some single ladies."

Dragoti, a native New Yorker, was an advertising executive—he created the famous "I Love New York" ad campaign in the 1970s to boost tourism—and a successful feature film director whom I knew from Elaine's. It was all over the news when on his way to the 1979 Cannes Film Festival, he was caught trying to smuggle twenty-one grams of cocaine through the Frankfurt, Germany, airport. Told a judge that he'd been driven to drugs by an affair that his then-wife, Cheryl Tiegs, was having with famed photographer Peter Beard. Stan spent eight weeks in jail before a judge released him and suspended his twenty-one-month sentence.

"Where?" I said to Paul. "What time?"

"Thursday," Paul said. "Seven-thirty upstairs at Bruno's on East Fifty-eighth Street."

"Who else is going?"

"I invited Donald and Marla," Paul said.

"They RSVP?"

"Not yet."

"They'll never show. Not after that *National Enquirer* article."

"You're probably right."

The tabloid had recently broken a story about Marla being caught by Florida cops under a lifeguard stand on Delray Beach, in the middle of the night, in a compromising position with a Trump bodyguard. Donald called BS on the story. Threatened to sue the paper.

"Do you think she did it?" Donald asked me immediately after he talked to an *Enquirer* reporter who was asking him to comment. "Was she screwing around?"

Knowing Marla the way I did, knowing that her marriage to Donald was rocky, remembering her wholly inappropriate conduct with Donald's bodyguard Scott Cummings back in the Atlantic City days, I wouldn't put it past her. But I didn't want to stir the pot.

"No," I said. "The *Enquirer* is full of shit."

A tuxedo-clad band was playing an old Glenn Miller tune when I arrived at Bruno's crowded second-floor dining room. The dance floor was crowded with upscale couples. I walked across the floor and entered the private party room, a dark, romantic space. Paul greeted me as soon as I walked in. I slipped off my Burberry trench coat, hung it on a hook. Straightened my black silk-knit tie, said happy birthday to Stan Dragoti—I think he was turning sixty-four years old and looked ten years younger. Got myself a cocktail, sat down with Stan and Paul, and checked out the talent.

There were about thirty people, five women to each guy. One or two of the women looked familiar. I think I'd seen them over the years on modeling go-sees or TV commercial auditions. The others were strangers who I'd wager were new in town. I spotted a gorgeous redhead who appeared to be coming back from the ladies' room. I eased to my feet, flashed my best smile as I approached, and attempted to introduce myself. But she scowled angrily and pushed past me.

Ouch.

I spotted two model types sitting in a dark alcove across the room who were laughing and chatting away. I got within earshot and heard one girl tell the other that the very act of giving a guy oral sex made her orgasm. Interesting. I thought about trying to join in on the conversation, but decided to lay back. Play it cool. I didn't feel like getting shot down by any more angry women that night.

I found myself sitting alone in a corner ten minutes later. Sipping my drink, listening to the live music, thinking about how early I could leave, take a cab up to Elaine's, without offending Paul or Stan.

"Coach," Paul was standing over me. "What's wrong?"

"I'm good, Paul."

"Why aren't you mingling with the girls?"

How to explain?

Fact was, I felt that I was wasting my time being at that party. Sure, it was good to see Paul and the birthday boy. But the whole party scene wasn't fun for me anymore. Granted, I didn't like being alone. But it was better than being with someone I had no connection to. And it had become disheartening—one of the reasons I'd married Sheila —putting myself out there night after night. Going through the endless grind of trying to meet and connect with someone. Getting to know them. Finding out that, for whatever reason, you were not a good match.

"You sure you're okay, coach?"

Three stunning women filed into the room. Ford model Julie Gordon, who I'd modeled with for *Modern Bride* magazine, saw me, dashed across the room, and jumped on my lap. Things were looking up. After smothering each other with hugs and cheek pecks, Julie introduced me to Cheryl V., another Ford model I recalled seeing several times at both McMullen's and Herlihy's. Cheryl and I shook hands.

"And this," Julie said, "is Cheryl's sister Wendy."

Wendy stepped out from behind her sister. She was petite, a beautiful brunette with even features, full lips, and large, catlike blue-green eyes. She reminded me of the actress Anne Archer, only more attractive.

"Hi, Wendy."

"Let's dance." She grabbed my hand.

"I don't dance."

"Why not?"

"I'm as graceful," I said, "as an alligator falling out of a tree."

"Funny," she said and dragged me out to the main dining room and onto the dance floor. Little did I know that that alpha female was to be the next and last great love of my life.

At the end of the evening, I agreed to escort the three women back to Julie's apartment on Lexington Avenue, a few blocks away from my own residence. As I delivered the women safely to the doorman, Wendy and I made plans to meet the next day for lunch before she and her sister headed to JFK to catch a flight back home to San Diego. We rendezvoused at 12:30 at Victory Café on Third Avenue and Ninetieth Street. Flirted over Bloody Marys.

"Tell me about yourself, Wendy."

"What would you like to know?"

"Everything."

Wendy smiled. Said she'd grown up in Bel Air, California, across the street from producer Aaron Spelling. Besides her sister, she had a brother. She'd married her high school sweetheart, who she'd been with for fourteen years until he decided that he didn't want to be married anymore.

"Were there other people involved?" My way of asking if she or her ex had an affair.

"No. Brad and I married too young." Wendy went on to say that they had two young daughters and owned three restaurants with her ex: two in Del Mar—Cilantro and Epazote— and a fast-food taco place in downtown San Diego. "Brad's the one who wanted to be single," Wendy said. "I was happy being married."

We found ourselves holding hands over two more Bloody Marys. Agreed that long-distance relationships were impossible.

But we exchanged phone numbers just the same. I paid the check. Held Wendy's hand as we walked back to Julie's apartment.

"Thanks for the drinks," Wendy said as we entered the building lobby, walked past a distracted doorman, his face buried in the *Daily News*. Wendy pushed the *up* button on the elevator. Turned and looked up into my eyes. I pulled her to me, slid my arms around her tiny waist, and kissed her full lips—a kiss filled with surprising emotion and heat. I had to stop and catch my breath. The elevator door opened. Wendy broke the embrace, smiled seductively. "Be seeing you, handsome." She entered the elevator. Pushed a button. The doors closed in my face.

Our relationship blossomed slowly with the help of email. She asked me if I'd email her some of my short stories, which I did. One of her favorites was "The Paranoid Elite"—a short story I'd recently written about working for the mercurial billionaire Ron Perelman.

Sure, we spoke on the phone most days, but emails gave us the chance to get to know each other in a unique way. (The Tom Hanks and Meg Ryan romantic comedy, *You've Got Mail*, wouldn't be released for another year or two.) Through those daily emails, I discovered that Wendy was romantic, intelligent, aware, hardworking, a devoted parent with an abundance of rare, down-to-earth common sense.

A few weeks later, I flew out west for a star-studded party at Larry Hagman's Malibu beach house. Got to meet Patrick Duffy, Linda Gray, Steve Kanaly, Charlene Tilton, Victoria Principal—basically the cast of the TV series *Dallas,* among others. Stayed the weekend. Then I drove south. Got a room at the Marina del Ray hotel. Asked Wendy to join me. That was where we really connected.

Remember when O.J. Simpson and I were standing on the balcony at Studio 54 and had agreed that our type of woman was whoever was nice to us? Well, Wendy was nice to me. There was no attitude, games, or, even after several cocktails, no drama or nutty behavior. Sparks flew, then burst into flame. After that weekend, I knew that I wanted and needed Wendy in my life.

I began to fly out to Del Mar and rent short-term apartments. Since Wendy had custody of her girls Monday through Friday, she and I spent weekends together.

It took a while for me to get to know the two girls, and for them to get to know me. Lauryn and Faye were understandably standoffish at first, but gradually grew accustomed to my being around. My trained eye told me that both girls would blossom into world-class beauties one day. I told Wendy as much.

"You're going to have two heartbreakers on your hands."

Occasionally, I flew Wendy back to New York for long weekends, which as a nervous flyer—especially after a ValuJet crashed in Everglades, killing all 110 passengers and crew and then TWA Flight 800 exploded over waters of eastern Long Island, killing all 230 aboard—was becoming more challenging.

But Wendy loved the city. Enjoyed our predinner martinis at the Carlyle's Bemelmans Bar, fine dining, West Village jazz clubs, museums, and of course the shopping. And, oh yeah, she also got to meet Joni as well as my three sisters. They all liked Wendy. More importantly they liked her for me.

"She's a lot better," my sister Patricia said, "than the batshit crazy, jiggling jugheads you usually date."

Joni told me, "You're not so stupid." A high compliment coming from Joni. She and I were in a taxi, on our way to the Hilton Hotel on Sixth Avenue. We were attending a New York City Police Foundation annual fundraiser.

"Wendy's normal," Joni continued. "You've finally found a good one. Took you long enough."

"Look who's talking," I said, referring to the fact that six months ago she'd finally met and married a terrific guy. Larry L. was a retired Air Force B-52 pilot and currently an American Airlines pilot. Our taxi pulled to the curb.

Joni and I entered the hotel, took the up escalator. As we crossed a ballroom and headed to our reserved table, Donald, sans Marla, rushed into our path, shook my hand, kissed Joni on the cheek.

"Tom's a great guy," Donald said to Joni. "A great guy. A really great guy."

Joni smirked. "Define *great*."

"Tom kept his mouth shut in the old days. He's the only one. He's a great guy." Donald moved on to shake Ron Perelman's hand.

"What was that all about?" Joni said as we took our seats.

"I'm not sure. Maybe that I never betrayed him to the media?"

"So?" Joni said. "Neither did I."

"We were the only two," I said, referring to the fact that Marla's own mother, father, her guru Kim, and a dozen other "insiders" had all sold stories to the tabloids.

Chapter 41

THE BICOASTAL ROUTINE I WOUND up following was three months in Del Mar with Wendy and the girls. Three months in New York. Financially, it was stressful, since I was still paying for various short-term rentals in San Diego, plus my NYC apartment rent. Although a string of short-term, NYC roommates helped tremendously. Still, I had to work hard at earning cash to pay expenses.

I took a high-paying temporary gig bodyguarding a Saudi prince—since there are over four thousand, I don't recall which one—who was staying at New York's Waldorf Astoria Hotel.

Thanks to a TV commercial director friend, I booked an acting gig for Carnival Cruise Lines. A five-day shoot sailing on a ship out of Miami. Kathie Lee Gifford, under a long-term contract as the cruise line's spokesperson, was to be the principal star. Fitness guru Richard Simmons was also booked for the gig.

"Yes, of course I remember you," Kathie Lee said when I came on board. "You're Marla's ex." She turned to her husband. "You remember Thomas, right, Frank?"

Frank Gifford rolled his eyes.

Shortly after the Carnival Cruise shoot, I met with my police lieutenant father's former partner's son, Charles Rose, and told him I was looking for work. A Yorkville neighbor, Charles was a top-tier former federal prosecutor who'd fought classic courtroom battles with Mafia bosses—like Vincent (the Chin) Gigante and Colombia drug cartels. He'd left the US Attorney's office to become a partner at De Feis O'Connell & Rose. Law firms always needed investigators.

"You have any experience," Charles said, "with white-collar crime? Banking or securities fraud?"

I said I didn't.

We were sitting at the bar in the Carlow East, on the very same stools Jack Tupper and I had occupied just before Buddy Jacobson murdered him.

"Have you done much surveillance?" Charles said.

"Sure."

"There's a US Attorney friend that I can recommend you to. He's conducting an organized crime investigation. You might be a good fit."

"How so?"

"This is strictly confidential," Charles said. "The target is someone you know."

I thought I knew where this was going. "Grayman?"

"Grayman."

I shook my head. I'd always had a live-and-let-live attitude with the Yorkville hoods. And I must admit, although I didn't approve of how they made their living, I was fond of a few of them. Especially Grayman. "Thanks. But no thanks."

"I understand," Charles said. "We don't have anything right now, but I'll let you know if things change."

After that meeting, Charles seemed to withdraw from the social scene. I no longer saw him carousing at our usual haunts. He didn't return several phone calls. Unbeknownst to me, he had come down with brain cancer and would pass away two years later.

I got a call from a headhunting firm that placed bodyguards and took a gig driving Charles Koppelman, a music producer and businessman who founded SBK Records and held an executive position at EMI Records. The first day, which happened to be Christmas day, I drove "Mr. K" and his family to see the film *Nixon*, had the pleasure of meeting his lovely wife Bunny and a couple of their well-mannered children. But by the third day it was obvious that Koppelman had some sort of problem with me.

I can count on one hand the number of people I'd met in my life that I didn't get along with. Not that I thought everyone was a TF fan. But after being in the Navy and NYPD, I'd learned how to adapt, adjust, acclimate, compromise, do whatever it took to make a business relationship work. There was no getting along with Koppelman.

Although I had the feeling that for whatever reason I intimidated him, I never would know what Koppelman's problem was. Not that I cared. Sometimes things don't work out. I resigned a few days later.

It was difficult, but I managed to support my bicoastal lifestyle. To make money in Del Mar, besides working on my writing, I became a computer consultant of sorts. I was one of the few that had mastered the early computer operating system language called DOS. In those days, personal computers came blank more or less. You had to purchase software programs separately. Those programs had to be loaded onto the computer and the computer's system setup files—the autoexe.bat, config.sys—manually written using a DOS line editing program Edlin.

I looked for security work in San Diego. Didn't find anything that suited me. I started a criminal background-checking business, figuring that—what with so many local affluent households employing nannies and cooks and estate managers—there'd be a market. I was wrong about that. I tried to make friends with the San Diego cops, thinking that could lead to work. But the cops I met were not forthcoming. There wasn't any esprit de corps. From what I could gather, they were not close-knit like big city cops. They didn't have "cop bars" or restaurants that they frequented.

I did luck out when a bartender at an upscale hotel, L'Auberge's, told me about a transplanted New Yorker who'd retired from the New York City Fire Department. Wendy and I literally bumped into Danny Noonan at that same lobby bar a few weeks later. Discovered within minutes that we'd met before. Noonan had worked at the South Bronx's Engine Company 82, Ladder 31 on Intervale Avenue at the same time I worked as a cop with Richie G. in Fort Apache a few blocks away. (Another firefighter acquaintance, Dennis Smith, had written a bestselling book about that very busy firehouse, *Report from Engine Co. 82*.) Noonan, a writer, documentary filmmaker, and much sought-after speaker on fire-safety issues, had also co-owned a string of firefighter bars in New York City called Suspenders that I'd frequented over the years.

Danny and I became fast friends. He introduced me to everyone worth knowing in Del Mar. Although he couldn't help me land any security work, we would go on to write an article together titled "Red Star of Death"—the story of the 1975 telephone company building fire where over 700 unsuspecting firefighters encountered toxic, cancer-causing burning PCPs for the very first time. We would sell the story to *New York* magazine.

Eventually, Wendy and I rented a house together in Carmel Valley, next door to Del Mar. We attended an open house. Had to bid against a half-dozen interested renters. We lingered at the open house, cornered the Realtor and, although I didn't have much cash in the bank, I offered to pay the entire first year's rent in advance. The Realtor declined my offer, but rented us the house. One week later I rented a U-Haul. Wendy—who I affectionately nicknamed "the Little Boss"—organized and supervised the move. I did the grunt work. Then, with the help of a Navy SEAL I'd befriended, I built a professional home gym in our two-car garage.

Living with the love of my life and the girls in the 2,414-square-foot, 4-bedroom, 2.5 bath house, with a pool/hot-tub combo that looked like a giant penis, were to be the happiest, most peaceful days of my life. Wendy understood me and accepted me in a way that no one else ever had. As a result, I looked forward to every sunrise. Every sunset. Slept contentedly and dreamlessly at night. Although Wendy insisted that, during the week, I sleep in the office/bedroom downstairs. She and the girls' bedrooms were on the second floor.

We hosted Halloween parties, Christmases, and Thanksgiving dinners in that house. Invited local friends and friends from New York. Dominick Porco came to visit. As did Joni and her hubby Larry, Chuck Jones, Larry Hagman and Maj.

For someone from my background, I found it challenging adjusting to the quiet life in an idyllic, immaculately clean hamlet like Del Mar. No police or fire sirens woke me up in the middle of the night. No endlessly screeching car alarms. No calls for help. No gunshots, or city garbage trucks banging around, waking the neighborhood at 4:00 a.m. There were no squeegee men, homeless people relieving themselves in public, or aggressive beggars, or violent street gangs to evade. No one tried to shake down Wendy's thriving restaurants for protection money. No one stuck a gun in her face and demanded she empty out her safe. Street crime was nonexistent. And, unlike suspicious, belligerent, and often hostile New Yorkers, the people in Del Mar were open, warm, friendly.

However, I did pick out a few Mob types. To me they stuck out like a sore thumb: slick, shifty, incongruously dressed for the climate and environment. I didn't know if they were active in their nefarious professions or hiding out in the federal witness protection program. But I usually noticed them at restaurants close to the world-famous Del Mar racetrack. I always kept my distance.

Until this one evening.

Wendy and I were sitting at the busy bar in a classic, old-world-style steakhouse called Red Traction across the street from the track, sipping martinis while waiting for a table. An aging, central casting wiseguy-type character—sharkskin suit, thin tie, imported Italian shoes—sat at a stool beside us, ordered a Cutty and water. He turned to Wendy and introduced himself as Vito G.

"I love your accent," Wendy said.

"Yeah?" Vito said. "I'm from Brooklyn."

I glanced around and spotted Vito's 250-pound henchman standing by the entrance. The sharkskin-suited goon's beefy arms were folded across his massive chest. Alarm bells went off in my head. My instincts told me to get Wendy away from that active-duty mobster. But there was no way to make a move without causing a cringeworthy scene. Besides, our table would be ready soon and the old guy was being polite and quite charming.

"Youse two make a nice couple," Vito said. "Me? I was married for twenty-five-years. Had the best wife. She was perfect for me. She passed away two years ago."

The bartender served Vito's drink.

"I can't tell you how much I miss her. I miss her every day." Vito began to tear up. "I really loved her."

"Aw," Wendy sympathized. Reached out and patted the old guy's liver-spotted hand. "That's so sweet."

"I mean it." Vito sipped his drink. "I really loved her. Wanna know how much I loved her?"

Wendy nodded.

"All the years we waz together, I made certain that she never knew about my *goomah*."

Oh, shit.

"Pardon?" Wendy said.

"*Goomah*. You know, girlfriend. I usta have a lotta girlfriends. I made sure my wife never knew. That's how much I loved her."

Wendy went rigid. I knew what was coming.

"Some a the guys," Vito went on cluelessly, "they flaunted, shit where they ate. Not me. I loved my wife."

"You cheating son of a bitch!" Wendy shot to her feet.

Vito reared back. "What?"

"You're an asshole!"

The entire restaurant came to a standstill.

"What's your fuckin' problem, lady?"

Wendy got in the guy's face. The bartender raced down the bar, telling Wendy to "Calm down, miss." Next thing I knew Vito's goon was looming menacingly behind me. "Fuck is goin' on?"

"Wendy." I took her by the arm. "Stop." I pulled her away. Threw money on the bar. "We're leaving."

Chapter 42

Unlike many of the women I'd been involved with, Wendy was an avid reader. My first wife wasn't. My second and third wives read "chick lit" that they traded with girlfriends. Wendy chose her books from the *New York Times Book Review* and Oprah Winfrey's book club. We read and exchanged the same books, compared notes. Agreed on most.

Because of our sometimes spirited discussions about the veracity and importance of various literature, I became most impressed with Wendy's insights into people, dialogue, character, and plot development. Wendy read everything I wrote. Offered praise as well as constructive criticism. She was my beta reader. My most helpful and perceptive critic. My source of writing inspiration. My savage muse.

Our Sunday routine was to breakfast at Milton's Jewish deli in Del Mar, where we'd buy a copy of the *New York Times*. Flip though and organize the various sections. Discuss the book reviews, what we'd read next, while we ate. Then adjourn to Powerhouse Park, find an empty public bench, or spread a blanket on the grass under a tree, and read the paper. Something, because of the risk of being victimized by ambush predators, we'd never do in New York parks.

On one summer Sunday, we scored a bench on a high bluff overlooking the Pacific and divided up the *Times*. Sipped coffee from to-go cups. Traded sections back and forth.

I began to peruse a horrifying story about an earthquake in Izmit, Turkey, where over 17,000 were killed—I can't even imagine—and 44,000 injured when Wendy said, "Looks like your ex and Trump are finally divorced."

"I know." According to my sources, Marla had become unbearably controlling and pretentious during the marriage. They fought publicly and often. For the past six months the tabloids had featured pictures of Donald with various beautiful women. I hadn't seen or spoken to him much after the *National Enquirer* published the bodyguard tryst article. But I knew through the grapevine that he was still mortified. Especially after the bodyguard sold his story to a tabloid, finally admitting the affair. That, I knew, would be the final humiliation. The marriage death rattle. It was only a matter of time before Donald found another hottie to replace Marla. He'd work hard at it—which was why he'd recently founded a model agency, Trump Model Management.

"Disgusting," Wendy commented. "Looks like she lost him how she got him." Referring to the fact that Marla had stolen Donald away from Ivana. Now a new mistress or mistresses would take her place.

I had been planning to contact Donald, but I didn't know if congratulations or commiseration were in order. Or if he suspected that I was sympathetic to Marla. Which I was. And so, I procrastinated. Wished I hadn't. Because on June 25, 1999, Donald's father, Fred Trump, died. He was ninety-three years old. I attended the wake at Frank E. Campbell Funeral Chapel on Madison Avenue, a short walk from my apartment. Sent Donald a Gregorian Mass card. (Gregorian Masses consist of a series of thirty Masses offered on consecutive days for the soul of a deceased person.) Received a handwritten thank-you note and a phone call during which Donald and I planned to get together in the coming weeks. But I missed Wendy and the girls and flew back to San Diego. Was there a few months later when acquaintance JFK Jr., his wife Carolyn, and sister-in-law, en route to a Hyannis Port, Massachusetts wedding, died in a private-plane crash. I sent a Mass card to his former 20 North Moore

Street address in Tribeca figuring, since his mother died in 1994, that his sister Caroline would eventually receive it. I'm pretty sure John McCooey attended the invitation-only memorial service held at St. Thomas More Catholic Church, a parish that John-John had often attended with his mother and sister.

My life with Wendy in Del Mar—up early, driving the girls to and from school, to dance classes, soccer practices, to and from their friends' houses, helping Wendy with the catering end of the restaurant business—changed my life in New York. My world became more exclusive. I no longer frequented the trendy clubs every night or the hot new restaurants. Had no desire to stay out late and carouse with my friends. I was happy dining early in my neighborhood or alone at home. Spending time with my three sisters or Joni and her hubby, Larry. Emailing and speaking to Wendy on the phone. Concentrating on my writing and finding PI or bodyguard gigs. (I'd become overexposed in the TV commercial/modeling world and no longer auditioned.) Trying to earn enough money to maintain my lifestyle. Not an easy task.

I celebrated the new millennium with Wendy at a house party in Del Mar. We toasted with champagne and watched the record-setting crowds and ball-drop in Times Square. That spring Wendy and I had dinner at "21". I'd performed an in-depth forensic financial-background check on a potential restaurant investor for one of the owners and, in lieu of cash, had agreed to accept dinners as payment. Businessman Ron Perelman was seated with his fourth wife, actress Ellen Barkin, at a table across the main floor dining room. Film director and Trump Tower resident, Steven Spielberg, still riding high on the success of *Saving Private Ryan*, was seated with his second wife, Kate Capshaw, at a table to our left. I realized how starstruck Wendy was when she got all excited watching actress Julia Roberts walk past our table on her way out of the restaurant. I spotted Donald and his brother Robert and his wife Blaine coming in the front door. On his arm was a stunning model who I'd later learn was Melania Knauss. I hadn't laid eyes on Donald since his mother, Mary, died. Joni and I attended the service at Marble Collegiate Church on Fifth Avenue. I sent another Gregorian Mass card.

I waved to Donald. He waved back. Gestured that I should join them upstairs. But since Wendy had made it clear that she despised unfaithful men and had no respect for Donald, I knew better than to suggest that we join him.

Everyone remembers where they were on 9/11. I happened to be in New York. On the phone. Gazing out of my wide-open apartment windows, breathing in the fresh air, enjoying the crystal clear, sunny September day. Discussing the feasibility of taking on another stalker case with a gentleman who was in the collectable wristwatch business, a bicoastal San Diego-New York commuter like me. He was requesting that I deal with a twenty-one-year-old bartender who was stalking his nineteen-year-old daughter, a freshman at Marymount Manhattan on East Seventy-first Street. They'd dated a few times. The girl broke it off, but the boy wouldn't take no for an answer. The father had already filed a police report and there was an order of protection/restraining order in place.

"Technically, he's abiding by the terms of the restraining order," the exasperated father told me over the phone. "He hasn't tried to contact her. He keeps at least one hundred feet away—which is the issue. He's one hundred and ten feet away. Everywhere she goes. Day and night. He's there. Waiting. Watching. She's terrified."

"I'm not sure if I can help," I told the father. "If the guy doesn't violate the restraining order…"

"I'll pay you ten-thousand dollars cash to make him go away. Now. Today. I don't care how you do it. Put him in the hospital. Make him disappear for all I care. Just make him leave my kid alone." He broke the connection.

I hung up, stepped over to my open window, gazed out at LaGuardia Airport. Watched as a Continental Airlines twin-engine turboprop plane rose into the morning sky, heading east into the morning sun. I paced my apartment, tried to figure out how to earn that cash. Maybe I'd confront the stalker, get in his face. Try explaining that, although dumb Hollywood movies and romance novels teach men that when a woman says "no" she means "yes," that was not the real world. If that didn't work, I could always get into the guy's private life. Give him something to worry about besides a woman.

My phone rang. I snatched it up.

"What?"

"A plane just hit the World Trade Center," an ex-cop friend now living in Pompano Beach, Florida, said.

"So? It happens," I said, thinking of one of those single engine Piper Cubs like JFK Jr. had been killed in back in 1999. Or maybe a lighter-than-air aircraft had lost its way or been blown off course and into the building.

"No," my friend said. "It was an airliner."

"An airliner?"

I hung up. Turned on the news.

Saw that the north tower was burning. I was trying to figure out how that could possibly happen on a perfectly clear September day—a catastrophic navigational, mechanical malfunction?—when a second airliner crashed into the south tower. What the hell?

I phoned and woke Wendy. Told her what was happening. That I was safe. Told her to put on the news. A few minutes later, a newscaster said that all bridges and tunnels into Manhattan were closed, subways halted, isolating the island. Then all US airspace was shut down. All operating aircraft were ordered to land at the nearest airport.

I hung up with Wendy and phoned my brother and three sisters. Everyone was accounted for. Although my sister Maureen's son worked in the financial district. No one had heard from him that morning. But the phone circuits were being overloaded, so there was no need to panic. Yet.

At 9:59 the south tower collapsed.

My sister Maureen called. Her son was okay.

The north tower fell at 10:28.

Joni's husband Larry called around 1:00 and, after expressing our mutual outrage, said we should get to an ATM pronto, get cash just in case we had to stock up on food and bottled water. The streets were eerily quiet when I met Larry in front of my building and walked to a cash machine. The private ATMs were already out of cash, so we walked a few blocks west to a Citibank. Withdrew the maximum. Headed back home.

As we turned off East Ninety-first Street onto Third Avenue, we were startled by what we saw: A long line of ghostlike people covered head to toe with white ash, marching in utter silence north on the avenue. It was an unnerving sight. Something out of a movie portrayal of a zombie apocalypse. But since public transit was suspended, the bridges and tunnels closed, the people were being forced to walk off the island if they wanted to make it to their homes.

No one knew what to expect next. The TV newscasters said terrorists were behind the attack. Some speculated that, since the Russian military had admitted it lost track of upwards of 100 nuclear suitcase bombs, a nuclear attack could very well be the next. I was happy that Wendy and the girls were safe in Del Mar.

The airports reopened two days later, as did bridges and tunnels. Limited subway and bus service resumed. I phoned the collectible wristwatch dealer and declined the stalker job. Suggested that, as the girl's father, he confront the stalker himself. Have witnesses present. Videotape the encounter. Be sympathetic to the brokenhearted youth, but firm.

Then I booked the first flight I could back to San Diego. Found as soon as I landed that everything seemed disconcertingly normal. There was no outrage. People were going about their lives. There was little or no talk about the horror taking place in New York City. There was none of the systemic anger, shock, tears, and calls for bloody revenge that I'd left behind. This might not be fair to say, but the people I encountered during the next few weeks seemed unmoved by what happened on 9/11, as if it had taken place in a foreign land.

The next twelve months revealed that 2996 people had died in the 9/11 attacks. That the terrorists hijackers—nineteen men, fifteen of which were citizens of Saudi Arabia, were members of the militant Islamist group Al Qaeda. Which to me meant the end of al-Qaeda. I knew the USA would hunt them down. Stop at nothing to avenge 9/11.

"Ha-ha!" Wendy said. It was late on a Monday morning and we were sipping Starbucks coffees—I'm not a fan—sharing a table in one of our favorite hangouts, the Del Mar Public Library. I was flipping through a stack of news magazines. Wendy was reading a hardcover book.

"Ha-ha, what?"

"It says here," Wendy said, "that Trump's driver and bodyguard Thomas Fitzsimmons, a former cop, tried to convince him that he should run for president." Wendy looked at me. "I thought you never worked for Trump."

"I never did. And I don't remember ever talking to him about running for president. Mayor or governor? Maybe."

"So, why would the author write that?"

"Who's the author?"

Wendy held the book up. *Trump: The Deals and the Downfall* by Wayne Barrett.

"I don't know Wayne Barrett."

"It says here that you introduced Trump to Marla Maples," Wendy said accusingly. "Did you?"

Uh-oh. I saw where this was going. If I had introduced them, Wendy would see that as me helping Donald cheat on his wife. "More bullshit."

"It also says you sold Marla to Trump."

"What?"

Wendy read: *"Fitzsimmons had been dating Maples himself since she arrived in New York as an aspiring actress. In exchange for his 'relinquishing her to Trump' and serving as the couple's 'beard' on helicopter rides and at boxing matches, Trump indulged Fitzsimmons's Hollywood aspirations, paying $15,000 to commission a screenplay for a film called* Blue Gemini *that would star him, his twin brother, and Maples."*

"That's preposterous."

"What part?"

"All of it."

"Why would he write lies?"

"Because tabloid reporters make shit up. And they never understood my relationship with Donald. Why he'd befriend a lowly cop. So, they made up several fabrications they felt comfortable with. You wouldn't believe some of the crap I've read. You've gotta trust me on that."

Wendy regarded me skeptically.

Not that I blamed her.

It was all so surreal.

I glanced out a window, toward the blue Pacific, and had to admit that, in retrospect, being in the middle of the Donald-Marla relationship debacle had been a high-octane good time. Fleeing rabid paparazzi. Dodging amoral, high-paid tabloid reporters and their investigators and undercover agents. All in order to aid and abet the media fugitive, Marla Ann Maples.

And I'd led the high life for a few years. Sailed on Donald's yacht, flew on his helicopters. Enjoyed carte blanche at his hotels and casinos. I met the most interesting people: A-list actors, sports figures, singers, politicians, and businesspeople. I attended all the best parties, plays, concerts, and ate in the best restaurants. Then there was the fact that Donald always insisted that he pay for everything.

Of course, there had been a big letdown when it was all over. My phone stopped ringing. The paparazzi and reporters disappeared. I was no longer a pseudo-celebrity.

Not that I missed being close to Donald or Marla. We weren't estranged exactly, but what with all that had gone on, I didn't see us being close friends in the future.

Chapter 43

Michael Collyer called from New York in early October. I was in our Carmel Valley home, probably working on *Confessions of a Catholic Cop*, marvelling at the perfect weather. Another day in paradise.

"I have something you might be interested in. An A-list celebrity is being stalked. You available?"

I had to stop and think about that.

I wasn't due to fly back to New York for another month. I hated to leave Wendy and the girls. But we needed the money. As it was, Wendy was becoming impatient with my long absences and me trying to transition from being a PI/bodyguard to making a living as a writer. Still my biggest fan, she was frustrated and couldn't wrap her head around the fact that I was no closer to selling a book project or screenplay for big money than the day we met.

"It's not just about writing a good book," I'd explained to her. "It's connections. Timing. And above all, *luck*. Finding an agent or producer that's looking for my type of story."

"Thomas?" Collyer said. "You there?"

"I'm here. Yes, I'm available."

"I'm not at liberty to divulge the client's identity. But fax me a copy of your résumé, along with some references. I'll forward them. If they're interested, I'll arrange for you to meet their executive assistant. When are you back in town?"

"I'll fly back tomorrow."

Two days later, I slipped on a dark gray pinstripe business suit, black knit tie, and Gucci-like loafers and took a taxi to 825 Eighth Avenue, thirtieth floor. On the way into the lobby, I checked the building directory, perused the thirtieth-floor tenants. There was only one production company: Further Films. I found a lobby pay phone, called Joni. She'd recently switched jobs and was now working for a former FBI agent who was the director of security at Paine Webber, as his executive assistant.

"What do you want, dog breath?" Joni said.

"Do me a favor?" I said. "Look up who owns a production company, Further Films?"

"Sure. I've got nothing else to do with my time but stop everything and do you favors." Clicking of a computer keyboard. "Further Films," Joni said. "Offices at eight-twenty-five Eighth Avenue? Owner is the actor, Michael Douglas."

"Thanks."

"Thanks? That's it? Just 'thanks'?"

"I owe you a drink?"

"No one likes you very much," Joni said.

Julianne B., Michael Douglas's executive assistant, greeted me at the thirtieth-floor elevator, and led me into a rather large, bare-bones office. Like most production people I'd met over the years, the petite, attractive thirtysomething blonde was dressed ultracasual, jeans and a T-shirt. The interview was straightforward. Julianne had read my résumé and asked pertinent questions.

"Have you dealt with stalkers before?"

"Many times."

"Have you worked with A-list celebrities?"

"I have."

"Well," she said, glancing down at my résumé. "Your references are most impressive." I can't remember who I'd used as references, but since the potential employer was in showbiz, I most probably listed Larry Hagman, Carroll O'Connor, and Barbara Walters's hubby, movie mogul Merv Adelson.

Although she didn't mention names, Julianne proceeded to tell me a bit about her employer. At that point I realized that the person being stalked was not Michael Douglas (MD) but his wife, Catherine Zeta-Jones (CZJ). I did not let on that I'd exercised alongside MD at Mid-City Gym or that we'd conversed at Donald's *Art of the Deal* book party at Trump Tower and at the Directors Guild of America awards ceremony. Not that MD would remember me.

I got the call to return to Further Films a day later, where Julianne informed me that I'd been hired. She handed me some paperwork to fill out. I handed her xeroxed copies of my driver's license, NYS Department of State ID, as well my concealed-carry pistol license.

"I'll need your cell phone number," Julianne said.

"I don't have a cell phone."

"You'll need to get one ASAP."

"I'll get one today."

She then told me my new client's name. I acted duly impressed.

"Tell me about the stalker?"

Julianne said that an unknown person had sent CZJ more than two-dozen threatening letters and made repeated phone calls to her agents and hotels where the couple would stay, threatening to "slice her up and feed her to her dogs. Blow her brains out like JFK. Cut her throat the way that O.J. did to Nicole Simpson. Slice her up like Charles Manson did to Sharon Tate."

"I'm assuming they've filed a police report?"

"The LAPD is investigating."

"I'll need the name of the detective working the case." Julianne wrote down the information, handed it over. I was then told the location of the company SUV and given my first assignment. Pick up Catherine Zeta-Jones tomorrow at Teterboro Airport and escort her to the couple's twenty-million-dollar Central Park West apartment.

As soon as I got back to my apartment, I phoned the LAPD detective handling the stalker case and identified myself. The detective said they were making progress. They'd lifted fingerprints off several of the threatening letters and were in the process of running those prints though the FBI's database. I asked him to please keep me in the loop. Then I walked to the nearest Verizon store and purchased my very first cell phone. I phoned Julianne and gave her the number.

The following morning, I slipped into a bulletproof vest, pulled a white dress shirt over it, and tied my tie. Then I checked that my .38 Smith & Wesson Bodyguard gun was loaded. Clipped the weapon, along with a leather pouch containing extra rounds, to my belt. Pulled on my suit jacket and tan Burberry trench coat and drove to Teterboro.

I stood in the terminal as Michael and Catherine Douglas deplaned. I approached and introduced myself. Michael did a double take when he shook my hand, gave me a look of puzzled recognition. Catherine shook my hand and hit me with her million-dollar smile. She was one of the most beautiful women I'd ever seen.

Michael walked Catherine to the SUV as the skycaps placed her luggage in the back. He tipped them generously, kissed Catherine, said he loved her, and headed back to the airplane; he was flying on to another destination. I got Catherine settled in the back seat. She made and received several phone calls on our way to the city. I drove in silence. "Speak when spoken to" is a celebrity bodyguard's mantra. If and when Catherine wanted to talk, she'd let me know.

Basically, the gig was this: The Douglases' primary residence was on Bermuda, a ninety-minute flight from NYC. Michael's mother, Diana Love Webster Douglas, was born in Devonshire, Bermuda, allowing Michael dual citizenships: United States and the United Kingdom. They flew into New York approximately ten days each month, during which I was on call 24-7, ready to respond to their needs at a moment's notice. Working sixteen-hour days was not unusual. There were several twenty-hour days. Not that I'm complaining. The Douglases were dream clients; low maintenance. Polite. Considerate. And they paid overtime after eight hours.

But I was initially resented and treated with some disdain by CZJ's "controlling" PR people in LA for attempting to initiate security procedures that would prioritize her safety above all else. I was shocked by their willingness to risk her physical well-being for publicity. More than once I felt powerless to protect her when, against my vehement objections, they placed her life in the hands of swarming, aggressive fans who surrounded her and, on at least one occasion, nearly knocked her to the ground.

Then there were the various NY, LA, and Bermuda members of the Douglas family's rivalrous employees whose duplicity and jealousies—all trying to cull favor with MD and CZJ—caused occasional palace intrigue. I made it a point to stay out of all of it.

Carys Zeta Douglas weighed six pounds, twelve ounces when delivered early Easter morning, April 20, 2003, at Valley Hospital in Ridgewood, New Jersey, a suburb of New York City. The hospital was chosen to maintain privacy and keep the press—who'd staked out the CPW apartment in hopes of getting the first million-dollar photo of the newest Douglas child—at bay. Under cover of darkness, three days before she was scheduled to deliver, I snuck CZJ and MD out of the CPW apartment and drove them to Valley Hospital.

Best-laid plans ... twenty-four hours after the birth, the plan was for me to park in the hospital's rear lot. After making sure that no press was hanging around, meet CZJ, MD, and the infant at an obscure, locked NO ENTRANCE side door, and escort them to the SUV. But as I approached the door, someone opened it, a nurse dumped the infant into my arms, and slammed the door in my face. WTF?

Where were MD and CZJ? Was I expected to wait for them? Or secure the infant in the SUV? I decided on the latter. Carried Carys to the SUV, opened the rear door, and set her on the back seat.

"Well, Carys, darling. Welcome to the world."

She ignored me.

"I'll bet you'll grow up to be a princess and marry a handsome prince who will love your forever. What do you think about that?"

Carys gurgled.

MD and CZJ walked out of the hospital door.

The stalker, Dawnette Knight, was arrested June 3, 2004 at her Beverly Hills apartment and charged with one count of stalking and twenty-four counts of criminal threats dating to January 2, 2003. She was arraigned and held on $1 million bail.

At first, I thought that could very well be the end of my employment. What with the stalker now in police custody, and the continuing headbutting with CZJ's Los Angeles PR people, who I knew for a fact wanted me gone. But instead of being terminated, MD raised my salary.

Chapter 44

I WAS SITTING AT MY computer in my NYC apartment, answering emails from Wendy, making plans for her upcoming one-month visit, her longest yet, when Donald's executive assistant, Norma Foerderer, phoned me.

"Donald's having some people over tonight to watch the premiere of his reality TV show, *The Apprentice*. Can you make it?"

Although I'd never even seen a reality TV show before and hadn't heard anything about Donald staring in *The Apprentice*, I said, "I'd love to." I slipped off my computer glasses and glanced out the window into the morning sun. "But I've got business commitments this evening." I was scheduled to pick up MD at Teterboro Airport at 3:00 p.m. Take him to a business meeting, then a charity affair dinner at the Waldorf Astoria hotel. Tomorrow I was dropping him off at Teterboro, then picking up my Wendy at Newark Airport.

"Tell Donald I wish him good luck. Tell him I said to break a leg."

Around 1:00 the following afternoon, I was sitting in MD's SUV, outside his West Seventy-sixth Street apartment, reading mostly positive reviews of Donald's new TV show. I had to hand it to him. He never gave up on his pursuit of the limelight. Over the years I'd seen him in bit parts on half-a-dozen movies—*Home Alone 2: Lost in New York*— and TV shows—*Sex and the City*—usually playing himself. And now here he was starring in his own TV show.

I drove MD to Teterboro Airport. Then raced down I-95. Met Wendy in Delta Airline's baggage claim. Lugged her four heavy suitcases to the car.

After she'd unpacked and settled in at my apartment, I changed into a fresh dress shirt and tie. Wendy slipped into a sexy cocktail dress and four-inch heels. We took a taxi down to Bemelmans Bar in the Carlyle Hotel for a predinner martini. Then cabbed it down Second Avenue to the Palm II. Frank the bartender served us a drink at the tiny bar while we waited for our table. That was where I ran into William L.

"Just the man I wanted to see," William L. said after I introduced him to Wendy.

"You available next week?"

I said I was.

"I need you to bodyguard Gwyneth Paltrow."

Paltrow, who would one day be named *People* magazine's most beautiful woman, as well as being one of the world's most unpopular celebrities, was a former neighbor of mine. She lived with her parents, Tony Award–winning actress Blythe Danner and *St. Elsewhere* producer Bruce Paltrow, four blocks away. I recall seeing the family regularly in our hood. Noticed a blossoming Gwyneth and her privileged, underage Spence School classmates cocktailing at the infamous, Preppy Killer–famed Dorian's Red Hand.

William L. said Gwyneth had no specific threats, but that she'd be shooting a series of TV commercials at a new production facility located in the high-crime, 41st Precinct, Fort Apache in the Bronx. My former command.

"I'll take the gig," I told William L. He said he'd phone me with the details during the week and headed out the door.

"Your table is ready," the maître d' said and sat us at my favorite booth. I ordered a wine list and asked Wendy to marry me.

"Took you long enough." She beamed as I presented her with a diamond ring. I slid the ring on Wendy's finger. Told her

I'd love forever and a day. Was telling her that she was the most important person in my life, when a waiter interrupted.

"Excuse me," the waiter said and held up a bottle of very expensive champagne. "Compliments," he said, "of the gentleman at the bar."

I looked and saw Grayman raise his glass in a toast. I used my water glass to toast back and mouthed *thanks*. As the waiter set down two champagne flutes and popped the cork, I couldn't help but wonder how Grayman knew this was a special occasion. Then recalled I had told the maître d' when I made the reservation. But I never did introduce him to Donald like he asked. So, why champagne?

"Who's he?" Wendy said.

The waiter filled our glasses.

"A friend. Sort of."

"He looks like someone. I know! That 1940s actor who always played a gangster. They said he was a gangster in real life."

"George Raft."

"That's the one."

I picked up my champagne. "To us."

"To us," Wendy said.

We clinked glasses and drank.

At the time Wendy and I had been together for almost eight years. Had our ups and downs—what couple didn't—but we worked through the tough times. Became closer as a result. Not that we had a life plan yet. Although we'd considered several viable options.

Now that my security business was doing well, Wendy said she'd like to move to Manhattan. She thought the girls would love living in the city. Problem with that was that her ex-husband would have to go along with the move. And we'd have to relocate to a larger, much more expensive, apartment. Or move to the suburbs.

We ordered five-pound lobsters. Split a cheesecake. Just as I was about to ask for the check and suggest we head down to the

Village to a jazz club, Wendy said, "I want to go home." Uncharacteristic, to say the least. But I'd noticed some subtle changes the past few months. Normally the most consistent, measured person I'd ever known, she was tired most of the time, moody, and content to stay home. I was starting to become concerned. So worried that I asked the advice of my go-to authorities on all things female: my three sisters and Joni. "Could be early menopause," they all agreed.

Oy vey.

Gwyneth's Soho doorman announced me the following Monday morning. I rode the elevator to the penthouse floor. Knocked on her door. Gwyneth invited me in, introduced me to her children Moses and Apple. Offered me coffee, breakfast. I declined. We reviewed her schedule. Then she chatted me up for about twenty minutes. I mentioned that we'd once been neighbors. She studied my face.

"Oh, yes," she said graciously. "I remember seeing you in the neighborhood."

I knew she didn't.

Gwyneth told me where to find her Mercedes, which was parked in the building's basement garage. I was anxious to check the registration, inspection, gas level. I left her apartment, stepped out into the hall. The elevator door was closing.

"Hold the elevator, please?"

A hand shot out and touched the sensor on the door. The door sprung back open.

"Thanks," I said as I stepped inside. "Meryl?"

"I know you." Meryl Streep smiled warmly. "Don't I?"

I went to press the garage level button—it was already pressed—and explained that we'd met at various Screen Actors Guild functions, during press junkets for her movie *Postcards from the Edge,* and at a Robin Hood Foundation charity event. I did not mention that I'd had a crush on her after seeing her in the 1978 film *The Seduction of Joe Tynan.*

I walked Meryl to her car, opened and held her door for her. She thanked me and drove away. I located Gwyneth's vehicle and conducted an inspection.

That first week I spent with Gwyneth and Moses and Apple was thankfully uneventful and without drama. Although I'd heard the rumors about how difficult she could be, I found Gwyneth to be warm, friendly, approachable, and unaffected. Things went so smoothly that I was thinking I could add the Paltrow family to my steady client list when I blew it. Big-time.

I had driven her to pick up her daughter Apple at a dance class on Broome Street, where we were to meet up with her husband. Problem was I hadn't done my homework. Didn't know who she was married to. Never heard of the British rock band Coldplay. Never heard of Chris Martin.

I got Gwyneth and Apple settled in the Mercedes back seat, stood outside waiting for her husband. Figuring that, since Gwyneth was young and beautiful, I'd have no trouble identifying her significant other. That was when a greasy, homeless man approached the Mercedes.

I stiff-armed him, knocked him back a few feet. I didn't want to hurt the derelict, but if he tried to get past me, I was prepared to deck him.

"That's my husband," Gwyneth shouted out the Mercedes window.

"Where?" I looked past the derelict. There was a sharp-looking guy in a business suit, but he was way too young. There was a well-groomed Hispanic man, but he was way too old. Maybe the dark-skinned athletic guy coming down the street.

"Him," Gwyneth pointed at the derelict.

"Him?" I said in puzzled disbelief.

"Yeah. Me!" Chris Martin said angrily.

I would never work for Gwyneth again.

Chapter 45

"C'mon," I said to Wendy. "You'll meet me on the set. I'll introduce you as my assistant. You'll get to meet Catherine, Tom Hanks. Steven Spielberg."

"I'm tired," Wendy said. "I want to stay home."

I'd received a last-minute call from the Douglasses' office. I was to pick up CZJ at Teterboro at 4:30 and get her to Times Square by dusk. She was booked to shoot nighttime pickup shots for the feature film *The Terminal*.

"I understand," I said to Wendy, trying my best to mask my disappointment. Reminded myself once again that I was no longer dealing with the energetic, adventurous Wendy, but with a woman who might be suffering from menopause.

"I should be home by midnight." I tied my tie. Holstered my .38. Slipped on my suit jacket and a trench coat. Left Wendy sitting by a window, staring out toward LaGuardia Airport.

I picked CZJ up at Teterboro, escorted her to Times Square. The weather was clear, crisp. As expected, the area was swarming with thousands of festive tourists who were whipped into a frenzy by the fact a major motion picture, featuring A-list stars, was obviously being shot in their midst. There was a substantial police presence. The large wardrobe, makeup, camera, lighting and grip, fuel, catering, and sound trucks were parked on closed and blocked-off streets that ran east and west across Broadway.

I pulled alongside Stephen Spielberg's trailer, which was parked on West Forty-fourth Street. Ushered CZJ inside along with Tom Hanks, closed and made sure the door was secure behind them. I introduced myself to Hanks's and Spielberg's bodyguards. Spielberg's assistant informed us that we had time for coffee since the meeting would last at least half an hour. I took that opportunity to find CZJ's trailer, make sure it was secure.

It was not. Her plush star trailer, instead of being located on the closed side street where it belonged, had been parked off on its own on West Forty-ninth Street, which is very busy and open to pedestrian and vehicle traffic. Apparently, no one working on the production, or in CZJ's employ, had given any thought to her personal safety. Which meant that escorting her from the makeup trailer to the wardrobe trailer, then to the various sets, was going to be a logistical nightmare. Besides the fanatical paparazzi, A-list celebrities attract devoted and sometimes hysterical fans. But someone as stunningly beautiful as CZJ attracted a whole new level of crazy.

I scrambled to find the Teamster captain, asked him to please move CZJ's trailer to a secure location with the other production trailers. He assured me that by the time they did that, the shoot would be over. I prepared myself for a stressful night.

I got home around midnight, still tense from dealing with aggressive paparazzi and belligerent crowds who seemed to think that, as a movie star, CZJ owed them her time. I unlocked my apartment door, found that Wendy was still sitting in the same place, gazing out of a window toward LaGuardia Airport.

Weird.

"Hey, babe," I said as I hung up my trench coat and suit jacket and loosened my tie. I walked into the kitchen. Opened the refrigerator and got myself a beer. I checked the stove and sink, couldn't tell if Wendy had had anything to eat or drink.

"I want to go home," Wendy said. "I miss my girls."

I popped open the cold beer. Took a swig. "The Douglases are leaving at the end of next week. I'll go back with you then."

Wendy shook her head. "I want to go right away."

Okay, this was nutty behavior. She'd only been in the city for ten days and she was supposed to stay for at least another two weeks. But I kept my annoyance and frustration to myself. I called the airline. Booked her a ticket for the following afternoon. I drove her to the airport, pulled to a stop in front of the Delta terminal. We exchanged a long, passionate kiss. Then I fetched her bags from the trunk, checked them with the curbside skycap. We exchanged another kiss. I told her I'd miss her, that I'd see her soon, and watched her enter the terminal.

The Douglases stayed in the city longer than scheduled. But Wendy and I emailed and spoke on the phone every day. She kept me updated on the girls, our friends, and happenings in San Diego neighborhood. She seemed like herself again.

I escorted MD, sans CZJ, to the Jewish National Fund (JNF) charity event on one of the lower West Side piers. It was a well-attended affair. Donald was to be one of the featured speakers. He arrived surrounded by bodyguards—none of which I knew—about twenty minutes late and didn't notice me as he hurried through the crowd into the ballroom. I had no interest in the speeches or the rubber chicken dinner. Since the event was guarded by a competent event security company, I felt comfortable leaving MD in their capable hands. I walked outside, breathed in the fresh Hudson River air, and watched the ship traffic. Thought about Wendy. How I could best help her get through her change of life and all of its complications, not the least of which was decreased libido.

An hour later, I made my rounds, walked into the ballroom to check up on MD. He was enjoying himself, surrounded by people—he was a people person—as usual.

I moved across the room, saw that the desert buffet looked pretty good. I helped myself to an assortment. Was looking for a place to sit when Donald saw me and waved me to his table. Between mouthfuls of sweets and constant interruptions—seemed everyone wanted an audience with Donald—we made the usual small talk. Meaning Donald talked about Donald. Gushed about the Trump "brand." Boasted about his plans to take the Trump name worldwide. Open Trump hotels and golf courses in Scotland, Dubai, Russia. Deals he clearly thought I was familiar with. Like I had nothing else to do with my time than follow his career.

"Can you believe Trump Model Management? You have to come to the agency cocktail parties." Donald grinned conspiratorially, lowered his voice. "Meet some of the models. I have an agency full of tens. Nothing but tens. Ford and Elite used to be the biggest and the best agencies in the world. Trump is the best now."

As I listened to Donald prattle on, I realized our "friendship" had been based on womanizing. Starting at Maxwell's Plum back in the 1970s. We'd never progressed past that. But now that I was older, in love and in a committed relationship, our connection no longer worked. I thought about some of the baffling, foolish, and cruel things he'd done over the years. Not the least of which was allowing Marla to "trump up" the criminal charges against her former best friend and manager, Chuck Jones, and put him in prison.

Donald surprised me by saying, "How're you doing? You seeing anyone?"

"Going on eight years."

"Oh, right. The woman from…?"

"San Diego."

"Right. Get up to LA much?"

"We drive up every couple of months on our way to Napa."

"You see Marla?"

"Not since the Chuck Jones fiasco. You know how weird she can get."

"Know where she is now?"

"No."

"But you could find her if you wanted to. Right?"

Uh-oh. I thought I saw where this was going. Marla must have pulled one of her patented disappearing acts and Donald was asking me if I'd find her for him. Visions of tabloid headlines came flooding back. The fighting. The breakups. The make ups. Me the monkey in the middle. Just because they'd been divorced for five years, and he had a string of beautiful models, including Melania Knauss, at his beck and call, didn't mean the unpredictable billionaire wasn't still carrying a torch for Marla. Or maybe he was suing her, and he needed her location so a process server could serve her with papers. Not that I gave a rat's ass. There was no way I was going to become involved again.

"Right?" Donald said. "You could find her?"

I shook my head. "Not my circus, not my monkey."

Donald looked at me. "What does that even mean?"

I saw movement across the room. MD was on his feet, shaking hands, moving toward the exit. I swallowed some cheesecake. Put down my fork. Donald had no idea that I was working as a bodyguard, let alone working for MD.

"Gotta go."

"Call me," Donald said.

I said I would.

"I want to come back to New York," Wendy said over the phone a few days later. "I want you to come and get me."

"Get you? I'll be there soon. We'll come back together."

"I want you to come get me. Now."

"Why? You just left. What's going on?"

Wendy didn't answer.

"Okay, look, I'll get you a ticket. Hire a car service to take you to the airport. I'll meet you at baggage claim."

"Please come and get me?"

"But the cost of booking a flight last-minute? It makes no sense."

Wendy didn't respond.

I sighed, exasperated. "When do you want to come?"
"I'll let you know," she said and hung up.
I tried to call Wendy back. No answer.
I emailed her. No response.

Chapter 46

THE NEXT DAY, SUNDAY, November 14, retired FDNY firefighter Danny Noonan and I were in the Kinsale Irish pub on Third Avenue and East Ninety-fourth Street. Enjoying the traditional Irish music playing on the bar's sound system. Booked to teach a fire safety course at the New York City Fire Department Academy, Danny had flown in from San Diego the day before and was crashing at my apartment.

Two attractive, twentysomething women were sitting on the stools alongside us, bemoaning the cancelation of the HBO TV show, *Sex and the City*. I'd never seen the show, but I knew Sarah Jessica Parker, her husband Matthew Broderick, and "Mr. Big," Chris Noth from Elaine's. The women's husbands/boyfriends, who were standing behind them, were debating whether Alex Rodriguez, the newest New York Yankee, was worth $252 million.

Danny said, "I think 'Red Star of Death' would make a great movie." Referring to the short story we'd coauthored and sold to *New York* magazine. "There's countless cop movies out there, but only two about firefighters. It's a good story," Danny continued. "Well written. Everyone says so."

"Like I keep telling Wendy, it's not just about writing a good story. It's about connections and good old-fashioned luck."

Trying to get lucky, I'd already sent "Red Star" to Larry Hagman, Carroll O'Connor, Academy Award director Doug Wick, Merv Adelson, Steve Ross, and a few other Hollywood bigwigs and had yet to hear back. Not that I expected to. "Red Star" was a short story, not a fully developed screenplay or book. Submitting it was a shot in the dark, a Hail Mary. But, hey, we had nothing to lose.

"Did you show it to Michael Douglas?" Danny said.

"Not yet." I was trying to figure out a way to approach MD and his production company Further Films, but didn't think it appropriate. After all, he'd hired me to protect his family, and not as a writer.

Danny ordered us another round of drinks and my cell phone rang. I checked the caller ID. It was 858, a San Diego area code. I didn't recognize the number. But since only Wendy, my sisters, and the Douglases had my number, I decided to answer. I stuck a finger in my ear to block out the Irish music.

"Hello?"

Reception was lousy, the call was broken up. Someone was talking excitedly, something about the San Diego police department. But what with the bar's music, I couldn't make out what was being said. I walked out onto the sidewalk. Reception was no better.

Struggling to understand the caller, I panicked. What if something had happened to Wendy or the girls? My mind raced. I was pretty sure the next flight to San Diego left around 8:00 p.m. I had enough time to make a reservation and take a cab to the airport.

"Talk slower," I told the caller, but it was no use. "I have your number on my caller ID," I said, not knowing if the caller could hear me. "I'll call you back in five minutes." I pocketed the cell. Dodged traffic as I dashed across Third Avenue heading to my apartment. I used my key to unlock the door. Grabbed the closest portable phone. I took out my cell, looked at the caller ID, and dialed.

"Thomas?"

I recognized the voice. It was Wendy's ex-husband.

"Brad?"

"Wendy's dead," he cried. "She killed herself."

Chapter 47

I HAVE AGONIZED FOR ALMOST twenty years over whether to write about what it's like to lose the love of one's life. Decided I'm not capable of expressing myself coherently. Let's just say that I was gutted by Wendy's death. Yes, I'd suffered losses before—the death of my parents, other close relatives and friends from natural causes. Pals who'd joined the military and were killed in action. Police officers killed in the line of duty. But I'd never experienced the loss of a soulmate.

At first, the cop in me wondered if foul play was involved. That would explain everything. I mean, Wendy would never take her own life. She loved her daughters too much. I knew she was looking forward to their graduations, marriages, having grandchildren. We were engaged. Planning a life together. She had everything to live for. I got in touch with the San Diego PD. Read the official reports. Spoke to a detective. Much as I didn't want to believe it, nothing pointed to foul play.

The days, weeks, and months after Wendy's death were a blur. The shock, anger, grief, confusion, anxiety, loneliness, and feelings of abandonment were suffocating. I couldn't wrap my head around the fact that she was gone. Found myself searching for an old email from "the Little Boss" that I must have overlooked. Searched my computer's spam and trash folders. I checked my snail mailbox every day for months, expecting a letter—Wendy was a great letter writer—explaining what compelled her to commit the unthinkable. I couldn't sleep.

Began to experience sleep-deprived twilight visions. I always smelled her perfume first.

"Why didn't you come to get me when I asked?" Wendy always said. She'd sit on the end of my bed. So real I could reach out and touch her. "Why?"

"I wish I did," I told her time and again. "I'm sorry."

I felt crushing guilt. If only I'd done what she asked. Flown to San Diego and accompanied her back. She'd be alive today. I know she would.

To this day, I have never spoken to anyone about how Wendy's death devastated me. Not my sisters, brother, friends, priest, bartender, or shrink. Never sought any type of counseling. Didn't join any bereavement groups. Maybe I should have. But the men from my world don't ask for help. It's a sign of weakness. I bear the label of "suicide survivor" alone. And still think of Wendy the first thing every morning, the last thing every night.

I have learned to deal with the constant, never-ending feelings of loss by keeping busy: working, exercising, writing. In 2009 Macmillan published my novel, *Confessions of a Catholic Cop (City of Fire)*. Followed by *Confessions of a Suicidal Policewoman* and *Confessions of a Celebrity Bodyguard*. I wish my biggest fan and muse were alive to see that.

I continued to work for the Douglas family—I never told them about Wendy— almost exclusively for the next twenty years. Welcomed the always stressful sixteen-hour days.

I didn't date. Although I felt lonely at times, I didn't have an interest. Still don't. I did have two very short-term liaisons that ended rather badly. Not the women's fault. They weren't Wendy.

I keep in touch with Lauryn and Faye and their father Brad, though I don't see them as often as I'd like. It's taken me years to be able to visit Del Mar without slipping into a depression. As I predicted, the girls grew into world-class beauties and, after they learned to deal with the loss of their beloved mother, developed into well-adjusted, successful women with businesses and families of their own. They miss their mother terribly.

These days I find myself becoming closer to my family and the few friends I have left. Some I've simply lost touch with. Still others have moved on, their lives taking them in different directions. Like Marla, who moved to LA to raise her and Donald's daughter Tiffany. I haven't heard from her in a long time, but from what I hear she's as kooky as ever, with her silly New Age philosophies and ostentatious psychobabble. Then there's Donald, who went on to inexplicably become the forty-fifth president of the United States. I don't think anyone was more surprised than he when he won the election. Who would've thunk it?

Many of my dear friends have passed away, like my BFF Joni, Larry & Maj Hagman, Michael Collyer, David Broadnax, Paul Derounian, Alex Wasinski, Grayman, John McCooey, Tom Counihan, Bessy, and my sister Maureen just to name a few. Although we become more comfortable with loss as we age, I miss them all more than I can say. Which is one of the reasons I decided to write this memoir, tell my story. Recount, some have said, my extraordinary experiences. Commit my tale to paper. Dedicate it to all who've accompanied me on life's wild and crazy journey. Create my magnum opus. My last literary hurrah.

www.ingramcontent.com/pod-product-compliance
Lightning Source LLC
Chambersburg PA
CBHW051934290426
44110CB00015B/1972